START
love
REPEAT

START *love* REPEAT

HOW TO STAY IN LOVE WITH YOUR ENTREPRENEUR IN A CRAZY START-UP WORLD

DORCAS CHENG-TOZUN

CENTER
STREET

New York Nashville

Center Street
Hachette Book Group
1290 Avenue of the Americas, New York, NY 10104
centerstreet.com
twitter.com/centerstreet

First Edition: November 2017

Center Street is a division of Hachette Book Group, Inc. The Center Street name and logo are trademarks of Hachette Book Group, Inc.

The publisher is not responsible for websites (or their content) that are not owned by the publisher.

The Hachette Speakers Bureau provides a wide range of authors for speaking events. To find out more, go to www.HachetteSpeakersBureau.com or call (866) 376-6591.

Library of Congress Cataloging-in-Publication Data has been applied for.

ISBN: 978-1-4789-2074-8 (hardcover), 978-1-4789-2075-5 (ebook)

Printed in the United States of America

LSC-C

10 9 8 7 6 5 4 3 2 1

To Ned, my best friend, my partner, and the love of my life,
who taught me how to dream big.

And to our two boys, the brightest stars in our universe.

Contents

Foreword

by Meg Cadoux Hirshberg, former *Inc.* magazine columnist, and Gary Hirshberg, chairman and former CEO, Stonyfield Yogurt

Spouses of entrepreneurs, rejoice: Dorcas Cheng-Tozun has thrown you a life raft. Cleverly organized according to the typical stages of a start-up (market research, strategic planning, etc.), *Start, Love, Repeat* looks carefully and closely at the intimate relationship dynamics that occur when a business enters the family.

As a writer and the spouse of an entrepreneur, Dorcas is eminently qualified to give voice to the spouse's perspective on the concerns, struggles, and—yes—joys that typically occur in an entrepreneurial marriage, and she does so in clear and impassioned prose. My own entrepreneur husband and I often liken the spouse's journey to riding shotgun down a curvy stretch of road. Usually the driver—the one in control—is just fine. It's the passenger who feels sick.

When people start companies, they research the competition, market data, Small Business Administration loans, and the cost of office space. But they generally give little thought to how a business will affect their personal lives. The spouse may fret and worry a bit more about the insecurity of the venture for family, but generally both entrepreneur and spouse assume that they'll muddle through for the "year or two" it takes the company to gain traction. When things don't go as expected, and they rarely do, the cracks that exist in any marriage can grow into fissures, as the spouse's resentment blooms into full flower, and the entrepreneur comes to feel unfairly condemned and misunderstood.

A close reading of *Start, Love, Repeat* will go a long way toward dissolving those resentments before they start to build. Dorcas writes intimately and with great nuance about her own experience of being in an entrepreneurial marriage, and also includes illustrative stories of many other entrepreneur-spouse couples. Throughout the book, she cites fascinating research concerning entrepreneurship, as well as insights from therapists and executive coaches.

A common romantic image of the entrepreneur is of an exceptionally daring person who sallies forth—alone—with persistence and determination to realize a dream. While there is some truth to this vision, the unspoken reality is that an entrepreneurial venture sucks the entire family into its vortex. Dorcas details that reality, and acknowledges its potential danger to the couple's relationship. To better arm those who are along for this ride, she offers useful, practical, specific suggestions of actions the couple can take.

While Dorcas is sober about the challenges, she is equally clear about the tremendous potential upsides for a spouse in an entrepreneurial marriage. Much of it, she argues, is a question of perspective. She urges the spouse to consider: What is the opportunity in this?

As I opened page one of Dorcas's book, I wasn't sure I had much more to learn about the tribulations of marriage to an entrepreneur. First, I've been married to one of the tribe for more than thirty years. And as a former columnist for *Inc.* magazine, I had covered similar turf in my "Balancing Acts" columns for the magazine, as well as in my book *For Better or For Work: A Survival Guide for Entrepreneurs and Their Families*. Tearing through Dorcas's lively manuscript, I found her insights to be powerful, useful, and true.

Dorcas quotes author Brené Brown, who wrote that "Vulnerability sounds like truth and feels like courage." This is a perfect summary of *Start, Love, Repeat*. Dorcas's courage in making herself exquisitely vulnerable by speaking frankly about her own experience is quite clearly in service to her desire to help others who find themselves hitched to an entrepreneur's dream. The reason is simple. While the inevitable trials of an entrepreneurial marriage could have driven Dorcas apart from her husband, Ned, working through them has actually brought them much closer. "I don't want us to be lucky," she adds. "I want us to be typical."

—Meg Cadoux Hirshberg

*   *   *

Ever since Meg's book was published, I've advised every entrepreneur I know to read it with their spouse. It was the book I wish Meg and I had had when we got started on our crazy entrepreneurial ride growing our company, Stonyfield Yogurt.

Now I will have to add Dorcas's important book to my list of recommended reading. While she aims her thoughts and research directly to the spouses of entrepreneurs, this book is a must-read for entrepreneurs as well. Dorcas's insights into the entrepreneurial life and what is required of both spouses and entrepreneurs to survive and thrive on this journey should not be limited to spouses alone.

The essential quandary for entrepreneurial couples can be summarized this way: For a business to survive, the entrepreneur has to be all in, or the business doesn't stand a chance. The intense focus required by this passion project, aka the business, can be in conflict with the entrepreneur's passion for their intimates. Stimulated by the endless series of challenges, what feels to us entrepreneurs like a long series of sprints is often a lonely marathon for our mates.

I wholeheartedly agree with Dorcas about the importance of shared mission in keeping an entrepreneurial marriage alive. Meg and I found that our mutual commitment to growing the organic food sector helped get us through our darkest days with the business. Both spouse and entrepreneur must ask themselves and each other: What is our motivation? Why are we doing this? Ideally, the answer to that question can become a touchstone through the trials of growing a business.

Dorcas has great insight into the entrepreneurial personality, characterized by "that nagging yearning to start something." She understands that the entrepreneur perceives stress differently from the spouse. What's different, as Dorcas points out, is that an entrepreneur often perceives stressors as positive challenges. The spouse, not so much.

These and many other insights into the psyches of entrepreneurs and their spouses will not only give you tools you need to move forward and grow but will make you feel less alone in your struggles. Looking for a guaranteed good investment? Read this book.

—Gary Hirshberg

Introduction

When my husband, Ned, and I were expecting for the first time, I told everyone we were looking forward to the arrival of our first *human* child, but not our first child. That distinction went to my husband's latest and biggest start-up, which was conceived by Ned and several graduate school classmates just a few months after he and I married.

Our first child, also known as social enterprise d.light, has led to countless missed holidays and broken appointments; it has contributed to physical illness and emotional meltdowns for both of us; it even caused us to move to China for three years and to Kenya for seven months. Thanks to the demands of his business, Ned and I have had years-long disagreements about work-life balance, time management, and quality of life. We delayed any consideration about having real children until d.light was a little more grown up and independent. I have been in therapy several times and have even had to take antianxiety medication because of how deeply my husband's start-up affected my personal life.

Today d.light is a thriving multinational business with hundreds of employees across five continents—an outcome neither of us would have predicted in its wild, roller-coaster first years. Worldwide, about 80 million people are using d.light's solar products. Our lives have gotten a little easier as the company has matured, but the truth is that an entrepreneur never really stops being an entrepreneur. The challenges that we face as a couple, while morphing countless times over the past twelve years, continue to this day.

Along the way I kept hoping to find a resource or community of people who could explain the challenges of being with an entrepreneur and could tell me how to support my spouse's dreams without sacrificing my own. More often than not, my search led me to broken relationships or failed businesses.

Determined not to be another one of those statistics, Ned and I fought for our marriage even when doing so affected his business and both of our careers—and the outcome has been mostly positive for us. I know we're one of the lucky couples, as any foray into the lives of entrepreneurial spouses will quickly lead to stories of resentment, betrayal, and conflict. But I don't want us to be lucky. I want us to be typical.

We tend to stereotype entrepreneurs as uniformly young and single, but the truth is that nearly 70 percent of business founders have spouses, life partners, or children—all of whom, whether they like it or not, are living the start-up life.[1] Those who choose to be with entrepreneurs invite things into their lives they may never have wanted: financial instability, uncertainty, stress, and the nagging sense that they are always playing second fiddle to the greater lure of their partner's business.

In American lore, the entrepreneur that has most captured our imagination is the Steve Jobs–Mark Zuckerberg–Jeff Bezos–Elon Musk type. Someone who walks that fine line between brilliance and nuttiness, between the present and a future few can imagine. Someone from a humble background who eschews tradition, beats the odds, and through a fortuitous combination of ingenuity, perseverance, and good timing becomes a multibillionaire who changes the way the world works.

You may be in a committed relationship with one of these entrepreneurs, and to you I say, *Good luck*. Hopefully the years of striving and sacrifice will all be worth it when you can no longer keep track of the number of zeros in your bank account balance.

But the vast majority of entrepreneurs are a little more earthbound. Yes, they are creative and passionate, hardworking and motivated, but they also likely come from middle-class or upper-lower-class backgrounds.[2] They come from all different ethnic backgrounds and have varying levels of education. They have perhaps been gainfully employed for one or even two decades and may be around the age of forty (the median age of someone starting a first business).[3] Their reasons for wanting to start their own business will vary, of course, but most likely the list will be topped by their determination not to work for someone else, to be the masters of their own fate.

Ironically, your beloved's decision to be his or her own boss will likely impinge upon *your* ability to have full control of your life. Anyone who has been there knows that start-ups, at least at the outset, require what seems like a black hole's worth of two finite resources: time and money. Never seeing your significant other who is obsessively working to get his or her business off the ground will deeply affect a relationship. So will not having a regular source of income while savings disappear and debts pile up.

Or, if your business is among the nearly one-quarter of new

businesses that are co-managed by spouses, you are living and breathing the start-up life in every way imaginable.[4] There may be no clear boundary between your work life and home life—which, over time, creates its own challenges in the relationship.

But even if you aren't a *co-preneur*, it's likely that you're playing at least some role in your significant other's venture. My roles in Ned's multiple companies have ranged from envelope stuffer and proofreader, to circuit solderer and Santa-signature forger (more on that later), to human resources manager and director of communications.

Regardless of how involved you are in the venture, or how long you have been with your beloved entrepreneur, having a business in the family will affect you in innumerable ways—from your day-to-day schedule to your quality of life when you are old enough to join AARP. This book is for you.

This is the book I wish I had when Ned and I were preparing to say our wedding vows. I would still have married him, but understanding how deeply Ned's professional choices could affect me would have given me the chance to build my support network, gird my loins, find a really good therapist, and do whatever else I could to ensure that the pursuit of his dream wouldn't come at a cost I was not always confident I could bear. This book answers the questions that plagued me for years, from basic start-up information to relationship advice, including:

- What are the typical challenges faced by the spouses and partners of entrepreneurs?
- How can we minimize our financial risk before starting a new business?
- Is it possible for entrepreneurs to have work-life balance?
- How can I prevent my own identity from being subsumed by my spouse's larger-than-life work?

- Should we delay having children if we've started a business? Should we delay starting a business if we have young children?
- Is it ever reasonable to ask my significant other to walk away from the business for the sake of our family?

The content of this book follows the same trajectory as a (hopefully successful) start-up, beginning with market research on who in the world these entrepreneurs are; due diligence on understanding what you and your marriage need to be okay; strategic planning approaches to make your relationship and family life work; and ending with that hardest of questions: When is it time to call it quits, either in the business or the relationship, and start over with a clean slate?

Each section includes recent research findings and insights I have collected from professionals in the start-up ecosystem—business school professors, investors, executive coaches, experienced entrepreneurs—as well as advice from top marriage-family therapists. I have also been privileged to hear stories from dozens of entrepreneurial couples. In their hard-earned experiences, which I share throughout the book, are some of the most valuable lessons of all.

No research exists on how many entrepreneurs' marriages fail, but in one 2017 survey, 27 percent of business founders said that starting a company had negatively impacted their relationships and family life.[5] Ask anyone who has been in the start-up world for a while, and they'll tell you about the disproportionate number of broken relationships and divorces they've seen. Relationships, like businesses, take quite a bit of investment for them to last. They require our best energy and thinking, and our willingness to sacrifice and make adjustments. There may be only so much you can do to help your partner's business succeed, but there is plenty that you can do to help your partnership succeed, come hell or high water, or yet one more hundred-hour workweek.

Several therapists I've interviewed have said that someone faced with challenging or unexpected circumstances should ask this most powerful of questions: *What is the opportunity in this?* Our willingness to see everything that comes our way as a chance to learn and grow and try something new could be all we need to keep ourselves grounded and our relationships thriving. My hope is that this book will help you find your opportunities—for yourself and the ones you love most.

PART I

MARKET RESEARCH

Meet the Entrepreneur

My husband, Ned, entered college thinking he might like to major in music. Then he decided to be pre-med. Then he considered astronomy. Then audio engineering. Then physics. Electrical engineering. Environmental science. Computer science. Each time his major changed, he reorganized his entire class schedule, frantically adding and dropping courses right before the registration deadline. He usually ended up with an eclectic grab bag of classes, all of which he was already behind in. He would pull several all-nighters just to catch up in his classes and then push himself at full speed for the rest of the term to get good grades.

Ned and I became friends in the middle of our freshman year. "You're studying *what*?" I found myself asking him each quarter. "Why?" I was bewildered by Ned's behavior. I had come into college knowing that I wanted to study communications and was proceeding in a straight line toward completing my degree.

"Doesn't it sound fascinating?" he would reply. "I wanted to try it in case I want to be a doctor/scientist/astronomer/engineer/ musician/person who does something cool." Occasionally he shot back with a cheerful, "Why not?"

Watching Ned change majors and course loads more often than I changed my hairstyle drove me nuts. But I still fell head over heels for him, in large part because of his gentle persistence and infectious curiosity.

Yet some serious questions surfaced as I weighed our potential future together. What in the world would he end up doing after he graduated? Could he even keep a stable job? What would life be like with someone so lacking in focus and decisiveness?

The issue, we both realized much later, wasn't that Ned lacked focus. The challenge was that he wanted to focus on *everything*, to understand a bit of nearly every field. He worried about missing out on something better if he spent too much time and energy in one area. He actually enjoyed the rush of serially dating and dumping so many majors and classes. (Fortunately for me, he had no inclination to serially date and dump humans.)

We both should have known he was going to grow up to be an entrepreneur.

When Ned eventually graduated, he had earned two separate degrees: one in computer science and another in environmental science. He promptly found a job as an audio software engineer. I felt relieved that he was finally settling down. He had a real, stable, well-paying job, and he was getting ready to make a lifelong commitment to me. The wild days of his youth had passed.

Then, six months later, Ned quit his job. He had been miserable, his soul slowly suffocating under the weight of silent coding, socially awkward coworkers, and organizational politicking. He had no idea what he was going to do next. But he knew he didn't want to be an engineer.

Alarm bells began to ring in my head, triggered by everything my parents had ever taught me about being sensible. Ned should have been able to suck it up, I thought, to do what he needed to support himself and be a responsible member of society. Yet I was still madly in love with this unpredictable, unconventional young man. As someone who had always played by the rules, I admired Ned's willingness to buck expectations and plunge into new arenas without a second thought. He seemed fearless, bursting with confidence and hope that he could find work that was interesting, meaningful, and fun.

But I also worried there was something seriously wrong with him. If we ever merged our homes and our bank accounts, his free-wheeling, devil-may-care approach to life could very well screw up my orderly existence.

Ned wanted to do something creative with music and technology, and after a few months of brainstorming and experimenting, he and a couple of buddies decided to develop personalized children's music. They composed and recorded their own music, and developed an algorithm that seamlessly inserted each child's name into the songs. Their families fully funded the business. I did not put in a cent of my own money, but I contributed countless hours burning CDs (the height of audio technology in the early 2000s), sticking on labels, and stuffing envelopes.

Even then, I didn't quite know what to make of Ned's venture. Interesting, yes. Fun, yes. Perhaps meaningful for parents stuck on road trips with demanding youngsters. But I couldn't imagine him becoming a personalized children's music guru. Was he going to tour the country doing personalized concerts? What did success even look like in this industry? Most importantly, was he ever going to make any income?

By the time we got engaged a couple of years later, in 2003, Ned was on to his next business. He had realized the children's music market couldn't be profitable. The market was too niche, the distribution network too limited. Instead he was going to record and sell original mobile-phone ringtones.

I'm sure I gave him a look—one that has become quite familiar to both of us over the years. "They're huge in Europe and Asia," Ned explained defensively. "People there spend a ton of money on ringtones." He tried to convince me that even if I was content with the "Trio" and "Samba" ringtones that had come with my little flip cell phone, millions of other people in the world weren't.

You may be wondering how Ned and I addressed my ongoing concerns as we prepared for our wedding. We didn't. I didn't know how to tactfully raise the issue without sounding like I was questioning Ned's intelligence or character. And he, of course, didn't even realize there was a problem to be discussed.

Truthfully, my modern feminist self didn't mind the idea of being the stable breadwinner of the family. But I also didn't want to marry someone who would be dead weight. Despite Ned's excellent education and obvious talent, I thought this could be a real possibility—especially as he seemed to be running *away* from what he disliked (working for other people) more than he was running *toward* something he was passionate about. Children's music and ringtones were intriguing to him. But it seemed to me that his real motivation was to avoid being gainfully employed.

In this regard, Ned is actually like most entrepreneurs in the country: one of the top reasons company founders give for starting up is that they do not want to work for someone else.[1] As I've talked with entrepreneurs and their spouses around the country, I've found this to be a common story. Aaron Armstrong of Maple, Wisconsin, left his job because of an abusive, belligerent boss. He decided to open a music studio, from which he currently provides private lessons and trains church groups on building music ministries. Chris Bruno of Fort Collins, Colorado, was successfully leading an American nonprofit in Turkey until his vision outgrew that of the higher-ups. His day-to-day job became about fighting against the limitations placed on him, which was slowly killing his passion for building new things. He knew he had to leave, though he had no clear sense of where he was going next. He tried out a few different jobs until he discovered a passion for supporting the personal and spiritual development of men through counseling programs.

According to a number of studies, the other reasons why men and women choose to start a new venture are primarily opportunistic: they are unemployed or underemployed, or they've been working in an industry for ten to twenty years and feel confident enough to start their own venture in that same space.[2] Entrepreneurs have also reported being motivated by the opportunity to build wealth, to capitalize on a business idea, or to work in a start-up culture.[3]

Women are still greatly outnumbered in the start-up world, making up only 31 percent of business owners—a statistic that has increased only five percentage points in the last two decades.[4] But for females who choose to take the plunge, being their own boss may provide opportunities that working for someone else doesn't. Despite being more educated than the male population, women still make only 80 cents for every dollar earned by men and hold only 14.2 percent of executive positions within S&P 500 companies.[5]

For Lauren Schneidewind of Atlanta, Georgia, the lack of "equal pay for equal work" in her job at a chemical consulting business pushed her to venture out on her own. She was shocked and angered to discover that her annual salary had been $20,000 less than her male counterparts. "It was probably a 20 percent pay difference. It was not insignificant," she told me. "And they didn't want to make it right. I could see no path for success there. So I said, 'If you're not going to pay me, I'm going to do it myself.' " She decided to start her own consulting firm.

Beyond the numbers, though, many entrepreneurs seem unable to do anything but strike out on their own. *They just can't help themselves*, is what many have told me. That nagging yearning to start something often shows up early and can persist through changes in employment, income, marital status, and family planning. It's like an extra protein has been embedded in the DNA of 10–15 percent of the population, a protein that is all about creating something new and sharing it with the world. "It's just what they do," Dave Phillips, an executive mentor and coach who has worked with thousands of executives around the world, told me. "They're subject to their own poison. They're a wild bunch. They're unpredictable. That's why they're entrepreneurs: they can roll with the punches."

Dave Boyce of Provo, Utah, is a classic example of the consummate entrepreneur. Now in his forties, Dave paused for a moment when I asked him how many different jobs he has had. "I counted once for a presentation," he began, "and I counted forty-three different things I had been a part of in my life." From mowing lawns and delivering newspapers as a teen, to starting bands and an a cappella group in college, to serving as an executive or board member for several companies that have been acquired, Dave's life journey has been defined by his pursuit of new opportunities. This desire to try the novel, to provide something of value to others, has intrinsically been a part of who he is for as long as he can remember.

This tendency can show up even when someone has a clearly

defined job with a large company. Henry Gross had worked in sales for Bloomingdale's for twelve years and, throughout that time, he worked his job like it was a start-up. "He treated it like his own business, working long hours, traveling often, and doing whatever he had to do to get the job done," his wife, Nancy, told me.

They had been married for sixteen years when Henry finally decided to leave Bloomingdale's to start a specialty store in Princeton, New Jersey, the community where they lived. Nancy had just given birth to their first child. Despite her concerns with the timing, and the even greater stress and longer hours such a venture required, she didn't think to stand in Henry's way. "I worried that he would be miserable for the rest of his life if he didn't do this," she explained. "And it would be all my fault."

I felt the same way when Ned informed me just a few months before our wedding that he wanted to attend business school at Stanford University, the leading educational institution for entrepreneurship in the country. In college I had become a bit of a flaming liberal/environmentalist/social justice junkie, and the thought of being married to someone with an MBA, who was being groomed to flourish in our broken capitalist system, was horrifying to me. He might as well have told me he was running off to join the Taliban.

But I didn't feel like I could stand in the way of something that Ned was so excited about and would open up new opportunities for him. And he was more focused than I had ever seen him. So I gave him my blessing, even as I fretted over Ned's potentially shifting ideologies.

I realized soon after that my concerns were entirely misplaced. I should have been worrying about our marriage and our finances instead. My puny nonprofit salary forced us to live extremely frugally for the first two years of our marriage, even as Ned's school loan debts ballooned and his classmates regularly invited us out to hundred-dollar dinners. The only apartment near the Stanford campus we could afford was tiny, dilapidated, and owned by a cantankerous woman who was at least ninety years old. She liked to yell at us whenever we called to ask her a question, and she regularly let herself into our apartment to "fix" things.

On top of all this, I barely saw my husband for two years. The MBA has sometimes been called "the divorce degree," as the intensity of the experience and both the physical and emotional distances it creates have ended many a marital union.[6] A number of business schools now have programs and staff that cater to the needs of students' family members in hopes of stemming the tide.[7]

With its endless cycle of classes, group projects, student clubs, and pricey social events, business school was only the beginning for us. A couple of months into the school year, Ned began talking about a project he and his classmates called d.light, a play on the name of Stanford's design school (d.school for short), and their project goal: to create affordable lighting products for the developing world.

I loved the concept of d.light; I did not love what it required of Ned. The project quickly grew from an annoyance to a serious competitor for my husband's time and attention. d.light began seeping into all the cracks of extra time he had. Sometimes weeks would go by without our having a single meal together.

During the trying season that Ned was in business school, I forced myself to remember how Ned had fought for our relationship for years, even as I struggled to decide whether I could commit to someone so unconventional. Surely he wouldn't let the shininess of his schoolwork or his new business idea derail that. I also held on to his promise to find a paying job after he graduated. When he began interviewing for positions at large tech firms toward the end of his second year, I knew he was doing his part to honor that agreement.

In the late spring of 2007, I arrived home from work one day to find a large box nestled against the worn, creaky front door of our apartment. Not knowing what was inside, I dragged the package in the house and ripped it open. The box was filled to the brim with Google swag—a bright green athletic jacket, a rainbow cap, a blue Frisbee, pens, and other assorted tchotchkes. It was official. Ned had accepted a job with an excellent salary and great benefits at Google, that most giant of Silicon Valley companies. He would be managing an entrepreneurial team that developed new products and brought them to market. It was the best of both worlds: Ned would get to exorcise his entrepreneurial restlessness, and he would be paid handsomely to do so by someone else. I wanted to dance a celebratory jig as brightly colored Google health insurance and financial security rained down on me from the ceiling.

Even with his future cemented, though, Ned kept investing an inordinate amount of time in d.light—and the work he was doing had nothing to do with transitioning the business to someone else or closing it down.

A few weeks later, I arrived home to find another unexpected gift in our apartment: an oversize check for $250,000, made out to d.light from venture capital firm Draper Fisher Jurvetson. Ned and his four cofounders, a fellow business student and three engineers, had just won a major business plan competition that morning, resulting in more than enough start-up capital for d.light to become a reality. I was immensely proud of Ned, but I also braced myself for what was coming.

Sure enough, that same day, Ned carved a tiny bit of time out of his overflowing schedule to inform me that he was going to turn down the position at Google and work for d.light instead. We both knew he was de facto asking for my permission while assuming that I would give it to him. And he knew exactly how to push my social justice–junkie buttons.

"With this money, we'll be able to help thousands, maybe tens of thousands of families that are still using kerosene lamps," Ned explained, his voice rising in excitement as he waved his hands in large, sweeping circles. "I feel like we have to at least give it a shot."

I nodded in agreement, knowing that what he said was right even as my insides twisted in fear. I was now working for the housing department of a local county government, and my salary and benefits were better than they had been earlier in my career. But our family was still far from being financially stable. "How long will this money last you?" I had to ask.

"I'm not sure. Maybe a few months," Ned replied. "But we're going to leverage it to find other funding."

"Do you know if you'll be able to get more investment?"

"I don't know for sure, but there's a much better chance we can now."

He was right. Within six weeks, they had raised a total of $1.5 million from venture capital firms and social-impact funds, enough to launch the business and provide a decent salary for all five founders for at least a year. The company would provide no benefits, and Ned would be making less than half of what he would have made at Google. But in all the years I had known him, I had never seen him so animated. He was energized, motivated, driven—a man entirely confident in his calling to do this very business at this very moment. He was no longer running away from what he hated; he was running toward something that excited him and was, by every measure, incredibly meaningful. That had to be worth more than a huge paycheck, right?

Actually, yes. Though many of us assume that the very definition of a successful entrepreneur is the twenty-five-year-old semiretired billionaire, consider this surprising point: business experts—academics, investors, longtime practitioners—know that entrepreneurs motivated solely by money or the lure of success will likely not do well. For one thing, the chances of financial success, even moderate success, are relatively low. Only about one-third of owner-operated businesses earn more than $10,000 of profit annually, while the median profit for owner-operated firms is $39,000. The typical business owner actually earns 35 percent less over ten years than he would have earned working for someone else.[8]

That's not to say there aren't real-life stories of stunning financial success. In the investment industry they're called, appropriately, *unicorns*: start-ups with a valuation exceeding $1 billion. In high tech in particular, creating the next unicorn may not require more than a great idea and a few excellent coders. Think Instagram and WhatsApp, acquired by Facebook for $1 billion and $19 billion, respectively. But such businesses are extraordinarily rare; even those with a valuation in the millions are unusual.

And it takes an extraordinary amount of hard work to get there. Entrepreneurs motivated by money will likely become discouraged and give up, or they'll keep going but be miserable and hard to live with. If you're smart, hardworking, and ambitious, there are far easier ways to fill your bank account to bursting. (Also, striking it rich with a start-up isn't necessarily all it's cracked up to be. Sudden wealth and success can create their own host of problems, which we'll discuss in chapter 20.)

Entrepreneurs seeking status and public acclaim don't fare much better. Nancy Gross, the woman I mentioned earlier whose husband left Bloomingdale's to start the specialty store in Princeton all those years ago, now works for Stanford's Graduate School of Business and has seen all kinds of students with entrepreneurial ambitions come through her office. She says it doesn't take much to recognize the students who are drawn to the supposed glitz of entrepreneurship but have no idea what it entails. "They wanted to be fed. They wanted someone else to give them all the answers," she explained. "Sometimes they wouldn't even bring a pen and paper when they came in." Nancy and her colleagues instinctively knew that such entrepreneurs would never make it.

One reason why money- or status-driven entrepreneurs won't succeed is that they tend to make decisions that are bad for the business in the long run—though perhaps good for their own ego, image, or bank account in the short term. A woman I'll call Erin challenged her then-husband when he said he wanted to start a company making products for low-income families. "I knew he didn't give a shit about the people he was serving," she told me. "I know that sounds harsh, but it's true. He just wanted to start the next big thing and become famous. And because of that, I knew he would never succeed." She watched as he refused investors' calls to bring in more experienced leadership and alienated his employees with his top-down management style. Eventually, his intense need for control and obsession with the business (among other factors) caused their marriage to falter as well.

The risks of chasing money and fame exist in the arena of venture capital–funded start-ups as well. One Silicon Valley venture capitalist always attempts to discover an entrepreneur's core motivation before making a funding decision. He thinks of it this way: Is the entrepreneur motivated by money, fame, or a desire to change the world? It's not a question most of us would answer honestly, especially to someone from whom we'd like to collect a huge check. But over decades of funding start-ups, this investor has found that only those who want to change the world will persevere through the great challenges of building a company. So this investor typically gets the entrepreneur in a relaxed environment, maybe buys him or her a few drinks, and then probes gently around this question of motivation until he's found his answer.

Guy Kawasaki, who was the chief evangelist for Apple in the 1980s before he cofounded venture capital firm Garage Technology Ventures and became a bestselling author, puts it this way: "The best reason to start an organization is to make meaning—to create a product or service that makes the world a better place."[9] Today the archetypal example of this kind of world-changing dreamer is Elon Musk, cofounder of Tesla and founder of SpaceX. A recent biography of Musk called him "the possessed genius on the grandest quest anyone has ever concocted. . . . Where Mark Zuckerberg wants to help you share your baby photos, Musk wants to . . . well . . . save the human race from self-imposed or accidental annihilation."[10]

Entrepreneurs who seek to create something meaningful for the world, even if it's on a slightly smaller scale than saving humanity, gain something far more precious than finances: contentment. It turns out that entrepreneurs consistently report higher job satisfaction and overall happiness than those employed by someone else.[11] In fact, a global study of 197,000 entrepreneurs found that they have relatively higher rates of subjective well-being than their non-entrepreneurial peers, regardless of country or culture.[12] (It probably helps that entrepreneurs have a tendency to be optimistic about their own chances of success. One survey found that entrepreneurs could easily list challenges that a company founder would face, but often did not apply those same challenges to themselves.)[13]

That's not to say that entrepreneurs who have the right motivations will have perfectly rosy experiences starting their businesses.

Despite their greater job satisfaction, business founders work significantly longer hours and report higher levels of stress than those who work for someone else.[14] Another thing I've heard from entrepreneurs, Ned included: it's lonely work. Entrepreneurs bear a lot of responsibility and often do so alone. As much as they love controlling their own destiny, it's wearying to know that the buck always stops with them and no one else.

But that's where we as the significant others come in. Of the limited studies that have been conducted on entrepreneurial support networks, the consistent findings have been that having a strong network of supporters gives entrepreneurs a significant leg up. And the most critical source of support? Spouses, of course.[15]

While society already assumes that entrepreneurs are exceptional, I want to assure you that their spouses and partners are as well. It takes remarkable people like you to support the creative, independently minded, can't-help-themselves entrepreneurs we love. What I have discovered over the nineteen-plus years of my relationship with Ned is that my role—no matter how invisible, overlooked, or overshadowed—is absolutely critical. His ability to succeed professionally and personally, to remain grounded and healthy, and to have the right perspective on life's greatest priorities is all dependent on my willingness to truly be his partner.

Of course, my ability to be a good partner to Ned is contingent upon my ability to understand what in the world we're getting ourselves into. We'll talk next about that crazy, dynamic, resource-sucking organism commonly known as a *start-up*.

Meet the Start-up

O ver the years I've waffled between two definitions of a start-up: 1) a ticket to the greatest adventure of your life; or 2) a recipe for madness.

Perhaps it's a bit of both. I still can't say for sure.

When I agreed to support Ned in his pursuit of d.light, neither of us knew we would end up moving to China. From the beginning, Ned and his cofounders assumed they could manage all the company's operations through frequent travel. Ned oversaw their fledgling manufacturing processes in China, while his business school classmate Sam took on sales and marketing in India. The engineers managed product development and customer research, most of which took place in South Asia.

As soon as Ned graduated from business school, he began traveling more and more often to a city in China called Shenzhen. The Pearl River Delta region in which Shenzhen is based makes around 90 percent of the world's electronics—everything from calculators to laptops, and battery-operated toys to drones—leading many an entrepreneur to walk along its smoggy streets.[1] But, as we learned the hard way, manufacturing high-quality products in China doesn't just happen by itself. d.light's initial products were plagued with defects, quality issues, shipping challenges, and miscommunications with Chinese suppliers and manufacturers. To make matters worse, sales in India remained flat because we had trouble importing the products and developing strong relationships with distributors.

Things were clearly not working, and the team was burning through their funding fast.

After about eight months of working one-hundred-plus-hour weeks and traveling more than half the time, with few results to show for it, Ned and Sam had to do something to assure the investors breathing down their necks. They made the decision to move everything—including every*one*—overseas. Ned would go to China to open an office and build a local team there, Sam to India to do the same thing.

To his credit, Ned shared this very significant turn of events with me before he shared it with the rest of his cofounders. He knew this would never work without my support, but he also knew there was a fairly decent chance I would be willing to go all in with him. For years I had told Ned of my interest in living overseas and working in international development. And here he was, giving me the chance to prove the sincerity of my supposed dream by handing me the opportunity to live abroad and help change the world.

He gave me the hard sell, pitching the opportunity as seriously as if he were pitching to an investor. He showed me a series of photos he had taken on his recent trip to Shenzhen. The city was well developed, teeming with efficient public transportation systems and all the Starbucks, McDonald's, and KFC we could consume. "Just think how much we'll learn," he said fervently. "Think how interesting it'll be and the kinds of things we'll get to experience. And best of all, we'll get to do it together."

My lonely heart, which had spent far too many days without the company of my spouse, quickened at this promise of being *together*, of living unconventional lives *together*. But I still hesitated. I had never lived more than fifty miles from the town I grew up in, and, with a great job and a well-established social circle, I had plenty of reasons to stay. "What if we stayed here and you just traveled a lot?" I asked.

We did the math. Ned would likely need to travel two-thirds or even three-quarters of the time. But his current level of travel had already taken a toll on our relationship. Though we had been married for less than three years, our individual lives were already seriously diverging. Some of my friends had never even seen Ned and wondered about his existence. He was an actual, flesh-and-blood person, right? they'd ask. He wasn't a figment of my imagination?

During business school, we knew of a few of Ned's classmates who had maintained a long-distance marriage for the duration of the two-year program. Most of those couples ended up divorced. We agreed that if we wanted to stay married, we would have to spend most of our time in the same city. The only way Ned could stay with me in the Bay Area was if he left d.light—and we both knew that was not an option.

China it would be, then. That meant I had to resign from a meaningful job with plenty of advancement opportunities and say good-bye to the only home I had ever known. The mochas and burgers, I told Ned, had better be delicious.

Not everyone could make the same decision. Of the three

founding engineers, only one elected to move to China with us. The other two, including the only other founder who was married, decided to stay in the US and phase out of the company altogether.

I continued to doubt the wisdom and necessity of our move long after the decision had been finalized. "Are you absolutely sure you have to be overseas full-time?" I asked Ned at least once a week. In the relatively short time since d.light had become more than a concept, the company's business plan had changed so drastically and with such frequency—they were launching one product! No, three products! They would be AC-powered! No, solar-powered! No, both-powered!—that I couldn't be sure it wouldn't change again.

Unlike the other aspects of the business, Ned never budged on this decision. "Yes," he assured me over and over again. "We can't run the business from the US. It won't work and it's too expensive."

. In the spring of 2008, Ned and I broke the news to our family and friends. They responded with almost universal excitement: *How wonderful! What an adventure! Good for you!* Everyone in our Silicon Valley bubble loved the idea of a start-up, especially one trying to do social good, and couldn't imagine a more glamorous life than moving overseas to make our professional dreams come true. We were showered with gifts and well-wishes and farewell parties.

If only they knew what was to come. More importantly, if only *we* knew what was to come.

Despite being Chinese American, nothing in my upbringing had prepared me for life in mainland China. I had visited the country only once as a tourist and had never set foot in Shenzhen. But there was neither time nor money for me to take a scouting trip before we moved. Every day that we delayed meant more time in which the products were not being made in the right way nor distributed to the right people. The company was bleeding money, and any pleading I made about needing more time to pack or say good-bye or rethink this life-changing decision felt insignificant in the face of a dream on the cusp of cardiac arrest.

I was planning a new life in a country I knew almost nothing about, banking on a company that still had a very small chance of succeeding. I was no stranger to taking risks—I had been working in low-income communities for seven years, often attending meetings in which I was the youngest individual and the only Asian American in the room—but the degree to which we were staking our livelihoods on something that could implode at any moment boggled my mind a bit.

Even more alarming was the frequency with which I had to answer well-meaning questions from friends with the words *I don't know*.

"How long will you be there?"

I don't know.

"What will you do there?"

I don't know.

"Will you be able to find friends?"

I don't know.

"What will it be like to live in a Communist country?"

I don't know.

As I started to experience heart palpitations and bouts of anxiety about the transition, friends tried to offer helpful advice. Maybe *the company* could hire packers or movers. *The company* could cover our moving costs. *The company* could have someone in Shenzhen set up our apartment before we arrived. *The company* could take care of our visas. *The company* could send someone to meet us at the airport. *The company* could provide an assistant or interpreter to help us get settled.

"There is no 'the company,' " I tried to explain over and over again. "*We* are the company." Any work that had to be done would come from our own labor, sweat, and late nights. Anything that had to be paid for would come out of our own limited savings. When we arrived in China, any setting up or settling down would be our own responsibility, despite the fact that we were ignorant, illiterate, and friendless.

I didn't know it at the time, but I was experiencing two of the classic characteristics of start-up life: uncertainty and going it alone.

These are some of the things that don't typically exist in start-ups, at least in the beginning: paychecks, health insurance, job descriptions, assistants, business phone lines, office space, office supplies, tech support, reimbursements, vacation days, sick days, comp time, delegation, boundaries, work-life balance, timelines, guarantees, and answers. Believe me, I know. I asked Ned about every single one of these—especially health insurance, timelines, and answers. I prayed fervently for guarantees, but those weren't coming either.

Most start-ups begin with this: one person, or maybe two or three, and a home office, which could be anything from a kitchen table or garage workbench to a desk or a dedicated room. Those who live in cities with high real estate prices, like San Francisco or New York City, might spend a few hundred dollars a month to rent a desk in a coworking space. Ned's company resided on a cofounder's dining table for months before they could afford office space. The cofounder and his wife were relegated to eating on the couch. Luckily for them, this lasted for only a few months. One study found that fewer than 5 percent of home-based businesses moved out of the home within a five-year period.[2]

Perhaps even more surprising, not all businesses begin as a fully formed idea. An astonishing 42 percent of new business founders start a company before they have identified a business idea, and nearly half of them change their business idea at least once.[3] There is nothing about the start-up life, not even its inception or its purpose, that is predictably linear.

As you might expect, the conceptual phase (or lack thereof) is where problems between significant others can already begin. In the 2014–15 academic year, Ryann Price oversaw a two-quarter course at the Stanford Graduate School of Business called Startup Garage. The course simulates the start-up experience and lays the groundwork for students to launch new ventures when they graduate. Entrepreneurship is becoming increasingly popular with each incoming cohort, which is why Startup Garage attracted more than 25 percent of the school's second-year MBA students that fall. But by the start of the second quarter, the number of students in the class had dropped from 140 to only 50.

According to Ryann, the majority of those who left the class had finally wrapped their minds around the "emotional risk" that pursuing a start-up involved. When the dream began to turn into a reality they weren't sure they wanted to live, they left. For those with significant others, their partners' protests played a major role in their leaving.

When I asked Ryann what the difference was between significant others who supported their entrepreneurs and those that didn't, she immediately replied, "The nos come from spouses when the entrepreneurs are still exploring. If they can't communicate a clear vision or goal, then their spouses can't get on board."

An insatiable passion for the business, however, can certainly win over the reluctant significant other. Vanessa Quigley of Provo, Utah, had many reasons not to support her husband Nate's decision to pursue a start-up. Even as he was finishing up his

MBA program, she was caring for their three young children and expecting a fourth. They were saddled with large school debts. But instead of returning to a cushy management consulting job, Nate wanted to team up with some friends to create a software company aimed at helping distributors get their products into convenience stores.

I asked Vanessa why she supported this decision when their life circumstances seemed to indicate it wasn't the wisest choice. "It was a leap of faith for me. But I believed that he wanted this badly enough, and so it was going to work out," she explained. "We didn't draw a list of pros and cons. It was just clear that this was where his passion was. As a student he spent way more time on business plans than reading cases. It was obvious that he was supposed to do this."

But even with all the vision and passion in the world, no entrepreneur can avoid taking risks, especially financial risks. It just comes with the territory. The typical new business requires about $30,000 to get off the ground, though a more ambitious business plan could require a significantly higher investment.[4] The majority of entrepreneurs provide these funds on their own—by charging their credit cards, or pulling money out of their savings, retirement funds, kids' college funds, or getting a second mortgage. A smaller number secure bank loans or borrow from family members and friends, and an even tinier portion seek venture capital funding. Women entrepreneurs remain at a significant disadvantage when it comes to outside investment: in 2016, male-run companies received more than sixteen times more venture capital funding than female-run companies, which received only 2.19 percent of all venture capital funding in the US.[5] This may be why female entrepreneurs are almost two times more likely than their male counterparts to seek early-stage funding from business partners.[6]

In recent years, crowdfunding has also become an increasingly popular option for entrepreneurs from all industries, funding everything from the latest skateboard and video game to an entire feature film or musical album. Launching a successful crowd-funding campaign isn't necessarily as easy as it sounds, however, as marketing the campaign and managing hundreds, if not thousands, of backers can suck up significant time and resources. As of May 2017, Kickstarter, the most popular crowdfunding platform, reported that only 35.83 percent of its campaigns were successfully funded. And more than two-thirds of the successful campaigns raised less than $10,000.[7]

Regardless of where the money comes from, that initial investment likely won't make its way back into the entrepreneurs' pockets anytime soon. Only 11 percent of new businesses are able to make a single sale by the end of their first month of operation.[8] Unfortunately, living with debt or a minimal budget is a concept that almost all company founders—and their families—are uncomfortably familiar with.

From personal experience, I can say that financial stresses don't go away when a business has secured outside investment. Even though d.light was a venture-backed company from early on, the vast majority of that money went into business operations rather than salaries, reimbursements, and decent health insurance. Whenever the business had severe cash flow problems—which happened several times—the first things that Ned and his business partner axed were their own salaries. (Each time this happened, I felt both great respect for and great frustration at Ned.)

Unsurprisingly, the conceptual instability and financial uncertainty so common to start-ups can bleed over into almost every area of life. Without a clear sense of your joint income, it's hard to establish a budget. When your significant other is working in the home at all hours, she never actually leaves her job and has limited, if any, time for you or your family. Planning a night out becomes challenging, let alone a weekend away or a vacation. Family members may question what she is doing: "When is she going to get a *real* job?"

If you are anything like me—and I consider myself fairly typical in this regard—then you will have some trouble with this uncertainty, especially when it seems self-inflicted. *What do you mean, you're rewriting your entire business plan? Why in the world are you making a new product when you still haven't sold the old one? And when are you going to start giving yourself a paycheck?* But such is the start-up life: It grows in fits and starts. It develops through pivots and learning from mistakes. It succeeds through big risks, flexibility, and educated guesses.

Because I enjoy a well-defined, predictable life, I have struggled for years to understand this reality. Why? Why does it have to be this way?

Investor and billionaire Howard Marks, cofounder of global asset management firm Oaktree Capital Management, is well positioned to answer this question. After thirty-plus years as a remarkably successful investor, he has developed a two-by-two matrix to demonstrate when investors can expect outstanding returns.[9] For me, this matrix also begins to explain why the start-up life cycle has to be so zigzaggy and tumultuous. According to Marks, all business ideas are either driven by conventional or unconventional behavior. Both can lead to either favorable or unfavorable outcomes. But he draws a distinction between so-so favorable outcomes, like a modest return on investment, and what investors really want: the big, flashy, 10x-factor "above-average good results."

	Conventional Behavior	Unconventional Behavior
Favorable Outcomes	Average good results	Above-average good results
Unfavorable Outcomes	Average bad results	Below-average results

Even if making money isn't what's driving your entrepreneur, Marks's model is still applicable. Every entrepreneur I have ever met, regardless of their deepest motivations, wants positive results—whether it be by providing for his family, creating a useful product, impacting an industry, or changing systems and lives. To meet any of these goals, the venture has to generate revenue. As Guy Kawasaki writes, "You can't change the world if you're dead, and when you're out of money you're dead."[10]

Some business owners are content to live in the conventional behavior/favorable outcomes box if their primary objectives are to have a flexible schedule and earn just enough to support themselves. This usually involves starting something in a well-established industry with a proven, robust market, such as educational apps for children or fashion accessories for women. I have great respect for entrepreneurs who pursue what's commonly called *lifestyle businesses* and make it work for them. By definition, though, these are not the entrepreneurs who are willing to risk a lot for their businesses; they are also probably not the entrepreneurs who drive their significant others batty. They may actually enjoy relatively placid family lives.

But not so for those of us in bed with entrepreneurs who dream of succeeding big. The success that they are seeking (however they define it for themselves) most likely requires a deep foray into the unconventional behavior side of the matrix. Now we can begin to see why the start-up life is a bit crazy making. Your entrepreneur may have a fantastic, world-changing idea, but few people, if any, will recognize it. They will question her. They will challenge him. They will refuse to invest in her. They will not work for him. They will need a lot of convincing to buy her product.

Put another way, a great but unconventional idea hasn't been successfully implemented before. No one, your beloved entrepreneur included, really knows how to pursue this dream. The entire process to get there, let alone the end product or service itself, remains untested and unproven. Major triumphs—like securing funding or signing a big customer—rarely offer relief but instead lead to more pressure and more challenges. You may not have the processes and controls to manage the funding you just received. You can't deliver the products quickly enough for your new customers. You have no idea if you can meet the targets that you are now accountable for to an ever-growing list of stakeholders with competing interests. No wonder, then, that only 45 percent of new firms last five years, and only 29 percent last ten years.[11]

At a Kauffman Foundation training for aspiring entrepreneurs a few years back, a venture capitalist warned, "There will be a moment in time, if the start-up takes off, that will be like drinking out of a fire hose." And that's if things go *well*.

Assuming you can tolerate the short-term pressures—and not everyone can—the chances of long-term success remain pretty small. Only one-third of those who set out to start businesses have something "up and running" within *seven* years.[12] Even Y Combinator, the much-touted Silicon Valley start-up incubator, reported that 93 percent of its ventures—selected through a highly competitive process—eventually failed.[13]

A decade after its founding, Ned's company has hundreds of employees and millions in monthly revenue. It doesn't look like a new business anymore. But I can't think of a significant period of time in the last ten years in which it didn't feel like a start-up. If anything, the stakes have only gotten higher as more and more people become dependent on d.light for employment and the services it offers.

Given the low odds of success that all new companies have to contend with, any substantial effort to make a business work—especially before someone else makes it big with the same idea—requires substantial resources. That includes money, of course. But it also includes time. In his national bestseller *Outliers: The Story of Success*, Malcolm Gladwell relays how every exceptional artist, athlete, innovator, and intellectual we know—from the Beatles and Mozart to Bill Gates and chess grandmaster Bobby Fischer—had to invest ten thousand hours of practice in order to master a skill. Gladwell calls it "the magic number of greatness."[14]

The same time commitment, and perhaps even more, may be required of the nascent entrepreneur, who is trying to become proficient in multiple areas of expertise as quickly as possible: how to run a business, how to do every job in the company, how to develop and disseminate a product or service, how to succeed in a particular industry, and more. To meet that ten thousand hours, your significant other would need to work ten hours a day, every single day, for nearly three years.

The most dogged entrepreneurs I've seen are willing to do anything and everything, whenever it's required, to optimize the chances of success. A company founder who is going at it alone and requires minimal capital needs to spend one year of full-time effort just to get his new business started; for larger teams with more complex and costly business models, this could take significantly longer. Some experts estimate that it may take six to seven years for a start-up to become an established firm.[15]

Several years operating at maximum capacity on a full sprint with no guarantees? That's a lot to ask of anyone.

When Ned and I moved to China, we were only at the beginning of that sprint. But, without anyone to help us, I was quickly overwhelmed by how much there was to do—and how much we had to sacrifice for the sake of the company. We applied for our own visas and bought our own one-way plane tickets. A few weeks before our move, Ned traveled to Shenzhen, found an apartment and an office, and opened a bank account. We packed no more than what we could fit into four large suitcases, with no idea as to whether that would be enough to build a new life in a new country. After we arrived, we shopped and paid for all the household and personal items we needed. We carried Chinese-English dictionaries with us everywhere we went. We converted a significant chunk of our personal savings into Chinese *renminbi* and deposited it into a local bank.

On the business side, Ned and his engineer cofounder did all the business negotiations themselves. They spent many nights building business relationships over lavish Chinese banquets and drank far too many glasses of *baijiu*, a disgustingly strong Chinese alcoholic beverage. Ned signed endless contracts written solely in Chinese, hoping against hope that his suppliers weren't trying to take advantage of him. I started working full-time for Ned's company because he desperately needed the help, and I, frankly, didn't have any other good options for how to spend my time. I oversaw the company's public relations, communications, and human resources, with little idea of what I was doing.

We were putting all our chips in the unconventional behavior side of the matrix. If I thought Ned's previous children's music and ringtone businesses had impacted my life, it was nothing compared to how much my life was about to change now. I felt exhilarated and terrified, all at once, during almost every waking moment. I thought we were living the craziest lives imaginable.

Oddly enough, we weren't. The move to China aside, we were actually living pretty typical start-up lives. The financial risk, the big lifestyle changes, the infinite workload, the way in which Ned's company had taken over our lives—for better or worse, these are actually pretty normal circumstances when it comes to life with an entrepreneur.

3

The Entrepreneurial Life

L et's get to the bad news right away: it is normal and expected for entrepreneurs to work ridiculously long hours.

In one UK survey, entrepreneurs reported working 63 percent longer each week than the average worker.[1] In the US, more than 40 percent of founders surveyed said that they are on the clock for fifty or more hours a week.[2] Many entrepreneurs I know regularly work up to and even beyond eighty hours a week.

The constant connectivity enabled by smartphones, tablets, and laptops sure isn't helping. A recent study by the American Psychological Association's Center for Organizational Excellence found that more than 50 percent of working adults check their email before and after work, on weekends, and even when they're home sick. If your entrepreneur is male, the tendency to log in after hours is even greater.[3] One reason could be the *telepressure*— or, "the urge to respond immediately to work-related messages, no matter when they come"—that many American professionals experience today.[4] Entrepreneurs, whose companies are their babies and whose homes are often their offices, live with telepressure in spades.

When you look more closely, it's easy to see how the hours add up. Entrepreneurs officially work at least fifty hours a week, probably more. Then they go home, laptops in one hand and smartphones in the other, and keep working. They're making phone calls, responding to emails, strategizing in their free time. And then there's the travel.

Studies haven't been done on how much entrepreneurs travel, but almost every entrepreneur I know has to travel. As our world becomes smaller, this will probably become more and more commonplace. Investors may be scattered around the globe. Suppliers will be in one corner of the planet, distributors in another. IT support could be outsourced to one country and accounting to another. Customers might be spread across six continents. In 2016 alone, Americans logged 457.4 million person-trips for business.[5] Ned estimates that he's flown 1.5 million miles for the business over the past ten years, which, in some circles, is considered pretty run-of-the-mill. Perhaps your mate has traveled just as much, if not more, for his or her company.

It's no wonder, then, that venture capitalists have been accused of having an age bias when selecting their investees. Young, single entrepreneurs, unencumbered with any other responsibilities, are the ideal workhorses. Michael Moritz, a venture capitalist with Sequoia Capital, one of the most prestigious investment firms in the world, has famously said that he's "an incredibly enthusiastic fan of very talented twentysomethings starting companies." Why? "They have great passion. They don't have distractions like families and children and other things that get in the way."[6]

While few in the investment community would dare say it so

baldly, the vast majority retain sky-high expectations of an entrepreneur's commitment, regardless of personal circumstances.
Married or not, with kids or not: the company founder who wants
to be taken seriously must prioritize the business—heart, soul,
body, and mind.

   This is definitely not a recipe for a healthy marriage or a robust
personal life. But there's a reason why this is the norm in the
start-up world: few new businesses can succeed without extensive
investments of time and energy. That's why entrepreneurs, many
of whom started a business to have more say over their own lives,
often end up having *less* control over what they do and when they
do it. Meg Cadoux Hirshberg, wife of Gary Hirshberg, the first
CEO of Stonyfield Farm, has written extensively about her experience of being hitched to her husband's dream. She explains that
"businesses are like babies: they need you when they need you.
And they *always* need you—your time, your attention, and your
energy."[7]

   Every entrepreneur I've met feels the pressure to prioritize the
business first, and it shows in their behavior and their decisions.
Ned's business partner, Sam, was riding his bike to work one day
when a bike coming from the opposite direction suddenly clipped
his. Sam went flying and crashed into the ground—hard. One of
his arms was in excruciating pain, at least sprained, possibly broken, he guessed.

   At that moment his cell phone rang. Sam saw that it was a
potential investor that was still doing due diligence on d.light but
seemed on the cusp of investing. Sam braced his aching arm and
took the call.

   The investor, noticing that Sam's voice sounded strained, asked
him if he was okay.

"I just got in a bike accident," Sam replied honestly.

"Do you want to talk later?" the investor offered.

"No, I'm fine. Let's talk now," Sam said. It seemed like a logical choice at the time. Answer investor questions first, go to the hospital later.

Clearly impressed, the investor paused for a moment—and then launched into his latest round of questions about the business. Shortly after that conversation, the investor agreed to put money into d.light, citing the founders' total commitment to the company as a factor in his decision.

The start-up may require this kind of hyperactive devotion for several years before it evolves into a more established firm (assuming it survives that long). And I can't overemphasize the intensity of the experience—thus the previous analogy of drinking out of a fire hose.

Well, people who drink out of fire hoses for prolonged periods of time rarely come out unscathed.

In the Silicon Valley circles that surround me, entrepreneurs are universally admired. Say the names *Steve Jobs* or *Mark Zuckerberg*, and it's not unusual to see people's faces begin to glow. Even the entrepreneurs who fail big—like those who started Webvan or Pets.com before the dot-com bust at the turn of the millennium—are revered. They did it. They lived the dream. They had the chutzpah to chase their ambitions, even if they flamed out.

But here's what we almost never hear in the romantic yarns about pursuing start-up dreams: being an entrepreneur is out-of-this-world stressful. When I met Ned in college, he was one of the most lighthearted, carefree people I had ever known. Today, nineteen years later, his head is full of gray hair. He regularly goes through periods when he can't sleep, doesn't exercise, barely remembers to eat, and oozes anxiety like sweat. He unquestionably loves what he does, but the frequent ups and downs and loop-the-loops have taken a huge toll on him.

One entrepreneur uses this analogy to explain what it's like: Imagine a man riding a lion. Others look at him and think, "This guy's really got it together! He's brave!" But the man on the lion is thinking: "How the hell did I get on a lion, and how do I keep from getting eaten?"[8]

Kelly McGonigal, a leading health psychologist who teaches at the Stanford University School of Medicine, defines *stress* this way: "Stress is what arises when something you care about is at stake."[9] In everyday life, the list of things we care about ranges from the mundane (being on time for an appointment) to the earth-shattering (the survival of a loved one). For company founders, the birth of a new business creates a host of new things that are at stake:

- The idea
- The product or service
- The business model
- The cofounders
- The funding
- The investors
- The employees and their families
- The customers
- Other stakeholders (external partners, advisers, advocates, lenders, etc.)

And that's on top of the personal things that entrepreneurs risk when they strike out on their own:

- Their dreams and ideals
- Their reputation

- Their competence
- Their financial situation
- Their family's well-being
- Their career trajectory
- Their confidence
- Their identity

These are not trivial things that entrepreneurs are laying on the line. No wonder building a business can sometimes feel like a life-and-death venture. And no wonder entrepreneurs' stress levels can seem monumental. If your beloved is right in the middle of the start-up process, he's probably feeling that stress with every breath.

While we may think of stress as uniformly negative, psychologists actually separate stress into two subcategories: *eustress* and *distress*. Eustress, first explored by pioneering psychologist Richard Lazarus in the 1960s, is stress that is good for you.[10] Eustress invigorates you, pushes you to achieve a goal, and often leads to feelings of fulfillment.[11] Distress, on the other hand, leads to the negative impacts that we more commonly associate with stress, including anxiety, impaired thinking, and illness.[12] Most interestingly, what causes us to feel eustress or distress is not the specific stressor, but our *perception* of that stressor: Is it a positive challenge or a negative threat?[13]

Unsurprisingly, entrepreneurs seem to experience copious amounts of both kinds of stress. You've probably already seen the effects of eustress on your significant other: that light in her eyes; that fire in his belly; that insatiable excitement to do something new, different, and challenging. Some people come alive when faced with the challenge of starting up a new venture. A friend of ours, who recently started his own investment firm, called it "the most stressful fun" he's ever had.

Leanor Ortega Till of Denver, Colorado, has seen astonishing changes in her husband, Stephen, since he started his screenprinting business in 2010. Many people around them—herself included—weren't convinced he could do it. "I was against it from the beginning," she admitted. "I told him, 'I've never seen you lead anything.' " But Stephen took those doubts and questions and used them as motivation. "When people say you can't do this . . . that gives him a burst of inspiration like no other," she explained to me. "Now he's one of the best bosses I've ever seen." Stephen used his loved ones' critiques and doubts to fuel eustress instead of distress.

For all my concerns and complaints about Ned's entrepreneurial ambitions, I've clearly seen how pursuing a start-up fed his spirit and stretched his intellect like nothing else. It isn't something I've ever wanted to stand in the way of, especially given how Ned felt in that audio software engineering job he had right after college. A decade and a half later, this is how he describes it: "Every day I went there, I felt like I was dying. It was a soul-killing experience for me." Or, to put it more clinically, he was not experiencing eustress. There was nothing driving him to do better or be better.

Compare that to what happened when Ned and his business partner, Sam, had to pitch d.light in the Draper Fisher Jurvetson business plan competition I mentioned in chapter 1. Here's the behind-the-scenes story of how that $250,000 check ended up in our living room.

With all the work they were juggling as second-year MBA students, Ned and Sam actually forgot about the competition until eleven o'clock the night before. They haphazardly threw together a presentation with just a few hours to spare. Only after giving the presentation before a panel of judges at the competition did they realize they were supposed to have prepared a second, even longer presentation. They created it on the spot, taking the sixty-minute lunch break to put together a PowerPoint and come up with talking points. While the other competitors enjoyed filet mignon and quinoa salad, Ned and Sam—sweating and starving—paced outside in the parking lot and practiced, practiced, practiced. When they returned, they gave what Ned considers the best presentation they have ever given in the history of d.light. They successfully won over the most skeptical judge and even moved some audience members to tears.

That $250,000 prize launched the entire company. This is eustress at its best.

But when does eustress turn into distress? According to the American Psychological Association, "an extreme amount of stress can have health consequences and adversely affect the immune, cardiovascular, neuroendocrine and central nervous systems."[14] The point at which these negative effects kick in will differ for everyone, of course, given our individual capacities to cope with challenging circumstances. It's likely that entrepreneurs, renowned for their expansive sense of optimism, have a higher capacity for perceiving stressors as positive challenges. However, the start-up path is so demanding that even the most buoyant entrepreneur will experience some distress.

For one thing, distress is more likely to come about when stress becomes chronic. Evolutionarily, stress was designed to help us survive occasional threats like bear attacks and flash floods. But when stress goes on for months or years, without any time in between to recover, the structures of our brains actually change in response. We live in a constant fight-or-flight mode, causing our brains to function less efficiently and become more vulnerable to mental disease.[15] We become less resilient and less able to cope with stress, not more. Human beings—whether entrepreneurs or not—are not built to be under high degrees of stress, nonstop, for years on end.

Then there's the sheer number of stressors entrepreneurs experience. When I asked Bill Reichert, managing director of venture capital firm Garage Technology Ventures, what he would most want the partners of entrepreneurs to know, he replied, "What's hard for a spouse to appreciate is all the different pressures that a founder is under. It's hard to communicate this. There's pressure from the team, from investors, from customers, and others."

This pressure can come in many forms, from difficult personalities and relational conflicts to deadlines and financial challenges. Investors almost always push business founders to accomplish more in a shorter amount of time. Team members demand to be heard, respected, affirmed, and included. Customers ask for higher quality, lower prices, and responsive service. It's easy to see how the entrepreneur may feel like she is constantly and simultaneously juggling the needs, opinions, and demands of multiple stakeholders—and how she will likely feel that she is failing to please anyone in the process. On top of all this, she is probably doing the work of at least five people.

For those of you who think more quantitatively, here's another way of weighing the stress caused by a start-up. You may have heard of the Holmes and Rahe stress scale, a list of stressful life events that can contribute to illness. It was developed by psychiatrists Thomas Holmes and Richard Rahe back in the 1960s, and scientific research on the immense physical toll of stress has only reinforced it in the fifty years since. Of the forty-three items on the list, I can conservatively count at least a dozen that will likely affect a household at the start of a new business, including: taking on a mortgage or loan; major change in responsibilities at work; major changes in working hours or conditions; major change in type and/or amount of recreation; and major change in sleeping habits. Add all these life changes together, and it's actually quite easy to exceed the scale's threshold score of three hundred for someone at high risk of illness.[16]

These high levels of stress exist even when everything is going right. If something goes wrong—and your entrepreneur would have to live an extraordinarily charmed existence not to have something go wrong—there are no limits on the amount of stress he may experience.

Jake and Hillary Denham of Denver, Colorado, have been running their own carpet cleaning and water damage restoration business since 2008. Today the company is doing great, but that's only because it survived what Jake calls "the winter from hell." In late 2013, the Denver area was hit by a freak rainstorm that caused flooding across the city. The Denhams responded to the sudden spike in demand by hiring another full-time employee and spending $25,000 on additional equipment. That month they restored more than forty flooded properties, a 400 percent increase over a typical month. But the following month, the number of calls they got inexplicably dropped to 80 percent below their average—and stayed there for the next eight months. "I spent $120,000 over four months to keep the company going. I used every line of credit I could," Jake recounted. "Our employees were leaving. We had no money. We didn't even have money to buy food for the kids. We were hopeless and depressed."

At the height of the winter from hell, Hillary found out she was expecting a third child. She sobbed as she broke the news to her husband: "Jake, I'm so sorry! I'm pregnant!" Jake remembers going out to the porch, sitting down, and being unable to move or speak for at least an hour. "We were barely surviving, and now we had another human being coming into the world," he explained.

It took ten excruciating months of cutting expenses, laying off employees, and doing everything on their own again, along with extremely frugal living, for the Denhams to climb back out of that hole.

Needless to say, Jake and Hillary were feeling distress, not eustress, throughout that season. The number of things they cared about that were at stake and the volume of external challenges that they couldn't control were overwhelming. In such a situation, running the business together may have hurt them more than it helped. When both partners experience the same stressors at the same time, it's extremely difficult to shore one another up. Jake and Hillary's marriage survived—but not without a lot of work to prioritize the relationship before their dreams of building a big and successful business.

After we moved to China, Ned and I experienced our own parade of horribles, which tested our relationship and our individual mental health to the breaking point. (I broke. Ned didn't. That's why he's the entrepreneur in the family.) I had naively thought that moving the company overseas would solve its most pressing problems. But the challenges that came our way after we moved to China were far, far worse. Here is a sampling of the greatest stressors we experienced in the first six months after we moved:

- Feeling overly ambitious, we tried to launch three products at once. But two of the products were hastily designed and did not fit the market. We ended up having to cut those two products before they launched, costing the company significant time and money.
- Ned and Sam had to work desperately to secure a new round of funding. They had already deferred their own salaries to keep

the company alive as investors hemmed and hawed over the decision. The day the investors finally signed the term sheets and began wiring the money to d.light's account was the same day in 2008 that Lehman Brothers collapsed, marking the dramatic beginning of the worldwide Great Recession. If the deal had been delayed by even twenty-four hours, the entire thing would likely have fallen through and spelled the death of the company.

- We received our very first container order—a tremendous victory for the still-young business—and filled the container with 6,300 products that had a 100 percent failure rate. Of course, we didn't discover this until the container was already in the middle of the Indian Ocean, halfway to East Africa. Another container, sent to the team in India, was full of the same defective products. A couple of team members from China went to India to rework all the units, but they couldn't do it fast enough to fulfill orders. They had to hire an entire team of temporary workers to work around the clock for one week.

Talk to almost any entrepreneur and you will hear similar stories: living under six figures of debt; losing key investors, customers, or business partners; dealing with crashing websites and malfunctioning products at the worst possible moment. No doubt your entrepreneur has experienced something like this already. Any of these circumstances would create a huge amount of stress—and that stress has an impact.

In a recent Gallup-Healthways Well-Being Index, 34 percent of entrepreneurs reported feeling worried, and 45 percent said they were stressed. In both instances, these numbers were several percentage points higher than that of other kinds of workers.[17] In another study, conducted by researchers across several California universities, *72 percent* of entrepreneurs self-reported mental health concerns. About one-half of the study's 242 participants said they had one or more lifetime mental health conditions. A sizable number reported struggling with depression (30 percent), ADHD (29 percent), and substance use conditions (12 percent).[18] In contrast, the Centers for Disease Control and Prevention has found that about 7.6 percent of the general population over the age of twelve are depressed, the majority of them women.[19]

It's possible that some of these numbers might be attributable to the well-documented link between creative genius and mental illness.[20] But the brutal start-up environment certainly can't be helping.

Ben Horowitz, an entrepreneur-turned-investor who was one of Netscape's first product managers, has blogged frankly about the monumental challenges that come up over and over again when one is following the entrepreneurial path. He calls it "the Struggle" in a passage that would be beautifully poetic if it didn't make start-up life sound like one of the nine circles of hell. Here's an excerpt: "The Struggle is when you are surrounded by people and you are all alone. The Struggle has no mercy. The Struggle is the land of broken promises and crushed dreams. The Struggle is a cold sweat. The Struggle is where your guts boil so much that you feel like you are going to spit blood."[21]

I don't know about you, but reading that makes me want to curl up in a ball and call my mother.

It's no wonder, then, that entrepreneurs seem particularly susceptible to burnout. Drena Fagen, an art therapist and social worker in New York City who specializes in burnout, defines it as "the gap that exists between our expectations and what is actually possible."[22] For our perpetually dreaming entrepreneurs, this gap could be as wide as the Grand Canyon. "We occupy the land of the unknown—each of us is an inventor and innovator in our own ways," writes author and businesswoman Adelaide Lancaster. "There are no maps, no guidebooks, and no pre-defined expectations." But then she goes on to say: "No one knows what is possible, and that's what is exciting."[23]

Are our beloved entrepreneurs gluttons for punishment? It's tempting to think this, but it may be more accurate to think of them as gluttons for a challenging, thrilling adventure. Taking the risk to pursue a passion, to overcome seemingly insurmountable odds, to create something with lasting value for society, can give an adrenaline rush like nothing else. Just ask the 550,000 Americans who are flocking to start their own businesses every single *month*.[24]

If launching a new venture were easy, it probably wouldn't be nearly as fun or satisfying. Richard Branson, the billionaire founder of Virgin Group, is known for saying (with his typical swagger), "If you want swashbuckling action in your life, become an entrepreneur and give it a go."[25] Even the very down-to-earth Apple cofounder Steve Wozniak, whose favorite haunt is Outback Steakhouse, can't resist encouraging aspiring entrepreneurs to take the plunge. "If you love what you do and are willing to do what it takes, it's within your reach," he writes in his memoir. "And it'll be worth every minute you spend alone at night, thinking and thinking about what it is you want to design or build. It'll be worth it, I promise."[26]

The allure of an adventurous, fulfilling, and inspirational life is something that few of us are immune to. But the entrepreneurial path exacts a cost, almost all of which is personal. Entrepreneurs live at the epicenter of the Struggle and breathe and bleed every high and low. This inevitably affects their health, their character, their priorities—and their loved ones.

Even if you have the most solid relationship in the world, and you yourself are healthy and well-adjusted and content with your life, the stresses of your significant other's new business will impact you. Recent studies have found that stress is as contagious as the common cold. Being around a stressed individual or even just seeing him or her on video—beware video chats!—will elevate your own cortisol levels.[27] In addition, stress caused by factors wholly outside the relationship can deeply affect marriages. Social scientists call this phenomenon *stress spillover*, and it can do everything from increase marital conflict to cause you to like your spouse less.[28]

And no wonder. In my research and the interviews I've conducted, I've come across the same metaphors again and again to describe a start-up: It's like a child. A lover. An obsession. The center of your beloved's universe. And life in this strange threesome—you, your entrepreneur, and the business—is its own unique adventure.

4

The Entrepreneurial Relationship

If I asked you to conjure up an image of Steve Jobs, chances are that you would picture him wearing a black turtleneck. He wore that rather bland garment every single day in his later years—whether in the office, at home, or before thousands of adoring fans at Apple's annual Worldwide Developers Conference. This might seem like an odd quirk of a particularly brilliant man, but he's not the only one. Mark Zuckerberg dons the same gray T-shirt in television interviews, business meetings, and family photos with his wife and baby. Other well-known people who have stuck with such banal uniforms include Albert Einstein, Segway inventor Dean Kamen, and even President Barack Obama.[1]

Fashion icons they are not, but their commitment to wearing the same clothes is deliberate. And it provides an important clue for understanding what life with an entrepreneur is like.

At his first-ever public Q&A in 2014, Zuckerberg explained why he wore the same T-shirt every day: "I really want to clear my life to make it so that I have to make as few decisions as possible about anything except how to best serve this community."[2] Even small decisions like choosing what to wear or deciding what to eat for lunch take too much mental energy. After all, he's a little busy running the world's largest social network.

Neuroscientist and psychologist Daniel Levitin, author of *The Organized Mind: Thinking Straight in the Age of Information Overload*, says we all practice this, called *satisficing*, to some degree. *Satisficing*, a term coined by Nobel Prize winner Herbert Simon, refers to the strategy of making a decision that is not optimal but is sufficient enough to satisfy us. When we pull into a gas station that doesn't have the best price but is convenient, or we put on the first jacket we see in the closet, we are satisficing. As Levitin explains, "Satisficing is one of the foundations of productive human behavior; it prevails when we don't waste time on decisions that don't matter, or more accurately, when we don't waste time trying to find improvements that are not going to make a significant difference in our happiness or satisfaction."[3]

For the most part, satisficing is a healthy and helpful practice. Entrepreneurs, who typically make hundreds of decisions daily, must practice satisficing simply to survive. In a typical week your beloved may be making high-level judgments on strategy, expenses, designs, and target markets—while juggling those alongside menial choices such as what kind of pen to buy, what brand of paper to order, and what salutation to use in an email.

That is quite a bit of information for a single human brain to process, even if that brain belongs to a creative genius. Our conscious brains can process only about 120 bits of information per second. It takes 60 bits of processing power to listen to one person speaking to you. Add in another person talking to you at the same time, and your brain is already maxed out.[4]

To make things worse, neuroscientists have found that our brains don't automatically know how to differentiate between more important or less important decisions.[5] It takes additional processing power to prioritize which decisions need to be made, which can be postponed, and which can be ignored altogether.

The end result? Your entrepreneur's brain is very, very full from business-related matters alone. He will likely begin satisficing to a degree that increasingly limits the mental energy he has left for personal matters. If it gets bad enough, he may even begin satisficing *you*.

Cheng-Ling Chen of San Francisco, California, has known her husband, Andy, since they were sophomores in high school. Their relationship was his top priority during their high school, college, and grad school years. But then, as Andy was finishing his PhD, he and three friends started a company that developed and sold debugging software. Cheng-Ling's close relationship with him changed dramatically in the years that followed. "What enabled him to be so focused on what he does and be successful is because he's so single-minded. He pushes everything else to the side," Cheng-Ling reflected. "We were used to a certain level of closeness and connection that his obsession with his company didn't allow for. Before then *I* was what he was focused on." Andy's satisficing had practical and emotional ramifications for their marriage. "There were times in the past when he could have or should have reached out, but he didn't have the mental capacity for it, so he didn't do it. I couldn't understand that and couldn't forgive it for a long time."

Andy's company was acquired in 2014, providing the successful exit that many entrepreneurs dream of. But that success doesn't mean that he and Cheng-Ling have figured out how to balance their relationship with the time and space he needs if he pursues another start-up. "One thing we're continuing to work on is, how can he still turn toward me without losing that single focus? How can I feel included in his world?" More than ten years after Andy started his company, they're still struggling to find a solution that works for both of them.

When I asked Julian Gorodsky, a clinical psychologist in Silicon Valley for nearly four decades, how he would characterize the experience of being with an entrepreneur, he didn't mince any words. "The start-up can be like a lover," he said. Gorodsky has a gray beard and kind eyes that make you want to confide in him. He has counseled many high-powered couples in the Valley and has seen firsthand the pressure that a start-up puts on a relationship. "The entrepreneur is intensely involved in this other," he continued. "As with extramarital affairs, some marriages break up because of it, and others don't."

According to Gorodsky, the difference between the couples who stay together and those who don't is whether there is a true affirmation of love and a deep understanding of what it means to love unconditionally.

Unconditional love isn't easy under any circumstances, and it's certainly not easy when your partner's venture takes over her brain and begins affecting multiple areas of *your* life—finances, schedules, quality of life, geographical location, emotional health, children, and more. As much as you might try to buttress your personal lives against the turbulent waves of the business, it won't be possible to avoid some kind of impact. As a result, you may find yourself doing things or putting up with things that you never expected.

Meg Cadoux Hirshberg moved into the Stonyfield farmhouse

after marrying her husband, Gary, in 1986. The farmhouse had no central heat, no insulation, and no locks on the doors. It also doubled as the yogurt company's office. She went to bed each night with "the sickening odor of fermenting curds and whey." She could never take a bath for fear an employee would wander into the bathroom. She even gave birth to two of her children there, employees roaming the hallways as she moaned through labor.[6]

Eleanor Williams[7] found herself moving from California to Togo, a tiny West African nation, shortly after she married. Her husband, Andrew, had worked there a few years earlier. She had visited Togo only briefly before, yet now she was relocating her entire life to help him start a business in one of the poorest countries in the world.[8] On Eleanor's first visit to Togo, she lived in a village for a week with no running water and no electricity. She rode an overcrowded ferry that ended up crushing a passenger against the dock. The whole experience was quite a shock for someone born and raised in the San Francisco Bay Area.

Others may experience more common but no less challenging circumstances when their significant others are consumed by their ventures. Heather Caliri of San Diego, California, was not expecting to have to operate like a single parent when her first child was born. But when the stop-motion-animation software project her engineer husband, Dyami, had been doing as a side project suddenly began to take off, he told her that he wanted to quit his job and work on the business full-time. Realizing this was a train she couldn't stop, Heather gave Dyami her support—even as she dealt with postpartum depression and their aging kitchen literally fell apart around them. The 2008 Great Recession hit soon after, and they lost most of their savings and had to move back in with Heather's parents.

It takes a significant level of commitment to stick with our mates through such challenging circumstances. Even more so when we are faced with the reality that they have voluntarily created greater chaos and stress for us—while simultaneously having a diminished capacity to help manage that chaos and stress. You may feel like your partner is the bull who destroys everything in the china shop and then splits, leaving you to clean up the mess.

To their credit, it's probably not intentional. Our significant others are simply protecting their brains from decision overload by limiting the number of things they need to worry about or act on.

This can start off innocuously enough. If your beloved begins wearing the same clothes or eating the same meal for breakfast every day, that's no big deal. If he begins to forget to put his dirty dishes in the sink or to fill up the gas tank in the car, that's annoying but manageable.

From there, assuming his business is becoming increasingly complex and demanding, the brainpower he has left for the rest of life will only dwindle. He may stop paying attention to what he eats altogether. He may forget important dates and events. He won't remember to do chores around the house. He won't think to schedule time to see family or friends. He'll lose track of the kids' activities and the names of their friends.

And the fate of all those daily life decisions that fall through the cracks of your entrepreneur's overtasked brain? Unless your family has its own personal assistant, they will land squarely in your lap—whether or not you want the job.

Outside of the direct support I have offered to Ned and his company, the list of indirect support I have had to give him—sometimes happily, sometimes less so—is long and continues to grow even now. I do most of the household chores. I pay our bills. I plan our date nights and pack for our vacations. I schedule our medical checkups. I buy the groceries and cook all our meals. I run most of the errands that need to be taken care of during business hours. I'm the first line of defense for fixing stuff around the house. I oversee our social calendar and maintain our friendships.

If I include everything I do to take care of our son, especially when Ned is traveling or working late, the list grows even longer.

The concept of a *lead parent* is espoused by Anne-Marie Slaughter, the scholar and policy analyst who shot to national fame in 2012 after writing about how women "still can't have it all" in *The Atlantic*. Many modern couples, Ned and myself included, have fully bought into the ideals of co-parenting, but Slaughter and her husband, Andrew Moravcsik, make the argument that this isn't necessarily feasible. Unless the couple has perfectly complementary and flexible schedules, one parent will almost always have to take the lead in caring for the children. This is how Moravcsik, who has played this role for several years, explains it: "Lead parenting is being on the front lines of everyday life. In my years as lead parent, I have gotten the kids out of the house in the morning; enforced bedtimes at night; monitored computer and TV use; attempted to ensure that homework got done right; encouraged involvement in sports and music; attended the baseball games, piano lessons, plays, and concerts that resulted; and kept tabs on social lives. To this day, I am listed first on emergency forms; I am the parent who drops everything in the event of a crisis."[9]

Moravcsik admits that this list is significantly shorter because he and Slaughter have the financial resources to hire plenty of help. For middle- or lower-class families, the lead parent has even more responsibilities.

If your mate is an entrepreneur and you have children together, the chances that you will be the lead parent are pretty much 100 percent. I have been the lead parent for our son for the entire five and a half years of his existence, and I don't expect that to change anytime soon. I track everything from his doctor's appointments and meals to his social activities and physical development. Some days I feel like I'm struggling with decision overload just from taking care of everything that Ned can't. And that's before I've paid attention to any of my own personal or professional needs.

For all the responsibilities that your entrepreneur has at work, you, as his or her partner, will have to take on as many responsibilities at home. You will be the CEO of your home and your family, of your children and your marriage. You will be the primary advocate for your personal lives, ensuring that you, your partner, and your children remain emotionally and physically healthy, and that your relationships stay strong. It is very possible that your own career prospects will suffer, or at least be limited by, the proportionally greater responsibilities you need to take on at home.

The truth is that your contributions—behind-the-scenes, unglamorous, and often unrecognized—are what allow your entrepreneur to pursue his or her dreams. This is why your support of your partner's venture is so vital. If you don't genuinely buy into this journey, all the effort and sacrifices that will inevitably be required of you will be a ticket straight to resentment purgatory. And resentment, if left to fester and grow, can be the beginning of the end for relationships.

Resentment "is the persistent feeling that you're being treated unfairly—not getting due respect, appreciation, affection, help, apology, consideration, praise, or reward." Unlike anger or rage, which require physical and psychological energy that we can't sustain for long periods of time, resentment can be easily maintained for years on end. After a while, resentment becomes "more of a mood than an emotional state, and the behaviors it motivates are more habit than choice."[10]

Resentment is a risk and a reality in the entrepreneurial life.

One Silicon Valley investor I spoke with, who has worked with start-ups for more than a decade, has seen plenty of entrepreneurs split from their spouses. The primary reasons? "Resentment and infidelity," he told me without hesitation. "The spouses spend so much time apart that resentment can build up in either of them. It could be on the part of the entrepreneur, who feels like he or she is not being supported, or the spouse, who feels like he or she is not being acknowledged. That's when you want to blame your spouse or find someone better."

It's not realistic, of course, to simply will yourself not to feel resentful. Over the years I have felt far more resentment toward Ned and d.light than I would like to admit, dating all the way back to the second Christmas after we married. Back then the company was just a months-old school project. Ned decided to go to Myanmar to do field research for d.light during winter break—the same winter break I had been expecting to spend with the husband I'd barely seen since the summer. But he chose to spend the holiday volunteering his time with a project in a random foreign country with people he had never met instead of choosing *me*. And it hurt—deeply.

Over time, the d.light project began to fill up every extra bit of bandwidth that he, as a full-time graduate student, had. When he needed more margin, he created some by reducing the time he spent with me and other people. He worked on d.light whenever he wasn't doing homework, and he went on business trips whenever he had a break from school. When he graduated, all the time he had dedicated to attending classes and doing homework was seamlessly and completely absorbed by what had become a full-fledged business.

In just a couple of years, Ned went from being my new husband, to a roommate who was sometimes around to eat and help clean up, to a phantom that emerged only occasionally. Just as the theory of satisficing would predict, Ned stopped helping with errands and chores around the house. He rarely attended social events with me. Any date night we put on the calendar was usually rescheduled, and rescheduled again, until it was inevitably canceled at the last minute. Worst of all, even when Ned was with me, he wasn't fully *there* anymore. I often had trouble getting him to look me in the eye or listen to an entire sentence I spoke. Ned had been completely captured—intellectually, emotionally, and physically—by his venture. The other love of his life was taking over, and I had been relegated to making do with the crumbs of attention he occasionally threw my way. Resentment and I became well acquainted during those years.

But the truth is that resentment doesn't help Ned or me, in large part because it adds emotional strain without spurring us into action. When I am in the throes of resentment, Ned feels more guilty and I feel more stressed. Yet we're no closer to finding actionable, helpful solutions. Our relationship, and we as individuals, are far better served when I channel my resentful energy toward doing things differently. This begins with more realistic expectations, is fueled by a sense of empowerment, and is facilitated through strategies like proactive communication and intentional time spent together. (We'll get to all of these strategies later in the book.)

For the couple that is doing business together, the challenges of finding the mental capacity for managing your personal lives can be even greater. You will both need to learn how to create the time and energy for priorities outside of work. If you have children, you will need to negotiate what co-parenting looks like, or if one of you can take on the role of lead parent. You will both need to be advocates for your relationship and your family.

But what, exactly, does that advocacy look like? Part of the answer, I believe, can be found in the wisdom of the late business guru Stephen Covey. If you've been around the business world at all, you've probably been exposed to Stephen Covey's quadrant of time management. Covey made the case that all our tasks can be labeled as urgent or not urgent, and important or not important. They will then fit into one of these four boxes:[11]

I. Urgent and Important	II. Not Urgent and Important
III. Urgent and Not Important	IV. Not Urgent and Not Important

At first glance, the table looks simple enough to put into practice. Do everything in quadrant I first. Then move to quadrant II. Only when you've finished those tasks should you even consider the items in quadrants III and IV.

Unfortunately, the reality is that many of us spend a disproportionate amount of time in quadrant III, on things that feel urgent but don't really matter. That's a problem for entrepreneurs and their significant others, given their greatly limited time and mental capacity.

In his classic book *First Things First*, Covey explains how many of us have an urgency addiction: "Some of us get so used to the adrenaline rush of handling crises that we become dependent on it for a sense of excitement and energy." That sense of urgency can be so exhilarating and satisfying—contributing to the eustress that we discussed in the last chapter—that we begin to equate urgency with importance. "Then when the importance isn't there, the urgency fix is so powerful we are drawn to do anything urgent, just to stay in motion. . . . It's become a status symbol in our society—if we're busy, we're important; we're almost embarrassed to admit it. Busyness is where we get our security. It's validating, popular, and pleasing."[12]

What helps us feel busy and important? Making decisions, big and small, about a business. Checking things off a to-do list. Attending meetings. Creating documents. Replying to emails. And what feels like a less productive use of time? Chatting with our significant others. Playing with our children. Hiking. Reading a good book. Sleeping.

Your family and your relationship are the epitome of what it means to be in quadrant II. You are no doubt very important to your entrepreneur, but you're certainly not urgent. You will still be there if she works a fourteen-hour day, just as you will be there if she works an eight-hour day. You will be there if he travels 70 percent of the time or if he never leaves home. The challenge for both of you will be gaining clarity on what is paramount in your life and allocating your time accordingly. Together you'll need to develop the discipline to ask questions like: Is this task important or is it just urgent? Can I make that decision tomorrow? Is finishing this actually essential to the business?

We tend to avoid such questions because making these decisions takes work and consumes valuable processing power. But when we don't do the work of understanding what is truly important, the siren call of urgency can lure us in. If your entrepreneur always answers that call, and you enable him or her to do so, you and your family will come second—or third or fourth—every day. And when your relationship is put on the back burner for too long, the simmering affection you have for one another may eventually fizzle.

The top reasons for divorce in the US, while differing slightly across surveys, always include the following: financial problems, infidelity, poor communication, and growing apart.[13] It's pretty easy to see how being with an entrepreneur could exacerbate all these factors. The stress and uncertainty alone could strain your relationship. If you're also constantly getting the message that you are not as deserving of time, attention, and energy as the business—well, it's understandable why some mates might struggle to stick around.

My hope is that, if you're reading this book, you *want* to stick around despite the challenges. If your beloved is a decent human being who loves you but just happens to be consumed with a business, it makes a lot of sense for you to fight for your relationship. Even if you think the start-up is taking over your marriage and your family life, it need not be that way forever. Some measure of hardship is normal in start-up life, but that is not a predictor of how the rest of your life will turn out. Things *can* get better. Remember the three women whose stories I highlighted earlier in the chapter? Consider where they are now:

After surviving a hellish few years, Meg Cadoux Hirshberg saw her husband lead Stonyfield Farm to become the bestselling brand of organic yogurt in the country. As a result, I'm pretty sure she is no longer living in a farmhouse and now has locks on her bathrooms.

Eleanor survived a couple of eventful years overseas before

returning to the US with a much clearer picture of her own needs and sense of vocation. Her experience equipped her to have a frank discussion with her husband when he wanted to move abroad for another venture a few years later. Together they decided to remain in the US so she could work and take care of their new baby. Her husband was then able to start a locally based company.

After a harrowing year and a half for Heather and her family, her husband's stop-motion-animation software company took off. Their software has been used in major studio films ranging from the Claymation hit *Shaun the Sheep* to *Star Wars: The Force Awakens*. The family has been living comfortably off the income of the company for more than a decade, and she and her husband have attended some pretty fabulous VIP movie screenings. Dyami has attained the life that most entrepreneurs hope for: he's working less than forty hours a week, earning more than he did in his previous jobs, and has a flexible schedule that allows him to spend lots of time with his wife and children.

There's hope for entrepreneurial couples to get to the other side of the craziness as stronger individuals with deeper, more grounded relationships. I know that's been the case for Ned and me.

When the professional and personal challenges overwhelmed us after we moved to China, Ned and I rallied to one another's side. We advised one another, vented together, celebrated together, and cheered one another on. We poured the best of our intellects and skills and hearts into d.light—and grew profoundly in our respect and love for each other as a result. I'm convinced that our marriage is more resilient and our level of trust in each other far deeper than if we had remained in our comfortably predictable lives.

That being said, the whole start-up thing was still a lot harder than it needed to be. If we had prepared better for the experience, we could have saved ourselves a lot of misery, conflict, and burn-out. If I had made the effort to better understand myself and Ned, to know my greatest needs and greatest stressors, we probably could have arrived at the same place we are today with fewer battle scars and a lot less baggage.

In the next section, we'll cover these areas in hopes that you won't need to repeat my mistakes.

PART II

DUE DILIGENCE

5

Knowing Yourself and Your Partner

Less than two years after Ned and I married, I found myself in therapy. Unlike when I sought grief counseling after the death of my father, this time I couldn't explain how or why I had ended up on a therapist's couch. One day, I had been my usual hyperproductive, overachieving self. The next, I was a depressed, weepy individual who could barely get out of bed. I didn't know what was wrong with me—and I was terrified.

My therapist solved the mystery within minutes. "It sounds like you're suffering from burnout," she suggested gently after I explained to her how much I had been working and what my work environment was like.

"Really?" I was surprised at her diagnosis. As a twenty-seven-year-old, I had assumed burnout wasn't a legitimate thing. And if it was, it only happened to old men with receding hairlines who had overworked themselves for decades. "Why? What would cause that?"

"Well, for starters, it seems like you have trouble saying no to others," she replied. "Is people-pleasing important to you?"

I hesitated. "I guess so," I said reluctantly.

"What do you think would happen if you started saying no to people and started setting boundaries?" she pressed.

My insides clenched, my skin tingling with horror. If I began saying no, surely all of humanity would hate me. The earth would break apart into tiny little pieces and get sucked up by the universe. But I chose to give a milder response. "Other people would be disappointed in me. I could lose the respect of my friends and coworkers."

"Are you sure that's true? Is that how you feel when other people say no to you?"

"No," I admitted with a heavy sigh. I had really been hoping to blame someone else for my depression and dysfunction. Unfortunately, as is often the case, the root issue was my own.

But Ned's entrepreneurial pursuits were part of the equation too. The stress and strain it had put on our marriage helped create fertile ground for some of my worst character traits to emerge.

When d.light became the time-suck of all time-sucks for Ned, I responded in a way that surprised even me. Yes, I felt the usual hurt, loneliness, and resentment. But I also experienced a peculiar need to prove that I could keep up with my dream-big husband. A competitive fire within me, which I thought had been extinguished when I was beaned in the head with a dodge ball in fourth grade, came surging back with unexpected vigor.

If Ned was going to dedicate his whole life to his work, so could I. If Ned was going to give his heart and soul to his company, then I would give my heart and soul to my job organizing programs and community service opportunities at our church. If Ned was going to be too busy for me, then I would be too busy for him. He worked very long days and most nights and weekends. I tried to outdo him by scheduling meetings every night and every weekend on top of my extended daytime hours.

I'm going to go ahead and say what you are already thinking: this was not a good or healthy response. It was bad for our marriage, of course, as we went from seeing one another a tiny percentage of the time to not seeing one another at all. We were acting more like competitors than partners. (Admittedly, the competition was totally one-sided. Ned was too busy to pay attention to the fact that I was trying to compete with him.) And it was terrible for my personal health, as evidenced by my emergency visit to a therapist's office—and my eventual resignation from a job that I could no longer sustain.

My therapist's insights broke open the protective shell behind which I had been hiding for years—even from myself. I now recognized that I had been a bona fide people-pleaser for as long as I could remember. I could never say no to anyone or set any personal boundaries. I babysat my boss's three young kids for an entire night on a moment's notice. I went ninety minutes out of my way to drive home someone I barely knew. I was available for meetings and phone calls anytime, anywhere.

It had been a long time since I had reserved any time or energy for taking care of myself or having fun. I had pushed myself far past the point of exhaustion, ignoring any physical and emotional cues my body tried to give me, determined to prove that I could be as important and hardworking as my husband. No wonder, then, that my body and mind completely shut down. It was the only way to force me to exit my self-inflicted rat race.

For your sake, I hope you don't struggle with people-pleasing and boundary-setting as much as I do. Trust me, it's not fun. But chances are you struggle with *something*—and that something will be triggered, possibly to epic proportions, by the stress of being with an entrepreneur.

And you wouldn't be the only one. There's more than enough space for two to tango on this dance floor. It's likely that your beloved will also begin exhibiting different or unexpected behaviors in response to the stress of creating a new business. (Not to state the obvious, but *every* human being has issues. If your partner ever tries to make the claim that you are the only one with neuroses that need to be addressed, take comfort in knowing that you have just identified one of his or her issues.)

A woman I'll call Cindy had saved up a comfortable nest egg with her husband when he first joined a relative's start-up. They had several children, but their financial situation was stable enough and the potential of the product high enough that their personal risk in the venture seemed minimal.

But a year later, when the seed funding dried out and with no substantial sales on the horizon, things went quickly downhill for them. Her husband stopped receiving a salary, yet continued to spend most of his time out of state for the start-up. Cindy was left behind to care for their children, including two toddlers and two autistic preteens, on her own. She begged her husband to find another job; instead he extended his contract with the start-up without consulting her. When their car stopped working, he bought a car from his business partner but told his wife he was just borrowing it.

Within two years, their financial reserves and their children's college funds had disappeared entirely. Cindy kept asking her husband to find other work nearby or to stay home to care for the children so she could get a job. He refused to listen to her pleading.

Instead he retorted, "You can't tell me what to do. You're not the boss of me."

The state of their finances and their family relationships continued to deteriorate. Their home was eventually foreclosed on, and Cindy and the kids had to move in with a family member. Only then was her husband willing to reconsider his employment options, eventually finding another job with an established company.

When Cindy shared these events with me, several years after the fact, her tone was incredulous. "He was a good and caring man," she assured me several times. "But working on that company totally changed him." Their financial challenges had been painful, but far more excruciating had been how her husband became someone she couldn't recognize or fully trust. He no longer prioritized the needs of his wife and children; he willingly risked everything his family had for a failing business; he lied and made major decisions without asking for her input.

I asked Cindy why she thought her husband had changed so much.

"I think he wanted to see the company succeed so badly, he felt the ends—a huge financial windfall—would eventually justify the means," she replied. "But once you start ignoring your conscience, I think it gets easier and easier to do things that you never would have considered before."

Executive coach Dave Phillips would probably add that Cindy's husband already had these behavioral tendencies within him; they just hadn't had the opportunity to manifest themselves. Phillips uses the Birkman Method—a multidimensional assessment of behavioral, motivational, and occupational data—to guide his clients toward healthier, more productive careers and family lives. "Lots of people don't like behavioral assessments," he told me. "But they allow us to understand our natural predispositions and understand the animal we've been created to be. We need to understand that the enemy is *us*." (For the record, Phillips was able to diagnose my off-the-charts competitive spirit after just a quick glance at the results of my Birkman evaluation.)

For hundreds of years, we humans have tried to develop different ways of understanding and categorizing ourselves, from ancient astrological signs to the twentieth-century codification of the Myers-Briggs Type Indicator.[1] Philosophers, spiritual leaders, and psychologists all make the case that self-awareness is necessary for personal health and development. In the last few decades, scientific research has helped us better understand that self-consciousness and the willingness to disclose what we're learning about ourselves to others actually allows us to be more effective leaders and to have stronger, more satisfying relationships.[2] According to the authors of one psychology study, which showed that asking a series of personal questions could accelerate intimacy in a relationship, "One key pattern associated with the development of a close relationship among peers is sustained, escalating, reciprocal, personal self-disclosure."[3]

This self-awareness is particularly key when venturing down the entrepreneurial path, which is guaranteed to be fraught with challenges and stress. None of us are our best selves under such circumstances. "The more stress people get under, the more their time horizons narrow, the less far they can see into the future," Dave Phillips explained. "They will not see the natural consequences of their actions."

The transformation you might see in your beloved doesn't have to be as extreme as what Cindy witnessed. For example, most days I cohabitate with normal, everyday Ned, who happens to be one of the most even-keeled, good-humored, and kind individuals I know.

But, occasionally, overly-stressed-entrepreneur Ned emerges. He is exasperated and snappy, distracted and cold. When this version of Ned comes into the house, I feel my own cortisol levels rising. I snap back at him. I keep my distance. And, ultimately, our relationship suffers.

When I speak with entrepreneurs' significant others, I almost always ask the question, *What do you wish you had known before this whole thing started?* The question is intentionally broad, leaving space for people to talk about business or marriage or anything else. Frequently the responses I receive have to do with personality or character. Here's a sampling of the statements I've heard:

- "I wish I had known about my desire to control everything."
- "I wish I had learned how to set better boundaries."
- "I couldn't admit to myself how selfish my husband actually was."
- "I should've understood that she didn't think about the practical matters in life."
- "I wish I had known that I didn't want a single moment of financial exposure."
- "I didn't know we would drive each other crazy while working together."
- "I didn't realize what a good listener my spouse is, so I didn't take advantage of that earlier."
- "I wish I had known how much I would struggle with my own sense of identity and purpose."
- "It took me a long time to realize how much I internalize stress, and how harmful that can be if I don't have a good outlet."
- "We should've played to our strengths more, dividing up the responsibilities of the business based on what we are each good at."

This wide range of regrets points to the same truth: the more we understand ourselves and our partners, the better prepared we will be for the challenges of maintaining a relationship and building a start-up at the same time. If we can anticipate how we will respond to immense stress and uncertainty, we can better understand how best to cope and support one another.

Renowned psychologist John Gottman has researched married couples for more than twenty years. He emphasizes the importance of emotional intelligence in a successful relationship: "The more emotionally intelligent a couple—the better able they are to understand, honor, and respect each other and their marriages—the more likely that they will indeed live happily ever after."[4]

A significant part of this emotional intelligence is developing detailed "love maps" of one another, or the mental file cabinet where we track everything important to our partner: his or her likes, dislikes, pet peeves, past experiences, fears, hopes, goals, and more. "Couples who have detailed love maps of each other's world are far better prepared to cope with stressful events and conflict," Gottman explains.[5] These love maps, so long as we continuously update them, help us stay intimately connected with our partners regardless of the swirling, unpredictable challenges that come our way. Put another way, all the seemingly insignificant tidbits of information I've learned about Ned over the years (dislikes jazz, hates shopping, loves Thai food, passionate about astronomy, enjoys making Excel spreadsheets) actually do matter.

This is especially true for couples that work together. Julie Holly, who ran a real estate business with her husband in Modesto, California, explained, "It can be rough. It's not like you can go home and gripe about your boss. If something goes wrong at work and you blame your spouse for it, you're not going to want to be all snuggly with the same person you're mad at." The keys for Julie and her husband were finding one another's personal and professional strengths, dividing roles and responsibilities accordingly, and then respecting and trusting one another to carry out those responsibilities well. "We've had to develop a healthy level of trust and certainty. Now we know one another well enough to know when we can go ahead and push the button without consulting the other." It's taken them several years of missteps and conflict to get to this point, but they're finally seeing the fruit of their efforts.

Fortunately for today's entrepreneurs and their partners, we live in an age full of self-assessment tools and resources. Just take a peek inside your local bookstore or online retailer and you will find everything from *What Color Is Your Parachute?* to *StrengthsFinder* and the latest essential guide to Myers-Briggs. Those of us who are verbal processors can call upon all sorts of wise and well-trained people to help us untangle our inner workings, including mentors, life coaches, spiritual leaders, and therapists. I have learned more about myself through therapy and spiritual direction (a cross between counseling and spiritual mentorship) than I ever could have learned through self-reflection or journaling alone. There are even exercises couples can do together, like "The 36 Questions That Lead to Love," which went viral in 2015 after being published by the *New York Times*.[6] (If you happened to miss it, just Google it to find the quiz.)

Despite all these great resources, it takes work—and a lot of time—to decrypt ourselves. We are fluid beings living in fluid environments that become particularly dynamic and challenging when there's a start-up involved. Julie has certainly found this to be true. "I feel like entrepreneurs change at a much faster rate because we always have to make very broad moves very quickly. We have to contort ourselves so much more to realize our dreams."

In Ned's case, the contortions he made seemed part and parcel of the entrepreneurial journey. He worked hard—really hard—but what entrepreneur doesn't? Only years later did we recognize that Ned was struggling with workaholism. He was addicted to the highs that work provided him, and it was a dependence that couldn't be broken without help.

I should have seen this back in college, when Ned was taking six classes each quarter, leading a student advocacy group, and serving as an academic adviser—while also playing in a band, singing in an a cappella group, and recording and mixing full-length albums for both. I thought he just liked being busy.

Family therapist Bryan E. Robinson, a leading expert on workaholism, defines it as "an obsessive-compulsive disorder that manifests itself through self-imposed demands, an inability to regulate work habits, and an overindulgence in work to the exclusion of most other life activities."[7] We both thought d.light was requiring this level of obsessive commitment from Ned, that it was the only way for the company to succeed. There was some truth to this, but Ned was also stretching the truth when he made the decision over and over again to choose his work over nearly everything else in his life. Robinson explains the difference between healthy workers and workaholics: "Healthy workers know when to close the briefcase, mentally switch gears, and be fully present. . . . Workaholics allow work to engulf all other quarters of life."[8]

At his workaholic worst, which was aggravated by his pursuit of a start-up, Ned ended up making decisions that he now regrets—missing weddings and birthday parties, neglecting friendships, disregarding his own health, casting aside hobbies and other interests, taking our marriage for granted. He let his venture turn him into a one-dimensional individual with only one clear goal in life: to make d.light work, at all costs. He no longer had a clear sense of what was most important to him.

Thankfully this isn't the version of Ned that I live with today. But it's been a long journey for him. Just as I have needed years to come to terms with my poor boundary-setting and stubborn people-pleasing, Ned has required an extensive amount of time to restructure his life such that work is only one part of who he is.

I'll be the first to admit that the process to uncover our deepest neuroses can be humbling in that painful, wanting-to-claw-your-own-face kind of way. Yet, in the end, it has been extraordinarily empowering for me to know who I truly am—obnoxiously large warts and all. This knowledge has allowed both Ned and me to focus our limited time and energy on the things that keep us grounded, healthy, and content. I've had much greater awareness of the expectations and priorities I bring into our relationship, and how that affects my response to the topsy-turvy journey we are on.

Only after I hit rock bottom and burned out did I realize how unrealistic my expectations of Ned were. Inspired by the romantic comedies I had grown up watching, I wanted him to be my *everything*. But he didn't want that role, and he certainly had no time or ability to fill it. I had to find emotional nourishment from other family and friends. My burnout also helped me understand how much I need balance for my well-being. That prompted me to invest significant time in counseling, journaling, good books, yoga, long walks, and rest. I encountered helpful resources like the classic book *Boundaries: When to Say Yes, How to Say No to Take Control of Your Life*, by Henry Cloud and John Townsend, and the Enneagram, an ancient system with Sufi and Christian roots that postulates nine different personality types. (I found this incredibly insightful, but not always easy. When I learned that I was a Four on the Enneagram—appropriately called "Tragic Romantics" for our pessimistic outlook and tendency toward despair—the first thing I did was cry.)

The knowledge I gained about myself and the practices I developed then, especially in building a broader support network and learning how to take care of myself, are practices I have relied on ever since. As a result, I am much better equipped to stay afloat even when our entrepreneurial journey gets stormy. And I have been able to pursue my professional and personal goals in a more balanced, soul-nourishing way.

Lisa Boyce of Provo, Utah, experienced this empowerment firsthand. (We met her husband, Dave, the consummate serial entrepreneur, in chapter 1.) A few years into being a new mom to several little ones, she was filled with bitterness at Dave's frequent business trips. He was sometimes gone as much as three out of every four weeks. Lisa found that she could power through those weeks of solo parenting, but as soon as Dave walked in the door after a trip, all of her suppressed resentment and frustration would come rushing out. "I felt mad and irritated because he didn't know my system. He didn't know how to do everything the way I wanted it," Lisa told me. "But, really, he could have screwed up or done everything perfectly, and I still would've been mad."

She later found out that Dave, in contrast, felt almost euphoric whenever he came home. He wanted nothing more than a warm, loving welcome from his beautiful family in his perfect, sweet-smelling house. "Just knowing he was wanting a welcome like that made me want to punch him in the throat," Lisa admitted, laughing.

As she grew more aware of her own emotional response and what she really needed after her husband's long business trips, the couple developed a new approach. The moment he returned home from the airport—whether early in the morning, late at night, or any other time of day—she would immediately walk out the door and stay out of the house for a couple of hours. "We wouldn't even talk. We would just high-five each other and I'd get in the car, whether or not I had somewhere to go." Sometimes Lisa would find a girlfriend to hang out with; other times she'd take a walk or go browse the local bookstore. The strategy, while unorthodox, allowed the spouses to avoid unnecessary conflict and gave Lisa the break she desperately needed after caring for her family on her own for so long.

Of course, being aware of our personal needs and weaknesses isn't the only thing that will empower us. Knowing our strengths and unique capabilities can be just as, if not more, important. Angela Tam of San Jose, California, grew up with a mother who was ill and a father who was constantly sacrificing to care for his wife and two daughters. As a result, she's developed razor-sharp clarity on what matters to her and what doesn't, and hardly bats an eye at the idea of living with uncertainty. "I don't need control," she explained, her tone as relaxed as her words. "I can go with the flow." When her husband, Theo, expressed his desire to join a yearlong fellowship that would help him launch a start-up, she was comfortable with the risk he was taking. "I told him, 'It's okay if it takes one to two years to get this off the ground.' "

When Theo completed his fellowship and joined his second start-up, Angela's support remained unwavering, even as she worked a full-time job to pay the bills and cared for their two young children. For her, life is all about experiences, not material things or professional success. She wants her husband to try his hand at being his own boss and pursuing his passions. "It doesn't matter to me if he succeeds or fails. It's more important that he tries. I don't want him to regret not trying." She holds Theo accountable to spending time with her and the children, but as long as he keeps his commitments to them, she is happy to continue supporting his dreams.

I'll admit, I find myself envious of Angela's well-adjusted attitude. She's independent, flexible, low-maintenance, supportive, and very self-aware—all traits that seem to make her the perfect partner to an entrepreneur. But take it from this devotee of structure and certainty: we all have something positive to contribute to our beloved entrepreneurs and their start-up adventures. My more pessimistic approach to life has actually been a healthy counterbalance to Ned's fanciful, pie-in-the-entire-universe perspective. My stubborn need to have things scheduled has facilitated Ned's own boundary-setting with his work.

Understanding yourself and your partner provides another huge benefit: when everything goes to hell, and your resentment and anger are boiling over, you will hopefully be able to remember what you like best about him or her. Reminding struggling couples of this is a favorite tool of marriage counselors: *Why did you first fall in love with your partner? What characteristics and qualities most attracted you? What are your fondest memories of your relationship?*

These are among your "truths," as one therapist explained to me. Such truths will anchor you as individuals, and they will anchor your relationship through wild successes, spectacular failures, and whatever else may come your way. This is critical, because regardless of whether the business takes off or flatlines, you and your beloved will still have one another. The greater the distinction you can make between your own identities and the start-up, the better your chances of coming out of the experience with a richer, more mature partnership.

There's another set of truths that can help set you up for

relational longevity: recognizing the particular dynamics, both the glorious and the ugly, that define your relationship. We'll explore this next. Knowing how you operate as a couple can help you decide if your family can handle the rigors of the entrepreneurial journey, or if, perhaps, the risks are too great.

Knowing Your Relationship

Chances are that you've heard this line from your entrepreneur: "It's going to get better soon."

Ned has said this to me more times than I can count. It's been his favorite go-to assurance whenever I was certain that d.light was about to crumble, or I was overwhelmed with stress, or I fretted about the state of our relationship. He would look deep into my eyes as he said this, his voice calm, confident, and sincere. His workload would lessen as soon as he hired a few more people, he explained. His schedule would become freer after a new product was launched. We'd get to spend more time together as soon as a particular crisis passed.

Unfortunately, Ned was almost always wrong. The strain that the company placed on him and our relationship never abated. The more people Ned hired, the more work was required to train and manage all those people. When a product launched, he simply turned his attention from design and manufacturing to marketing and distribution. And as soon as one crisis was resolved, another one would rear its scary head.

Over the years Ned's resilient optimism has turned into a string of broken promises that fueled my disappointment and resentment. I never doubted, and still don't doubt, his sincerity. Every time he assured me that things would soon improve, I knew he meant it and he wanted it to be true as much as I did. But it wasn't realistic.

The false expectations he kept setting ended up being far more painful than if he had come right out and admitted, "It's going to stay really hard for another few years. I don't know when my schedule will get better." That would have been excruciating to hear, but at least I would have been better prepared.

In fairness, the questions that I asked month after month, in hopes of getting some concrete answers and deadlines, probably painted him into a corner. *When will you be home tonight? When are you traveling? How much are you going to travel this year? When will you stop working on weekends? Can you promise me we'll get to celebrate our anniversary? When are we ever going to have work-life balance? When is d.light going to be more self-sufficient?*

I asked because I simply wanted to know, but Ned heard my queries as, *Things better improve soon because I don't know how much longer I can take this.*

Ned has a high tolerance for my idiosyncrasies, but even he sometimes got fed up with my nagging. "I'm selling d.light all day, every day, to everyone around me," he'd say. "I don't want to have to sell it to you too." He needed me to be his number one fan and cheerleader, something that this stability-loving pessimist had a hard time doing.

You've probably already recognized that we had a basic problem in our relationship: we had mismatched expectations of one another. I wanted Ned to be a particular kind of husband, one who was more present and available for drawn-out dinners and weekend getaways. He wanted me to be all in with him and his venture—buoyant, adaptable, happy to join him on his wild ride and laugh about it along the way.

It's clear to me now that these were not realistic expectations— at least, not for our particular relationship. For most people, the desire to see your significant other for dinner or the belief that a planned and paid-for vacation will actually happen are reasonable assumptions. But those of us who are hitched to ambitious entrepreneurs live in something of a parallel universe. Not all the same relationship rules apply. And the sooner we're able to accept that, the easier it will be.

Through more than twelve years of my marriage, I've had to revise and re-revise my expectations of what our relationship and family would look like. I've had to remind myself that I love Ned for who he is, not for who I wish he could sometimes be. Ned is never going to become predictable or conventional; I am never going to feel comfortable with uncertainty and risk.

If the dynamics of our relationship sound familiar to you, it's because they are fairly common among entrepreneurial couples. Through the many Birkman assessments he has done with entrepreneurs and their spouses, executive coach Dave Phillips has found that "entrepreneurs often, but not always, marry their opposites. If they married someone like themselves, they'd go crazy. People who are entrepreneurial and wild need someone a little calmer. People who are chill and relaxed need someone to bring excitement into their lives."

Aside from the "chill and relaxed" part—I tend to be more neurotic and anxious—Phillips's description fits Ned and my relationship to a T. Our dissimilarities didn't matter much earlier in the relationship, when we were still in the honeymoon phase and had a lot of bandwidth in our lives to accommodate the other person's needs. But when d.light began taking up all our time and emotional resources, those differences quickly came center stage.

Here's the unfortunate reality for those of us who love entrepreneurs: just as the pressure of a start-up exacerbates our personal hang-ups, it can also amplify areas of tension in our relationship. Anything that has caused conflict in the past will most certainly cause more conflict once a new venture comes crashing into your existence.

When Lee Ott of Sunnyvale, California, launched his email-screening software company, he and his wife, Sophia, started arguing with greater and greater frequency. The business caused both of them a significant amount of stress, as did their three children under the age of two. (They had one set of twins, if you're wondering how the math adds up.) The ongoing sleep deprivation and ever-changing trajectory of Lee's company infected their relational dynamics.

"I remember it was New Year's Eve," Sophia told me. "We had the biggest fight we've ever had in ten years of marriage." They went into marriage counseling for three months, during which they made a surprising discovery: they weren't fighting about the company or the kids. "We were actually fighting with our moms, not each other," Sophia, a therapist herself, explained. "We were fighting about our attachment patterns from childhood." These dynamics had always been present in their relationship, but Lee and Sophia hadn't had to wrestle with them directly until their emotional resources had been drained by the collision of parenthood and start-up life.

At its best, having your unhealthy relational dynamics brought into such clear focus could be a catalyst for addressing them head-on. At worst, the foundational challenges the two of you have—those red flags that were always there but neither of you wanted to address—might gain enough of a foothold to destroy your relationship altogether.

In chapter 1, I mentioned a woman named Erin,[1] whose ex-husband had started a company that made products for low-income families. Here's the longer story of what happened to her.

She had married young, right out of college. Unfortunately, the union began exhibiting fissures almost immediately. Two weeks after the wedding, her husband decided to leave for a two-week out-of-state internship without consulting her. She threatened divorce just to get his attention. He called her bluff and left anyway.

At home, her husband refused to help with chores. Erin once decided to let the dirty dishes pile up in the sink until he washed them. After ten days of fruitless waiting, she could no longer stand the mess and the stench, and ended up washing the dishes herself.

Whenever Erin went to her husband with a concern or a request for something to change, he responded with anger. "Stop trying to change me," he'd say.

Two years after the wedding, he hit upon an idea for a product and decided to launch a company. There was one big problem, though: he and Erin had already mapped out their lives for the next few years, a plan that she was following to the letter. She had been hoping to leave a job she hated in order to stay home and raise the kids they had both said they wanted. Instead, her husband's new, high-risk business locked her into her current job *and* required her to get a second one to pay their bills. Children were definitely off the table.

Erin raised her many objections with her husband, including her belief that he was starting the company for fame and status rather than out of any real desire to help others. She begged him not to pursue it. Just like with the internship, he ignored her entreaties and went ahead with it. He worked crazy hours and maintained an even crazier travel schedule that got progressively worse. After a couple of years he decided to move to Bangladesh for the business and asked Erin to join him. She was extremely reluctant to move but agreed to visit Dhaka as a test run.

While there, Erin became violently ill for five days. She couldn't keep any food down and was so weak that she could only lie on the bathroom floor. In the middle of her illness, her husband announced that he needed to go to China to take care of a manufacturing emergency. He would be gone for ten days. Despite Erin's pleading with him to stay, he kissed her good-bye as she lay on the bathroom floor, and left. She did not have a phone or a taka to her name. She didn't know a soul in the entire country.

Realizing that she had to help herself, Erin peeled herself off the floor, checked into a five-star hotel down the street, and stayed there until her husband returned, at which point she declared that she wanted to live in the US.

But the long separations were hard on their relationship, so a year later she agreed to live in Bangladesh with her husband for part of the year and remain in the US the rest of the time. They stumbled along for a while—both under intense stress, neither of them happy in the marriage—until three years later, when Erin discovered a love letter to her husband from a female employee. The letter referred to an extramarital relationship that had been ongoing for two years.

Her husband was in Asia and she in the US, so she confronted him about it over Skype. He didn't deny it. Hoping against hope to salvage their marriage, she offered him forgiveness and a clean slate on two conditions: cut all ties with the other woman and start couples counseling with her.

He refused and said he wanted a divorce. She didn't offer any further protest, and the papers were filed within a month.

Erin realizes now that she should have seen this coming. "He's one of the most selfish people I have ever met, but I couldn't admit this to myself before," she told me. His unwillingness to change his behavior or respect her wishes, pretty much from day one, were major warning signs that she had ignored because she desperately wanted the relationship to work. She had also buried her own emotional response to the situation. "I got used to pushing aside my own thoughts," she admitted. "I learned to keep quiet in the marriage. I lost all sense of myself, my self-esteem, and was very depressed."

I spoke to Erin nearly a year after they had called it quits, by which time she had realized that splitting from her husband was exactly what she needed. She had moved to a new place, was working at a new job, and had a bounce in her voice that she said she never had when she was married. "When I finally let go of him, I really blossomed. I woke up one morning, took a deep breath, and felt my soul reenter my body," she told me. "I realize now how much denial I was in to make that marriage work."

I can't say whether Erin's marriage was destined to fail even if her husband had relinquished his entrepreneurial dreams. But it's clear that the start-up and all its baggage fast-tracked their relationship's demise. Life with a start-up was too full and moved too rapidly for them to invest the time and effort necessary to address the weaknesses in their marriage. The long periods spent apart and their rapidly diverging priorities made any intervention extremely difficult, if not impossible.

If your relationship has major cracks in it even without the stress of a start-up, you and your significant other may want to first figure out how to plug those cracks—or at least stop them from growing wider—before launching a new venture. Otherwise, the topsy-turvy entrepreneurial experience could turn those cracks into unassailable chasms.

But how can entrepreneurial couples know if their relationships are robust enough to hold together through the thrills and trials of start-up life?

A good place to start could be taking an honest assessment of your partnership. The United States Conference of Catholic Bishops has developed a tool for couples to rate the health of their relationships.[2] You don't have to be Catholic or even religious to use this tool, which simply asks you to rate your level of satisfaction (1–10, with 1 being the lowest and 10 the highest) in fifteen areas of your relationship. It's recommended that you and your significant other complete these ratings individually and then compare answers.

	You	*Your Partner*
1. Shared Values	_____	_____
2. Commitment to Each Other	_____	_____
3. Communication Skills	_____	_____
4. Conflict Resolution Skills	_____	_____
5. Intimacy/Sexuality	_____	_____
6. Spirituality/Faith	_____	_____
7. Money Management	_____	_____
8. Appreciation/Affection	_____	_____
9. Lifestyle	_____	_____
10. Recreation	_____	_____
11. Decision-Making	_____	_____
12. Parenthood	_____	_____
13. Household Chores/Gender Differences	_____	_____
14. Careers	_____	_____
15. Balancing Time	_____	_____

Scores of 8–10 show that you're happy with those areas of your relationship; scores of 4–7 indicate where your level of satisfaction could be improved; and scores of 1–3 point to areas of high dissatisfaction. When you compare your responses with your partner's, take note of any low scores or respective scores that differ by three or more points. Such low ratings and sizable discrepancies highlight the issues where you and your mate likely have tension.

This exercise can also help provide an overall snapshot of your relationship health. Do you and your partner have more areas of satisfaction than dissatisfaction, or is it the other way around? Is one of you happier in the relationship than the other? Do you have similar views on your relationship, or are there major differences? Are there one or two areas that you need to pay particular attention to?

There aren't many things in life that I can guarantee, but here's one: you and your beloved entrepreneur will argue, and probably more than you typically do, during the process of building a company. I have spoken with dozens of entrepreneurial couples, and every one of them has experienced conflict because of the business. Some couples keep quarreling about the same issue over and over again; others uncover multiple layers of friction and difference. But an important distinction is that some couples are able to hang together despite their disagreements, while other relationships fall apart because of them.

Psychologist John Gottman makes the case that *how* we argue is critical—and can make the difference between *con*structive conflict and *de*structive conflict. Among other factors, Gottman cites four forms of negativity so lethal to a relationship that he calls them the Four Horsemen of the Apocalypse: criticism, contempt, defensiveness, and stonewalling (or disengagement and avoidance).[3]

Most relationships can survive occasional brushes with these forms of negativity. But when they become permanent staples in your arsenal, so familiar that one or both of you wield them in your first line of attack, your relationship is at serious risk. If this is where you and your partner are at, proceeding down the road of entrepreneurship may not be the wisest option. Your relationship likely has far deeper issues to address than how much time you spend together or how much money you want to expend on a business.

If the two of you are able to keep the Four Horsemen of negativity mostly at bay, there's still work to be done. You can find productive ways of communicating your differences (which we'll discuss more in chapters 9 and 10), but it's also important to recognize when you can agree to disagree. After studying thousands of couples over several decades, Gottman has discovered that the majority of ongoing arguments in a marriage cannot be resolved. "Couples spend year after year trying to change each other's mind—but it can't be done. This is because most of their disagreements are rooted in fundamental differences of lifestyle, personality, and values. By fighting over these differences, all they succeed in doing is wasting their time and harming their marriage."[4] My persistent demands that Ned operate with a predictable schedule, and his ongoing expectations that I be completely tolerant of uncertainty in our lives, were never resolved despite years of conflict. In fact, focusing on these differences only drove us apart.

Here, then, is a crucial difference between how we treat our own personal foibles and how we deal with the problematic areas of our relationship: while it is always a good idea to address our personal shortcomings directly, we shouldn't expect to fix all the things that are amiss in our relationship.

If you and your partner had areas of dissatisfaction in the assessment above, you will need to decide how important these issues are to you. Perhaps one of these areas is particularly painful or sensitive to you, and you can't imagine surviving the tumult of a new business until it is resolved. Then, by all means, try couples counseling or other methods of conflict resolution to work through your challenges. But if something is less than make-or-break for you—an annoyance more than a fundamental concern—it's actually best if you can learn to let it go. That will allow you to focus your limited time together on bolstering the health of the partnership.

Here's another way to think about it: Anyone who has experienced a severe sprain or broken bone knows that overworking the point of injury in an attempt to help it heal or grow stronger will only make it worse. Instead, functionality is regained by strengthening the healthy muscles around the injury point and investing in the well-being of the overall system. The injured area will recover more quickly and effectively when everything around it is more robust and able to offer more support. Similarly, it is critical to invest in the strengths that you have as a couple. Your problem areas will become less substantial, and your overall relationship will become more hardy.

For many couples, their greatest strength is their friendship with one another. Gottman defines this friendship as "a mutual respect for and enjoyment of each other's company. . . . [Such couples] have an abiding regard for each other and express this fondness not just in big ways but in little ways day in and day out."[5] Couples who genuinely like one another as friends will be less likely to feel adversarial against one another and will be more likely to experience "positive sentiment override," when positive thoughts about one another are so pervasive that they can nullify negative thoughts.[6]

When Ned and I first met in college, we spent months just

hanging out—studying together, eating midnight snacks, playing good-natured pranks on Ned's roommate, commiserating about our respective dysfunctional dating partners. By the time the first spark of romance emerged between us, we had developed such a deep level of trust and camaraderie that dating felt like the natural next step. This foundational friendship has been a major source of resilience in our marriage through hyperactive schedules, unrecognized emotional needs, and, yes, even horribly mismatched expectations. When Ned and I drive each other crazy, there is still no one else with whom we'd rather watch a movie or share a joke.

Dr. Harville Hendrix, an educator, therapist, and author of the bestselling book *Getting the Love You Want*, calls this "safety" in a relationship, something that every couple needs in order to feel well connected. Each needs to trust that he or she is not going to have to constantly defend against attacks from the other; rather, they should be able to see each other as allies and partners.[7]

This sense of safety is built through time and experience, as we practice affirming our commitment to and affection for one another over and over again. But how this unfolds will be different for each couple. Ned and I had the luxury of being college kids who lived in the same dorm for four years and had way too much free time on our hands. Audrey Kalman of San Mateo, California, strengthened her relationship with her husband, Dave, through several major life transitions and the fiery rite of passage known as parenthood. Dave first brought up the idea of starting his own business when their two sons were only three and five years old. As Audrey remembers it, she "freaked out" and begged him to reconsider. "I had spent time working for start-ups myself and I pictured myself functioning as a single parent while he was off pouring himself into his new venture," she explained. Dave heard her concerns and decided to pursue consulting instead.

Then, just a few years ago, with one son in high school and the other in middle school, Dave once again expressed his desire to start a company. This time Audrey was ready and happy to support his dream. By then they had been married for more than twenty years, during which they underwent a cross-country move and made multiple career shifts, in addition to raising their two children. "Having kids will prepare you for a lot," Audrey told me. Enduring these transitions together and co-parenting two boys into adolescence was the perfect training ground for them to develop a strong level of partnership and trust. She could then fully support Dave's entrepreneurial pursuits, regardless of whether or not his venture succeeds.

Fortifying your relationship also involves figuring out what your partner most needs from you to feel loved, and then doing that to the best of your ability. Entrepreneur and business adviser Jim Warner, who has worked extensively with executives and entrepreneurs through the Young Presidents' Organization, encourages his clients to write down a list of ten specific ways in which he or she likes to be loved, and to ask their significant others to do the same. After exchanging the lists, each partner should take as many opportunities as possible to honor the requests of the other. But "don't keep score," warns Warner. It's not a competition. Instead it's about serving and caring for your mate in ways that are meaningful to him or her.

Dr. Gary Chapman, a minister, marriage counselor, and best-selling author, uses the analogy that we each have a "love tank" that needs to be filled up on an ongoing basis by our romantic partners. "When the love tank is full the world looks beautiful and we feel loved," he explains. "When the love tank is empty we feel discouraged and uncertain about ourselves and our relationships."[8] He postulates that people typically rely on five main expressions of affection, which he calls *love languages*: words of affirmation, quality time, giving and receiving gifts, acts of service, and physical touch. Each individual has one or two preferred love languages, or the ways in which we most feel loved. The secret is in knowing which love language is most important to your partner, and being willing to express that love language regularly.

Ned's favorite love language is words of affirmation. While I will never be free of concerns or questions about start-up life, I can still encourage him and celebrate his achievements. And Ned, to his credit, has made herculean efforts to give me the quality time that I need to feel loved. Neither of us does this perfectly. Words of affirmation were not spoken regularly in my family of origin, and Ned is still a workaholic at heart. But the effort that we each put into doing something purely for the sake of the other communicates quite a bit about our devotion to one another.

All of these activities—strengthening your friendship, creating safety and trust, proactively doing what your partner asks of you—require time and intentional effort. As such, it isn't always easy to invest in your relationship. But when (not if) you and your entrepreneur encounter a major challenge together, you'll be grateful for all the relational reserves you've built up over time.

This happened to Ned and me ten months after we moved to China. Things turned ugly when the endless work hours, the persistent threat of d.light's demise, and the isolation of living in a foreign city with few friends finally caught up to me. I burned out again and was overcome with depression and anxiety. Just the thought of leaving our flat each morning and contending with the crowded streets of Shenzhen nearly gave me panic attacks.

That season was one of the first times in our marriage that Ned didn't have an optimistic platitude to offer me. Instead, recognizing the urgency of the situation, he sprang into action to make things better for me. He pleaded with our friends in the US to reach out to me by email or Skype. He hired other people to take over my work responsibilities. He opened an office in Hong Kong—just across the border from Shenzhen but, culturally, a world away—in part so we could live there. We knew that Hong Kong would offer many more sources of support for me, including therapists, a vibrant expat community, and other job opportunities.

Ned was able to make a business case for these changes, but the truth is that he did them for me. It wasn't your typical romantic gesture, but I received it as an epic declaration of love to me, one that I will never forget. He proved that he was my partner first and an entrepreneur second.

Our move to Hong Kong also marked another significant turning point in our start-up journey: we were finally beginning to get our priorities straight. For too long we had prioritized the company's needs over our personal needs. We finally realized this wasn't a sustainable way forward for any of us, d.light included. The company couldn't survive if we killed ourselves in the process of trying to bring it to life. We needed to know—and actually live by—what mattered most to us.

Knowing Your Priorities

In 2009, a year after the Great Recession hit, Paul and Halee Scott decided to pursue a new start for their family in Denver, Colorado. After working as a therapist for several years, Paul was eager to pursue his dream of creating new resources on addiction recovery for churches and parachurches. Halee was caring for their infant daughter, Ellie, while completing a PhD program. She encouraged Paul in his ambitions and wanted to do whatever she could to support him.

And then one night, shortly after they moved, everything changed.

"The night before my daughter's first birthday, she was breathing funny and was fussy and wouldn't go to sleep," Halee recalled. "I called the pediatric nurse, but she didn't call back until after I had put Ellie down to sleep. The nurse asked me to put the phone next to her so she could hear her breathing. Right away, she said,

'She's not breathing enough. You have to go to the hospital right now.' "

Paul and Halee rushed their daughter to the emergency room. She was diagnosed with respiratory syncytial virus (RSV), a common virus that usually causes cold-like symptoms but can occasionally lead to severe complications for babies.

They found out later that it had been a close call. If they had let Ellie sleep for much longer, she probably would never have woken up.

Ellie remained in the hospital for more than a week before she was stabilized enough to go home. Able to afford only minimal health coverage, Paul and Halee saw their entire savings wiped out over the course of a few days. Paul's pursuit of his own business was no longer tenable. Instead, he accepted a standing job offer with a hospital in Holland, Michigan, and the family moved to a new state for the second time in a year.

"It took us four years to get back to where we were," Halee told me. "We had to live in Michigan for that amount of time before we could afford to go back to Denver." Only then could Paul begin developing the programs and resources he had hoped to create back in 2009, work that he continues to this day.

The Scotts learned that there are times when pursuing a start-up makes sense, there are times when it doesn't—and it's possible to flip from one to the other overnight. For Paul and Halee, the most prudent decision was pretty clear. With no financial resources and a young child to care for, at least one of them needed a full-time job that could provide a good salary and reliable benefits.

But what about when the possibilities before you aren't as clearly defined? What do you do when you have some choice in the matter, but you're uncertain what the best decision is? The answer, I believe, lies in knowing our priorities.

When Ned and I decided to leave everything we knew and move to China for the sake of a barely viable company, there was some logic to our madness. As twenty-nine-year-olds, we realized this could be the best time in our lives to try something like this. Among the realities we considered:

- We were young and physically healthy.
- We had minimal financial responsibilities.
- We had no children and were not planning to have children for several years.
- Our parents weren't elderly yet, so they didn't need us to care for them.
- We both wanted to try living overseas.
- We wanted to spend more time together.
- We felt confident in the health of our marriage.

And perhaps most important:

- We both believed wholeheartedly in the mission of d.light and felt that whatever we were sacrificing was worth it.

Even I had to admit we weren't taking that many risks. In the worst-case scenario I could think of—d.light goes belly-up in a few months and we move back to the US with our tails between our legs—our lives wouldn't look that different from what they had been before. We had very little savings and few assets to lose. We were both still early in our careers. We weren't responsible for anyone but ourselves.

On top of that, we were at a stage in our lives where the one thing that mattered most to us was pursuing our dreams. If it required us to put other priorities on hold, such as having kids or buying a house, so be it.

Your life may look nothing like this—remember, the median age for entrepreneurs starting their first company is forty—but that doesn't mean this isn't a good time in your life for a start-up. It all depends on who you are as individuals and as a family, and what matters the most to you in this season of your lives.

If you don't already know your top priorities, having a start-up in the family will probably drive you and your partner to figure them out. When your time, attention, and funds are in short supply, choices have to be made. And, if possible, being intentional in those choices is preferable to falling into them or having them forced on you.

In chapter 4, we discussed Stephen Covey's quadrant of time management, and how you and your entrepreneur need to figure out how to make time for the things in life that are important but not urgent. Once a start-up is born, everything related to it seems extremely urgent for the foreseeable future—making it even more critical that you have an unshakable understanding of what is most important to you. Whether your family is on the precipice of launching a new venture, or you've been walking this path for longer than you care to admit, taking the time to determine your life priorities will set the stage for critical decision-making now and in the future.

Action for Happiness, an international group patronized by the Dalai Lama that is "committed to building a happier and more caring society," recommends a list of eighteen common priorities from which to begin assessing what is most important to you:

- Family
- Friends
- Health and fitness
- Income

- Independence
- Influence and power
- Making use of talents
- Personal growth
- Positive impact on society
- Prestige and status
- Professional growth
- Security
- Spirituality/faith
- Spouse/partner
- Stimulating/rewarding work
- Time for leisure and relaxation
- Wealth/savings
- Where you live

They suggest taking some personal reflection time to rank these items from one to eighteen in order of importance to you. (No ties allowed.) The top six are "essentials"; the middle six are "nice to haves"; and the bottom six are "non essentials."[1]

Trust me—this is not an easy task. But we can't put our best energy into all or even most of these priorities at the same time. The hope, then, is that once you know what falls where, you can begin to make decisions on how to structure your life around your greatest priorities.

Or so goes the theory. Exercises like the above are definitely helpful, but the assumption that my highest values are static can make me feel a bit boxed in. What if I change my mind in a few years or even a few months? What if my priorities seem like they are constantly shifting? What about external circumstances that may force me to adjust my priorities? For example, just the simple fact that I am getting older has already changed my priorities. I actually have to think about my health and fitness these days, as opposed to the health that I used to merely wake up with when I was younger.

If you share these concerns, then it may help you to remember that the start-up cycle moves quickly. On average, new businesses that don't survive fizzle out about twenty months after their last round of funding.[2] That's not to say that your beloved's company will fail—I hope it doesn't!—but this gives a helpful marker in time when you and your significant other may have more information to reevaluate the future.

With this in mind, we can look at that list of eighteen priorities again with more defined parameters. Start with your own desires first; you can figure out your shared priorities as a couple later. Ask yourself: What are my six essential priorities in the next two years or so? Don't worry about ranking the remaining twelve items; in reality, you probably won't have much bandwidth to focus on them. (That being said, I've found it helpful to at least make note of the important things I'm choosing *not* to prioritize.)

Once you know your top six priorities, the next step is to get practical. What are your medium-term goals in each of these priorities? (Remember that the most effective goals are specific, measurable, and attainable.) And what are the practical implications of these goals on your two most limited resources—time and money? You may want to create a chart that looks something like this:

Priority	Goal	Time/Money Required to Meet Goal
Professional growth	Get promoted to manager	Work at least 45 hours a week; participate in monthly leadership trainings after work

| Family | Have a baby | Three-month maternity leave at reduced salary; cost for baby gear (clothing, diapers, etc.) and nanny/daycare |
| Wealth/ Savings | Save enough for a down payment on a house | Need to save $50,000; siphon off at least $2,000 of monthly income into savings account |

Now comes the tough part. Assuming that your significant other, if he were to also complete this exercise, had "start a new business" or "continue growing my business" listed among his goals, you'll need to consider whether your collective goals are compatible. With the huge financial and time investments that start-ups require, is it possible to achieve these goals in the same timeframe? Do you currently have enough resources between the two of you to sustain a new business, your relationship, *and* the things that matter most to each of you?

If not, you and your partner have a tough but crucial negotiation ahead of you. Together, you'll need to consider which priorities and goals can be moved down the list or postponed to make room for a start-up. Keep in mind that you're only thinking about the next two years, not the rest of your lives. But even then, it can be a painful process. You may both need to postpone something you care about, or one of you may feel like she is being asked to sacrifice more than the other.

This, of course, gets to one of the trickiest balancing acts in romantic relationships: taking care of yourself while also selflessly loving your partner. If your significant other wants to pursue a new business, this will inevitably require sacrifices. On the other hand, it's important not to sacrifice *everything* for the sake of his or her dreams. You need to hold on to at least a couple of things that will help you remain healthy, grounded, and somewhat balanced.

When I asked one longtime Silicon Valley marriage-family therapist about this kind of give-and-take between spouses, she explained, "You cannot achieve a mature marriage without power struggles." At some point, individuals in every couple will ask questions like, *Who will define this family more? How come he or she is not doing what I want?* and *Whose money is it?* It is normal, healthy, and necessary to struggle with these questions, and I've found that being with an entrepreneur can necessitate these discussions more quickly and urgently.

But how to draw the line between a healthy sacrifice for the sake of your partner or the family, and one that could be harmful? "Don't do things that will build resentment," the therapist warned me. "Ask yourself: What am I willing to do without resenting it?" For example, if you are worrying about your biological clock and do not want to wait another three years to have a child—and you think you may resent your spouse forever for asking you to wait— then this is probably a nonnegotiable priority for you.

It's possible that you may look at your priorities and decide that a start-up just can't work at this time. As a couple, you have too many other obligations, too many time-sensitive goals that can't be delayed. In this case, the sacrifice will need to come from your partner, who may need to let go of her entrepreneurial dreams— at least for a little while. But it's a big enough decision that you'll want to make it together, in hopes of staving off any bitterness or future regrets.

Elliott Rains[3] of Toronto, Canada, has had a bit of what his wife, Jen, calls "that entrepreneurial itch" throughout their twenty-year marriage. But he has yet to pursue a new venture for five very good reasons: they have five school-aged children, for whom Elliott and Jen would like to save enough for private college tuition. "If he didn't have me or the kids, he would definitely start a business," Jen told me. But they've both agreed that it's not a good time for a start-up. In addition to their parental duties, they have health concerns that require dependable insurance and two sets of aging parents to look after. "We have a lot of financial responsibilities. Elliott doesn't feel the freedom to jump off the ledge to jeopardize the security that we have."

Among all the entrepreneurs and their partners that I've interviewed, the issue of children seems to be a core determinant of the start-up life—if you want them, when you want them, if you have them, how many you have, how old they are, what special needs they might have. It's no wonder, given how drastically children change the family dynamic. In studies over the last decade, researchers have consistently found that the arrival of a first child can cause marital satisfaction and happiness to plummet. A second child often sends these numbers even lower. Blame that on the huge financial resources, personal energy, and time that children require, no matter how adorable they are. One Ohio State University study found that couples with a baby spend only one-third of the amount of time together that childless couples do.[4] If you have a new business *and* a new child, you probably won't be seeing much of your significant other.

In addition, nurturing children into adulthood is a shockingly expensive venture. According to the US Department of Agriculture, a baby born in 2015 will on average cost his or her family $233,610 up until the age of eighteen, or about $12,978 a year.[5] Childcare alone costs American families an average of $11,666 per year per child.[6] And that's not including the skyrocketing cost of higher education, which has consistently outpaced wages and inflation in recent years. We can all expect to spend a cool half million or more to prepare each of our children for a life of independence.[7] If you have one, two, or five children, your pocketbook will most definitely be impacted—now and for many years to come.

On the other end of the age spectrum, elderly parents or other aging relatives may also require expensive care. Assisted-living facilities can cost thousands of dollars a month; round-the-clock care for those with serious health issues can cost as much as $500 per day.[8] Folks who are in what's called the *sandwich generation*—caring for young children and elderly parents at the same time—may find their time, energy, and finances stretched extremely thin.

It can feel crass to discuss our loved ones in terms of how much they cost us, but these are exactly the kinds of realities that couples need to face before making an informed decision about starting a business. If you're like me and talking about money makes you squeamish, you may want to take a few sips of wine before considering this tough truth: like it or not, money is often the most pragmatic lens through which to consider what matters most to us. Unless you are so fabulously wealthy that you can afford everything you want, you will need to ask yourself: *What is important enough to me that I am willing to pay for it? And how much is it going to cost me?*

With these questions in mind, I went to David Cooper, a financial adviser with a major financial planning institution, to ask what advice he would give couples that are considering doing a start-up. "You have to have a clear understanding of what you're getting into, a believable pathway to success," he told me. "Both members of the family have to buy into this and believe in it. It's one thing if you have lots of money in the bank and lots of cushion. Then it might be okay to fail. But if you haven't made good headway on lifestyle and family goals, and if the entrepreneurial venture impacts those or prevents you from achieving them, then it's problematic if one of you isn't on board."

And what if the couple wants to start a business and pursue some other major financial investment, like having a child or buying a house, at the same time? "Don't do it," Cooper said immediately, and then laughed. "I'm saying that tongue-in-cheek, but those types of decisions are big, life-changing activities with long time horizons. You need to ask the question: Am I ready and willing to commit my energy and financial resources to starting a family or buying a home at a time when my income is highly uncertain? It's probably not the best timing that I could think of."

The unpredictable income—one of the hallmarks of the start-up life—is why the discussion about money is one that every entrepreneurial couple should have. If you or your partner enjoys the finer things in life and would be fairly miserable without them, then the entrepreneurial path may not be for you. Sacrifice is always going to be part of the package, at least for a while.

In the Startup Garage program at Stanford University, one team of students went so far as to create a detailed spreadsheet of lifestyle choices they would make based on how much funding they could raise. If they raised all the investment they were looking for, they could rent their own apartments and regularly eat out. Lower amounts of investment resulted in different scenarios, all the way down to living with their parents and subsisting on a daily diet of instant noodles if they couldn't raise any funding.

While I wouldn't recommend that anyone try to live off of cheap ramen—true story: the only person I ever heard of actually doing this broke out into painful boils after a few weeks—creating a detailed budget that breaks down your quality of life options is an excellent idea. Cooper recommends the following steps for families that are considering the entrepreneurial path:

1. Based on the business plan, set a timeline for the season of financial uncertainty.
2. Set a monthly line-itemed budget for the family, spending only as much as you can afford based on existing savings and anticipated income.
3. Before committing to the business, do a dry run on this budget for three months.
4. Evaluate how you did with the dry run, and adjust the budget as needed.

On the last two steps, Cooper explained, "It's one thing to say you can do it, it's another thing to actually do it." In other words, we'd all like to think we could tough it out for a while so our significant others can pursue their dreams. But it's hard to know how much we're really willing to sacrifice, and for how long, until we try it. "Prove that you can do it sustainably for an extended period of time," Cooper proposed.

One of the challenges with these kinds of conversations—about priorities, goals, life stage, lifestyle preference, and financial capacity—is that they won't always lead to a clear yes or no answer on pursuing a new business. If your significant other is like most entrepreneurs, she probably has a stubbornly persistent dream of starting something. As a result, the most relevant questions for the two of you will likely be *when* and *how*.

Paul Scott had to wait four years. Dave Kalman (from the previous chapter) waited more than a decade for his children to reach adolescence before founding a new company. For Elliott and Jen Rains, it's an ongoing discussion that they revisit at least once a year. "We both would say that the decision is still open," Jen explained. "When our last kids are out of college, Elliott will be in his mid-fifties. There's still more time for us to do other things."

But waiting isn't always what makes sense. Ned and I agreed that being in our late twenties was the ideal life stage for a start-up. Lee and Sophia Ott, who had those three children under the age of two, made the intentional decision to start the company at that time. They had saved up enough money to hire a full-time nanny, and Lee wanted to pursue his entrepreneurial ambitions while his children were too young to significantly miss his presence. The hope was that an intensive time investment in the start-up now could allow him to be more available when his kids were older and required greater emotional support and guidance.

The correct answer to the question of when will be different for everyone. It can only be answered by you, your significant other, your unique circumstances, and the priorities that you set together.

As for the question of *how*, the truth is that not all start-ups are created equal, and the kind of business your loved one pursues can and should be shaped by the other priorities in your shared life.

We didn't fully appreciate it at the time, but Ned chose a particularly challenging path with d.light. The company had a number of characteristics that increased the complexity, risk, and hardship involved. To name just a couple: the company was selling unproven products in unproven markets, and all major operations were happening in developing countries. Our lives would have turned out quite differently if Ned had chosen to program an app for American consumers.

For the aspiring entrepreneur who doesn't want to be completely consumed by his venture, lifestyle businesses are a viable option. They're more limited in scale and usually rely on the creativity, skills, and personality of the founder to sustain.[9] Ranging from opening a mom-and-pop shop to building a successful blog or selling your creations on Etsy, lifestyle businesses typically provide greater flexibility in time and energy.

Of course, lifestyle businesses aren't for everyone, especially if your entrepreneur wants to engineer macro-level changes in systems and industries. The good news is that she doesn't have to think small to pursue a start-up that allows for more margin in her personal life; she may just need to be a little more creative in how she goes about it.

Diana Rothschild of San Francisco, California, founded a coworking space with high-quality onsite childcare a few years ago. She's also married to a man who makes a habit of joining early-stage companies, and she is the mother of two girls under the age of six. Diana was just gearing up to launch her business when she discovered she was pregnant with her second child. Knowing that she needed to create more room in her life for family, Diana eventually chose to sell her company to another coworking business instead of continuing to run it on her own. "I gave up equity for this," she told me, "but it was worth it because I can have a life with my family and I can focus on the things I'm good at." She stayed on as the director of her coworking site and fast-tracked her hiring schedule so others could take over while she took a three-month maternity leave. When she returned from leave, she began flexing her hours as needed to help with the kids and manage the household, a practice she continued when she became CEO of the larger coworking firm shortly thereafter.

In all likelihood, your priorities will change as your personal circumstances change—and they probably should. One of the greatest mistakes I made in the early years of d.light was focusing only on my professional priorities, with a small nod to my marriage, and ignoring everything else.

When we moved to Hong Kong after I burned out, I organized my life around completely different priorities. Things like friends, personal growth, time for leisure and relaxation, and health and fitness suddenly became paramount. I had neglected my own well-being for so many years that these areas became necessary for my survival. In the years since, and especially after becoming a parent, I've learned that I need a robust balance of personal and professional priorities to operate sustainably. As strange as it may sound, I actually *need* to make sure I schedule quality time with friends, read good books, and occasionally eat some chocolate.

Other entrepreneurs' spouses I've met have faced the opposite challenge: they've spent so much time focusing on their family that they've neglected their professional interests. For these men and women, the best thing they could do for themselves might be to go back to school or to start a new job.

Being proactive about reexamining your priorities on a regular basis can hopefully save you from heartache and conflict later down the road. You and your partner could do this on a set schedule, such as every six to twelve months; you could also commit to revisiting this discussion with every major life change.

The business itself might even provide openings to reevaluate your priorities. Despite all the chaos that early-stage ventures create, they usually generate natural decision points around funding, product, and growth milestones. Perhaps you could make an explicit agreement about this with your significant other: *Each time you need to raise more funding, let's look at our priorities. When you want to start developing a new product, let's reconsider where we want to focus our time and money. When you've opened your second restaurant, let's revisit what's most important to us.*

Even when you've been in the start-up life for a while, it never hurts to have the conversation about what matters most. Not too

long ago, ten years into our marriage and shortly after d.light celebrated impacting fifty million people, Ned and I had some huge
decisions looming: whether to have a second child, when to try to
buy a house, where to settle down, and how all that related to what
was happening with the company and when Ned might be ready to
move on to something else.

Worried that Ned and I were veering in very different directions, I actually followed my own advice and proposed that we
map out our priorities and goals for the next two years. The result?
It wasn't the easiest of conversations, and there were a few tears
(mostly mine). But we discovered, much to my relief, that our
priorities were largely compatible. The main discrepancies were
around timing. We didn't resolve everything, but knowing that
Ned and I both wanted the same things for our family in the long
run gave me greater clarity and the assurance that we were still on
the same team.

That sense of teamwork, while critical for every marriage, is
especially important for entrepreneurs and their significant others. Whether I like it or not, whether it's official or not, I will be
on team d.light for as long as Ned is. But what, exactly, does that
entail? We'll explore your role as an entrepreneur's right-hand
partner in the next chapter.

8

Knowing Your Role

I met with Bill Reichert, managing director of Garage Technology Ventures, on a June afternoon that was scorching by Northern California standards. We sat inside a downtown Los Altos coffee shop, which was full of students, retired seniors, and a couple of aspiring entrepreneurs, judging by the conversations I overheard around us.

Bill founded four successful companies before becoming an investor. He has been with Garage for more than nineteen years. Knowing that he's probably seen a lot over the years from both sides of the table, I asked him what he saw as the most significant things entrepreneurs struggle with on a personal level.

He immediately listed off the obvious ones—challenges with time, availability, and stress—but then his response went in an unexpected direction. "Every founding team has an allocation of equity and salary. Often there is someone who feels like they're being treated unfairly," Bill told me. "And whenever that happens, in the background there is always a spouse saying, 'That's unfair!' Something in the allocation feels out of whack for the spouse."

As any entrepreneur can tell you, when one business partner has a complaint about his title or salary or equity, things can get really ugly really fast. From the look in Bill's eyes, I could guess that he had spent far too many hours trying to mediate such tensions between cofounders.

According to Bill, conflict that is fueled by spouses happens more frequently than you might think. And it's one of the worst things that a spouse can do to his or her entrepreneur. "It looks like the spouse is being supportive, but it's actually a criticism. 'You're letting yourself get taken advantage of. You need to stand up for yourself,' is what the entrepreneur hears," Bill explained.

I admit I was a little taken aback by what he said, both because it was the first time I'd heard someone mention this specific scenario and because this was a clear example of how we significant others may sometimes cause more harm than we realize. I could easily imagine a well-meaning spouse encouraging her entrepreneur to ask for what he deserves. I could also imagine a spouse, driven by fear and anxiety, pushing her entrepreneur to get a bigger slice of the pie, just in case.

Bill's scenario drove home two points for me: First, our roles as significant others absolutely matter. Whether or not it seems like it, we have a lot of influence over how our beloved entrepreneurs think and act. Second, figuring out what that role looks like, such that we're being genuinely supportive partners, can be a little complicated.

The role of an entrepreneur's number one fan can take many shapes and sizes, depending on your personalities, your relationship, and the venture in question. But there is no denying you will have some role. Sitting on the sidelines and pretending that your mate is a paper-pusher who works a regular nine-to-five isn't an option. As therapist Julian Gorodsky put it to me, "As the spouse, you're living the entrepreneurial life. How can you not?"

As an entrepreneurial partner, you can choose whether or not to get involved in the business itself. (We'll discuss this decision more in chapter 15.) But I would argue that offering other kinds of support isn't voluntary. There's the logistical support we discussed in chapter 4, including taking on management of the home and serving as the lead parent for your children. There's also emotional support, which I believe is the most foundational support you can offer on a regular basis. Our entrepreneurs rely on us to help shore up their psychological and spiritual scaffolding, for the survival of the company and for their own well-being.

If you've been around in the early stages of a venture, you'll know that the daily existence of a founder can seem like one sales pitch after another. If she's not pitching the business, she's pitching herself. If she's not pitching herself, she's pitching the product. Or the team. Or the strategy. Or the messaging.

Most of these pitches will probably not be successful. Some rejections will be accompanied by harsh criticism; others will be a respectful but still-painful no. Ten years later, Ned still remembers the investor who, as she was escorting him and his business partner from her office, told them in a kind but firm voice that they had absolutely no chance of succeeding and should just give up.

Female entrepreneurs, unfortunately, often face even more hurdles than their male counterparts. In its second season, the hit podcast StartUp dedicated an entire episode to the sexism and sexual harassment that female entrepreneurs face, from not being taken seriously to unwanted advances and groping.[1]

One female entrepreneur told me how, when she began pounding the pavement to raise venture capital for her company's first product, she encountered some stunning responses. "I've been propositioned by investors," she told me. "I've been mocked by investors." One investor went so far as to question the appropriateness of her desire to start a company. "What about your kids? Who's going to watch them when you have to travel?" he challenged her. Female investors, it turned out, were even harder to please. More than one critiqued her appearance and wardrobe in addition to her business plan.

These are the underlying messages that our entrepreneurs hear over and over again: You're not good enough. You're not smart enough. Your product's not unique enough. You're not in the right line of work. You're wrong. You'll fail.

And even though entrepreneurs tend to be more optimistic and self-confident than the average individual, such relentless critiques eventually take an emotional and even physical toll. You, as the person who knows and loves your entrepreneur best, are particularly well positioned to step in and offset the many rejections and failures she may experience. When so many forces are pulling her down, you can be the proverbial buoy that keeps her afloat and moving forward. *You are good enough*, you can say confidently. *You can do it*.

For artist Liz Grace of San Francisco, California, the support of her husband, Cameron, was essential to the launch of her company. "I'm very type A, very risk-averse," she told me. "And I was very aware of the emotional ups and downs that starting a company could bring." When she told her friends and family members about her business idea to create hand-drawn portraits from photographs, they questioned her rationale. "They asked me why I was doing this. They said it wasn't a real business."

But Cameron encouraged Liz to pursue her passion, one that she had been talking about for five years. They even went to business school together in hopes of making her dream a reality, and both started working on the company full-time in their second year as MBAs. "One thing I'm sure about: none of this would have happened without Cam," Liz explained. "He was the one who pushed me to do it. He would always say, 'You have to risk a lot to get a lot.' That goes for business and for our relationship."

As significant others, we are often our entrepreneurs' most steadfast allies. And in the lonely, uphill life of an entrepreneur, they need all the allies they can find. As *Entrepreneur* editor-at-large Ray Hennessey writes, "Along the entrepreneurial journey, there are a good number of successes to share with your team, with your stakeholders and your customers. But there are a ton more failures and setbacks. Few people around you share in those. That means you are essentially alone. You can only rely on yourself."[2]

With you in his life, your entrepreneur isn't alone. But that doesn't mean he won't feel alone, carrying the weight of all that he is risking and all that he is trying to build on his own two shoulders. Fortunately, there is much you can do to remind him that you are there for him.

Of course, being champion-in-chief is by no means a simple role. Along the way, you will likely have to wear many hats for your mate. You may need to be a cheerleader, encouraging her through rejection and celebrating any and all accomplishments. You may need to be a coach, pushing him to keep going and brainstorming new ideas and approaches. Or you may sometimes operate like a therapist, asking good questions and providing safe spaces for her to share and vent.

Perhaps most importantly, though, you need to be the one person who consistently expresses affirmation based not on how hard he works or the potential of his business plan. In words and actions, entrepreneurs need assurance from their mates that they are good enough. *Regardless of what venture capitalists or competitors may say, you are smart and capable. Even if your business doesn't make it, you are still a person of value. I love you for you, not for your earning potential, your pending patents, or the number of shares you own.*

The start-up world has enough ups and downs on its own; ideally, our affections for one another shouldn't be volatile in the same way.

In her book *Daring Greatly: How the Courage to Be Vulnerable Transforms the Way We Live, Love, Parent, and Lead*, nationally renowned shame researcher Brené Brown discusses the culture of scarcity, of never being enough, that has become pervasive in recent decades. One of the reasons why we are so susceptible to this way of thinking, Brown explains, is that "we are often comparing our lives, our families, and our communities to unattainable, media-driven versions of perfection, or we're holding up our reality against our own fictional account of how great someone else has it."[3]

This feeling of not being good enough is amplified to outsize proportions for our entrepreneurs. Just think about the accounts of successful company founders that we typically encounter in books and movies. They aren't just wildly rich and famous, but they are also vaulted into our institutional memory as people who forever transformed industries and societies. They changed how we spend our time and our money, and affected how our brains are wired. They revolutionized our very ways of living and being. They rewrote the history books.

If this is the standard by which our partners are measuring themselves, if they feel like they must be the next Sergey Brin or Jeff Bezos to be successful, then they are in dire need of voices in their lives that remind them they are enough. No matter how many rejections, failures, or challenges they encounter, they are still individuals of worth and value and love. They are far more than the sum of their entrepreneurial pursuits.

But, going back to the equity distribution scenario at the beginning of the chapter, when does supportive behavior become unhelpful or even harmful? And what does support look like when you have serious doubts about your spouse's business or her entrepreneurial ambitions?

To answer both of these questions, we should look at a category of support that is less about warm fuzzies and more about tough love. Being supportive doesn't mean saying yes to everything your entrepreneur desires or dreams about; chances are that he will occasionally want something that isn't wise or well thought out, or that requires more than your family can bear. In those moments, your support will need to come in the form of much-needed (and perhaps unwelcome) reality checks.

You may recall executive coach Dave Phillips's words from chapter 5: "The more stress people get under, the more their time horizons narrow, the less far they can see into the future. They will not see the natural consequences of their actions." If you are not playing a major role in the venture, you may be the one in the partnership with the clearer, longer-term perspective on how much the business is affecting each of you and your family as a whole. And even if you're working with your significant other in the company, you will likely see things that she won't.

For example, it's possible that you will notice negative health effects—sleeplessness, depression, poor eating choices, and lack of exercise, among others—in your beloved before he does. You may have greater awareness of the state of your relationship and the well-being of your family. You may be watching the family bank account and credit card bills more carefully.

Here's how Bill Reichert explains the significant other's role, based on advice he received from an experienced businessman: "It is a partner's responsibility to pull the other partner from the edge of the cliff when he is about to step off." If your entrepreneur, your marriage, your family, or the business is in serious trouble, it may be down to you to wave the red flag and call both of your energies back to what matters most. You may need to ask the hard questions about what you as a family are willing to sacrifice for the business, and where the line needs to be drawn.

I'll be honest: fulfilling this role isn't particularly enjoyable, and your mate probably won't be gushing with gratitude because of it. But its importance cannot be overstated.

Ned once mused that, if it weren't for me, he probably wouldn't have any friends left. We both laughed about it, but he may be right. I have been the unofficial social events manager in our family ever since d.light came into existence. For years, I've dragged Ned to outings with friends and meals with family members when he would have preferred to stay holed up at home, answering emails and building business models. I've made sure key events like weddings and parties and showers have a prominent place in Ned's calendar. On the home front, I've needled him about date nights, family time, and sharing household chores for as long as we've been together.

No doubt my meddling has been obnoxious to Ned at times, and I certainly haven't relished playing the role of the nagging spouse. But it was necessary, and, looking back, I'm glad I did it. After all, Ned wasn't going to do much of this on his own. When d.light was at its most demanding, he pretty much put a full stop on anything else in his life that wasn't work. No doctor's visits, no hobbies, no socializing, no date nights. And he would have kept going in that direction—except for my persistent insistence that his lived identity be broader than that of an entrepreneur.

No wonder, then, that scientific studies have consistently found that married people tend to be healthier than single individuals. Married people tend to get more preventative health checks and to give up unhealthy behaviors like smoking. And the health benefits actually increase with age and longevity of the relationship.[4] Sometimes nagging—if done in a loving way—really works.

I can't say my motives have always been pure; I have often demanded that Ned stop working because of my own neediness or insecurity. But other times I have seen the sallowness of his complexion and the bags under his eyes; I've sensed his heightened anxiety and heard the overwhelmed tone in his voice. And I've known that I had to intervene, even if Ned resented me for the intrusion. I wanted him to take care of himself well enough to grow old with me.

And that, I think, may be one of the most meaningful things that we significant others do for our entrepreneurs: we are the protectors of our shared future. We want our spouses to succeed, of course, but we want to balance that with long-term well-being. That includes physical health and financial stability, but also a strong marriage and meaningful relationships. And it includes caring for something far more lasting than a few headlines in the media or a big exit: their character. In the hyperactive rat race that building a business can be, it can sometimes be easy to lose sight of who our beloved entrepreneurs are at their very core, and whom they are becoming.

New York Times columnist and author David Brooks calls these "the eulogy virtues." "They're the virtues that get talked about at your funeral, the ones that exist at the core of your being—whether you are kind, brave, honest or faithful; what kind of relationships you formed," he writes in his bestseller *The Road to Character*.[5] We actually spend the bulk of our life's energy pursuing a different set of virtues, which Brooks calls "the résumé virtues." Many of us prioritize having an impressive list of achievements, titles, and skills that we can tout. But it is the eulogy virtues that will outlive most of our mates' start-ups—and will even outlive us.

That's not to say that your spouse shouldn't pursue the résumé virtues. He's actually going to need a significant scope of expertise and experience in order to succeed. But there are plenty of other voices out there telling him how he needs to learn a particular skill or gain a particular kind of know-how. Your beloved probably has an entire line of business partners, investors, customers, and others champing at the bit to tell him what he needs to do in his professional life and how to do it. Unfortunately, there are far fewer people reminding him about those important-but-not-urgent, often intangible priorities in life.

I once heard about a woman who liked to tell her entrepreneur husband, "You can do whatever you want. You're the CEO." She said this when he wrestled over a decision; when he wondered what others might think; when he accepted more modest perks and benefits to try to save the company money.

To Bill Reichert's point earlier, it's possible to read some hidden criticism in her words. She might have been telling her husband that he didn't have enough of a grasp of his own power, authority, or knowledge. She might have been implying that he wasn't doing a good enough job of asking for what he deserved.

But let's say we give her the benefit of the doubt and assume that she was only trying to express unequivocal affirmation and belief in her partner. Even with the best of intentions, I believe this kind of support is shortsighted and risky. Imagine what would happen if her husband began consistently operating with this mind-set. He might stop listening to others or taking their needs into account; he wouldn't seek advice or input; he wouldn't take the time to carefully consider his decisions or to learn from his mistakes. Such an approach could end up harming his start-up hopes, his character, and even their relationship.

As we discussed earlier, the typical entrepreneur is on a steep learning curve. She's trying to master business in general, a particular industry, and almost every role within the company at the same time. Assuring your beloved that she already knows everything she needs to know and is capable of everything she needs to do is a lovely sentiment, but it's simply not realistic. You may be inadvertently setting her up for failure. And you may be coaxing her toward a style of leadership that is ineffective and alienating to others.

Across the many entrepreneurs I've encountered, I've seen two character traits that have frequently gotten them and their businesses in trouble: arrogance and a need to control everything. Such entrepreneurs don't ask for help and drive away those who could help. They take on far more than they should, including things that they don't have the appropriate expertise in. They make poor decisions and stubbornly stick to them, even when they are clearly causing the company, its employees, and its customers harm. Such entrepreneurs almost always eventually become overwhelmed, let important matters fall through the cracks, and find themselves with very few allies who are willing to bail them out.

Occasionally I hear about an entrepreneur like this who still manages to build a hugely successful company, usually because he or she is independently wealthy or happened to have particularly fortuitous timing. But, on the whole, such entrepreneurs don't do well.

Unfortunately, when significant others offer unwavering affirmation to their entrepreneurs without any accountability or long-term vision, they are pushing them toward such narcissism and myopic thinking. They are, in essence, failing to intervene even when their beloved entrepreneurs are about to step off the cliff.

In all likelihood, you wouldn't want your mate to act with such impunity in your own relationship. If that were the case, she would make unilateral decisions without ever consulting you. She would control all the details of how you lived your life and organized your home. She would consistently do what was best for her without considering what was best for you. I know I wouldn't want to be in a relationship with a person like this. So why would we wish our entrepreneurs to conduct themselves in such a way in their businesses?

For me, meaningful and effective support of my entrepreneur spouse has two distinct but complementary approaches: First, I need to unconditionally love Ned, no matter what happens with his start-up or his career. He needs to know that I value him as a life partner and as my best friend outside of his identity as an entrepreneur. Second, I need to be willing to challenge him as much as is necessary.

Even as my commitment to Ned is unwavering, I'm willing to ask him tough questions. I hold him accountable to his responsibilities at home. When he's struggling over a decision, I offer differing perspectives. I push him to set boundaries and to prioritize things in his life other than work. I don't hesitate to call him out if I think he has overstepped or treated someone badly.

Because I truly want the best for Ned, I want to make sure he is conducting himself with integrity, treating others well, and continually growing into the finest version of himself. I want to nudge him toward actions that he won't regret, even for years to come. I want to encourage him to be as grounded, healthy, and well-rounded as possible. I want to do what I can to nurture his eulogy virtues, knowing that almost every other force in his life will pressure him to focus primarily on his résumé virtues.

If that's not enough to convince you or your entrepreneur, consider this: providing accountability and developing character will give his company a better chance of succeeding. They will equip him as an effective leader and a contributing member of society. And they will increase the chances that your relationship will last long enough for you to grow old together.

The accountability cuts both ways, of course. I expect Ned to be just as willing to challenge me. If I am becoming too resentful or pessimistic, if I am pulling away from him or not providing the support he needs, I want him to tell me. I want to know that he loves me enough to push me to keep growing and learning and becoming.

After all, during the high-stress moments in our start-up journey, I am just as susceptible to making poor decisions and thinking with a shorter time horizon. When we were living in China, it was Ned who recognized how burned out I truly was. He pushed me to quit my job at d.light and moved us to Hong Kong. And, once we were there, he gave me space to recover but he also encouraged me to seek counseling and take the time to truly figure out where I wanted to go next with my career.

It isn't easy for anyone to find the right balance of unconditional support and tough love. Exactly how this plays out will look a little different for each couple. But the depth of partnership and the growth in character that you'll both experience will make it well worth the effort. (We'll talk more about the great and long-term benefits of personal growth in chapter 18.)

But enough talk about lofty character virtues. You're no doubt itching to get practical, which is what's coming up next. What are the tangible, tried-and-true tools that can help you prioritize your personal well-being, your relationship, *and* your beloved's start-up ambition? In the next section, we'll explore the day-to-day practices and long-term strategies that can help you and your entrepreneur move forward with thoughtfulness, intentionality, and respect for one another. They are, I believe, the essential building blocks for creating an existence in which every member of your family can thrive.

PART III

STRATEGIC PLANNING

9

Developing Trust

One night in 2008, when Ned and I were preparing to move to China, my mother pulled me aside. "You need to be really careful," she said in Cantonese, her tone hushed and urgent. "Women in China might try to steal your husband."

I glanced at Ned on the other side of the room, checking email on his laptop, completely unaware that he was at risk of being pilfered.

"I'm sure it will be fine," I replied lightly, even as a sliver of unease slid into my stomach. My mom had always been overly cautious, bordering on paranoid, when it came to protecting my sister and me from the evils of the world. I knew this, and yet her anxiety was still infectious.

"And are you going to wear your wedding ring?" she continued. "There are a lot of thieves in Shenzhen, you know. They'll probably cut off your finger to steal your ring."

When I heard those words, I began to relax. This was just

another one of my mom's worst-case-scenario warning speeches, which always ended with someone dying a particularly horrific or tragic death. "Um, I think we'll be okay," I said, trying hard not to smile as I waited for the punch line.

My mom didn't disappoint. "Also, never go into a public restroom in Shenzhen. If you do, you'll never come out."

At that I laughed, unable to indulge her fears any longer. "I don't think that's going to happen."

Ned looked up at my laughter, and I saw a spark of humor in his eyes. Though he didn't understand her exact words, he knew my mom well enough to guess the gist of the discussion. "We'll be fine. Don't worry," he chimed in.

"Okay," she replied in English, looking resigned. When Ned looked away again, she muttered to me in Cantonese, "You'll see. That kind of stuff happens all the time in Shenzhen."

I just shook my head, knowing there was nothing I could say to change her mind. I could only go to Shenzhen and show her that the city was not the crime-ridden, black-market-driven underworld that she and other members of the Chinese diaspora assumed it was.

I'm happy to report that I had no trouble retaining all my fingers after we moved to Shenzhen. The public restrooms, while not ideal because of the prevalence of squatty potties, did not cause my demise.

But on one point, my mom was actually right. I had to keep an eye on my husband.

Unfortunately, Shenzhen has many factors that make it a haven for the proliferation of prostitution and mistresses: rich business-people, impoverished women, lax government oversight, porous borders, and unequal power dynamics across cultures and genders. While we were there, I watched as pimps solicited Ned and local women flirted with him. I heard stories of foreign men who hired prostitutes for business meetings and local factory owners who took their business partners out to sketchy karaoke bars late into the night. If ever a husband was going to be stolen, this would be the place for it to happen.

On top of that, Ned was often traveling alone to countries around the world that are known for sex trafficking and brothels, including India, Kenya, and Indonesia.[1]

If I hadn't trusted him, I likely would have driven myself crazy with paranoia. Even though I had moved to China to be with him, we still found ourselves spending weeks at a time in different countries. Other times he came home from the office after I was already in bed. Occasionally he even worked through the night on the factory line to help get a shipment out. In many of those instances, the only things I had to rely on were Ned's word and my confidence in his commitment to me.

Trust is a foundational component of any successful relationship, and it's what we most often seek in our partners. Across numerous studies, social scientists have consistently found that the top quality both men and women want in their partners is trustworthiness.[2] In a committed relationship, trust extends far beyond the question of sexual fidelity. We want to trust our partners with our emotions, our finances, our time, our children, our social interactions, our home, our belongings, our memories, and more. Trust leads to security and safety in a relationship; it's the gateway to meaningful communication and intimate connections. For entrepreneurs and their significant others—who often spend most of their time physically and emotionally occupying different realms—a high degree of trust is essential. Without it, heading down the path toward anger, resentment, anxiety, and infidelity is all too easy.

"If you trust your spouse, that's worth gold," one longtime marriage-family therapist, who has worked with many entrepreneurs, told me. "Then, even if he or she is busy, that's okay."

The sense that your spouse is trustworthy, though, does not happen automatically. It needs to be developed and maintained over time by the things we do and say to one another. Trust building requires us to get past the deceptions we often create about ourselves and our significant others when we first fall in love.

Renowned therapists Ellyn Bader and Peter Pearson founded and direct the Couples Institute in Menlo Park, California. Their office is situated about four miles from Sand Hill Road, home to many leading venture capital firms and the country's most expensive real estate.[3] Bader and Pearson believe that lies—not malicious lies, but lies that we ourselves want to believe—are among the greatest barriers to a healthy relationship. Some of the most common lies we tell ourselves in the honeymoon stage of a romance include: "I like everything about you" and "We like all the same things."[4] It is only when we take the risk to get past this stage—to acknowledge our differences and, yes, even the things we don't like about each other—and still remain committed that our relationship can grow. In their book *Tell Me No Lies: How to Stop Lying to Your Partner—and Yourself—in the 4 Stages of Marriage*, Bader and Pearson write, "The impetus for most marital lies does not stem from a wish to deceive the other, but rather from the wish to keep the relationship *as it is*. That's the incredible irony: *Couples lie to preserve their relationships, but it's those very lies that create dissent and leave the partners feelings stagnant, isolated, and alone.*"[5]

They make the case that both partners have a role in encouraging honesty. For every liar, there is a *lie invitee*: someone who doesn't want to hear the truth out of fear, anxiety, or insecurity.[6]

Only when both the liar and the lie invitee consent to airing and accepting the truth can a couple begin to break down the deceptions that have stagnated their relationship. In the past, when Ned told me that his workload would lighten in the near future, it was a deception we both desperately wanted to believe. When this assertion was proven wrong over and over again, my trust in him faltered. We both had to reject this lie in order to restore that trust. Ned had to stop being overly optimistic, and I had to challenge him to be honest with me instead of saying what I wanted to hear.

Rather than developing through a single grand gesture, trust grows through the small daily decisions we make to move toward honesty with our partners and ourselves. Bader and Pearson explain, "Several times each day you're faced with these choices: (1) to pursue a path of honesty or deception; and (2) as a listener, to encourage more truthfulness or to close down the avenues that could lead you to truth."[7]

Jenny Rae Armstrong of Maple, Wisconsin, held back her own anxiety about her husband's music business not to intentionally keep it from him, but because she didn't allow herself to be fully aware of how the up-and-down start-up life was affecting her. "Entrepreneurs are good salespeople and influencers. It's easy to get swept up in their passion and charisma," she told me. Thankfully her husband, Aaron, intentionally made time to check in with her and ask her how she felt. The more he created this space, the more comfortable she felt acknowledging and voicing her concerns.

Just as trust does not develop overnight, betrayal of trust does not usually come in the form of one cosmic-shifting event. We may instantly think of betrayal as infidelity—especially given its prevalence in the start-up world—but marriage researcher John Gottman calls it simply a "turning away from."[8] By this definition, life with an entrepreneur may very well feel like an unending series of betrayals, as our beloved chooses his or her company over us time and time again.

For partners who work together, mutual trust (or lack thereof) could have serious implications for the viability of the business. Every co-preneurial couple I've interviewed has mentioned trust as a key element in their professional and personal relationship. Each spouse needs to believe that the other will fulfill work responsibilities to the best of his or her abilities. Without this confidence in one another, work-related conflicts will likely be frequent and spill over into life at home. Lack of professional trust can lead to blowups that permanently sever a couple's ability to work together—even if they are still able to live together.

It may be tempting to look at your mate and think, *He's the one who needs to prove his trustworthiness to me, what with all his travel and long hours and prioritization of work over almost everything else in his life.* But the tricky thing about trust is that it's a two-way street. It is not just about your partner earning your trust by keeping appropriate boundaries and honoring commitments; you also need to demonstrate your trust of your partner through your willingness to be open, honest, and vulnerable.

As nationally renowned psychotherapist David Richo writes, "The first requirement for trust and commitment is telling the truth. We sometimes do not share our feelings and reactions with a partner because we sense that she [or he] cannot receive the truth from us."[9] Shutting your significant other out from your thoughts and feelings could be enough to signal that you do not trust her, which may prompt her to respond in kind—thus beginning a cycle of betrayal that could lead to far more damaging and possibly relationship-ending deceits. Remember how Cindy's husband made major decisions without consulting her (chapter 5) and Erin's husband cheated on her (chapter 6)? If you want your relationship to last, you don't want the cycle of betrayal to ever go that far.

The good news and the bad news is that betrayal usually happens in the little choices we make on a regular basis—choices we can make easily but may be so subtle that we don't think they matter. The reality is that I betray Ned when I choose to sit in silence over dinner instead of asking him how his day was, just as he betrays me when he checks his phone while I'm trying to talk to him. I betray Ned when I'm not honest about the hurt and resentment I feel at his frequent absences, and he betrays me when he books tickets for a business trip without first consulting me about the dates.

What looks like betrayal to me, of course, may not be betrayal for you. A key step for you and your significant other will be to define what you need to trust one another and avoid betrayal. Every marriage-family therapist and executive coach I interviewed used this word when referencing healthy relationship practices: *agreements*. I've come to see agreements as similar to setting expectations—with the important delineation that agreements are, well, agreed upon by both parties. Expectations can be, and often are, just one-sided.

"People need to make agreements," executive coach Dave Phillips explained. "But people don't make agreements in their relationships. They don't consider realistically what is actually going to happen. They don't get their agreements settled up front."

As you have probably figured out, Ned and I had no such agreements when we first married. We made no agreements when he was in business school, nor when he started d.light.

And then we discovered that we absolutely needed agreements.

Otherwise, we were each operating under different sets of expectations that were unspoken and mostly unrealistic. We were setting ourselves up to be constantly hurt, angered, and disappointed by one another. And we were, over and over again.

Figuring out and then voicing these agreements can feel awkward, but I can assure you that the alternative is far more painful. Agreements helped tether me to a tangible framework for what my marriage would look like, which was particularly helpful when Ned's business was sowing chaos and unpredictability deep into the foundation of our lives. Agreements became even more important after our son was born, when I felt like I had ceded all control in my life to our human child and our start-up child.

To ascertain what agreements you and your beloved entrepreneur need, you may need to ask yourself some tough questions, such as, *When do I trust my spouse and when don't I?* or *What kind of parameters do I need my spouse to set around work relations, work hours, or travel?* The responses to these questions will help determine what you need in the relationship to fuel trust in your partner, and what you need to ask of him.

For me, reexamining my tender spots and neuroses has been a good place to start to know where I most need Ned to be trustworthy. My primary love language, you may recall, is quality time. So it's essential that Ned and I have some kind of agreement about the time we spend together. I know I have a lot of anxiety about money and taking care of a young child on my own, so I can take only so much financial instability and travel. As a result, in these areas reside some of the most important agreements for the strength and stability of our marriage.

Here are some examples of agreements that you might ask your entrepreneur to make. The more specific and measurable you can make these statements, the better:

- When I need to work late, I will _____.
- I will set these parameters with friends, colleagues, and business partners of the opposite/same sex: _____.
- When _____ happens with the company, I will let you know right away.
- When I am traveling, I will call home _____.
- On the weekends, I will do _____ with the kids.
- If I need to make a large business purchase with personal funds, I will _____.

And here are some examples of agreements you might make:

- If I am feeling neglected or resentful, I will let you know by _____.
- If I need more time to pursue my own professional or personal interests, I will _____.
- I will set these parameters with friends, colleagues, and business partners of the opposite/same sex: _____.
- I will be responsible for taking care of the kids when _____.
- I will continue to support your pursuit of this business as long as _____.
- I will reserve _____ in my schedule as our date night.
- If something in our house needs major repairs, I will _____.

Though the process of developing these agreements will probably not make it into the highlight reel of your relationship, there's an important upside: creating these agreements can be a trust-building exercise in and of itself. Just engaging in the process requires that you be honest about your vulnerabilities and hopes, and be able to articulate what is most important to you and why. It also pushes you to hear your partner's vulnerabilities and hopes, and to give her the benefit of the doubt that she will do her best to honor these agreements.

The downside of making such agreements? If your significant other is human, he is going to break one—or perhaps even a few—of these agreements at some point. And so will you.

But betrayals will happen even if you don't make agreements with your partner. The difference is that both of you now have a clear, agreed-upon framework to reference. The aggrieved party has a basis for raising his or her concerns; the other party knows exactly what he or she did wrong and why it matters. Having agreements, then, allows your *dis*agreements to be more healthy and productive. They become opportunities to extend forgiveness, understanding, and trust—yes, that word again—to one another. In an article for *Psychology Today*, educator David Bedrick puts it this way, "This takes a new kind of trust—the trust in ourselves to be aware of our hurts, express our hurts, and address the injury and breach with our partner. Essentially, you are saying, 'I trust that there are times you will hurt me and I will hurt you. . . . However, I also trust that we can take steps to address these hurts and breaches and even turn the process, over time, into a strengthening of our relationship.' "[10]

Agreements can get us in trouble, however, if we wield them like a weapon, ready to be unleashed whenever we want to call out our significant other for the slightest misstep. If you are tempted to approach agreements with this punitive approach, your loved one will likely reciprocate. At that point, you are no longer partners but have become adversaries. (And it might be a good idea to revisit some of the strategies we discussed in chapter 6 for strengthening the foundation of your relationship.)

Thankfully, agreements are not meant to be carved in granite. They should be as dynamic as your relationship (hopefully) is, or as flexible as your partner's business plan (probably) is. Just as your beloved entrepreneur needs to respond to changes in the industry or the market, so should he respond to changes in you, your relationship, and your family situation. The arrival of a new child, the loss of a job, a health crisis, the death of a loved one, financial emergencies, major betrayals—these are all excellent reasons to reevaluate your agreements to see if they still work for you.

Just because you and your significant other have agreements, though, doesn't mean that you will automatically have trust. Perhaps you have been wounded in the past by a family member or loved one. Perhaps your spouse has already broken your trust through one significant act of betrayal or through a thousand tiny deceptions. How do you begin to build trust when you're starting from zero—or if your level of trust is in the red?

Executive consultant Jocelyn Kung specializes in working with Silicon Valley CEOs and other business leaders on developing the softer skills they need but often overlook: team building, empowerment, and trust. She has found trust between colleagues, partners, and spouses to be a huge challenge in the business world. "If a team has problems, the dysfunction can usually be traced back to relationships and to a lack of trust," she explained. Therefore, building trust is often one of the first areas she addresses with her clients. She has developed four steps for developing trust between people, based on business management expert Patrick Lencioni's research into workplace relationships.[11] Kung has used this paradigm successfully in her consulting work as well as her own personal relationships.

1. I understand you: I've taken the time to understand what your values are.
2. I appreciate you: I appreciate what you value. I will show this appreciation through affirmation and recognition.

3. I have your back: I have your best interests at heart and can articulate that in a way that is meaningful to you. I understand your fears and insecurities, and will do what I need to do to help you feel safe and loved.

4. I will tell you the truth: I will not deceive you or keep things from you. I will be honest and open about the hard truths.

According to Kung, the first three steps put money into the relationship bank, which is what allows the fourth step—the hardest step—to happen. We can understand one another by taking the time to really get to know each other, perhaps through one of the personality assessment tools we discussed in chapter 5. We show our appreciation of one another through words of affirmation or other forms of recognition. We have each other's backs by demonstrating our willingness to accommodate the other's needs and creating security in the relationship. If you've invested in each of these steps, your bond will be more resilient when a betrayal (perceived or real) occurs, or a hard conversation needs to happen.

One thing to be aware of: the process of building trust can sometimes lead to *increased* conflict. But this isn't necessarily a bad thing. Healthy conflict is good for a relationship. It means you're working through issues that need to be addressed—but you're doing it in a way that strengthens your bond rather than harms it.

When a conflict arises, Kung suggests using these four steps as a template for communicating with your significant other. For example, someone might say this to his or her entrepreneurial spouse: "I recognize how important this business is to you. I see how it's an incredible opportunity for you to pursue your dreams. I love how this has energized you in a way I haven't seen before. I want you to know that I believe in you, and I'm trying my best to take care of the kids and the house so you can have more time to work. But I'm having trouble managing everything right now, and I'm feeling lonely in my parenting. I'd like to see if you could set aside some more time to help out during the week and on weekends."

Within that short speech, it's easy to see how the foundational pieces of understanding, appreciation, and accommodation would make the hard truth easier to hear. If you've made the effort to understand your significant other's perspective, he will likely want to return the favor.

That's not to say that these kinds of conversations are easy. Giving your hurts and concerns into the care of someone else always feels risky. But if you have intentionally invested in the relationship through the above steps, you greatly increase the chance that such a risk will lead to positive outcomes for both of you.

In fact, even if you aren't feeling particularly inspired to trust your partner, just *acting* like you do can have significant benefits. Social psychology researchers at the University of North Carolina at Chapel Hill have found that one partner's "pro-relationship behaviors"—actions that are sacrificial and counter to their own self-interests—help sustain a cyclical pattern of increased commitment, dependence, and trust.[12] The more pro-relationship behaviors, the more commitment and trust. The more commitment and trust, the more pro-relationship behaviors.

I distinctly remember the time Ned returned from a business trip to China and told me that a prostitute had tried to force her way into his hotel room. She persisted for a while but eventually went away after he refused to open the door or engage with her. Ned didn't have to tell me this had happened; in fact, sharing this could have backfired pretty badly for him. But his desire to be completely transparent with me, even about something he knew I wouldn't like, caused me to trust him even more.

If you still feel like the idea of trust is too nebulous, then perhaps you can think of it in the same way therapist Chris Bruno does. As an entrepreneur himself, he understands well the challenges that entrepreneurial couples face. He prefers to use the word *loyalty* instead of *trust* when describing the foundational characteristic of a successful relationship. "At the base of the marital vow is the loyalty that you as my spouse are more important than anyone and anything else in my life," he told me. "As we make choices, we will always be, first and foremost, loyal to each other."

In my marriage to Ned, this has been one of my greatest struggles. When he is traveling half the time and working long hours the other half of the time, can I truly believe that I am more important to him than anything else in his life? He has had to remind me of this over and over—through agreements and honesty, but also just by telling me time and again. He is practicing open vulnerability by sharing how much I mean to him on a regular basis, and in return, I am choosing to trust him at his word. It doesn't feel like much in the short term, but, as we've seen, every little bit counts in the development of trust between significant others.

If we want our relationships to last, building and maintaining trust will always be among the most critical tasks we need to pursue on an ongoing basis. And one tool we all need to help keep trust strong? Healthy communication. In fact, one would be hard-pressed to exist without the other. But what does effective communication look like when life always seems to move just a little faster than our ability to keep up with it? We'll look next at the whats, whys, and hows of communicating—even over-communicating—with your beloved entrepreneur in the midst of start-up craziness.

10

Maintaining Communication

A couple I'll call Justin and Alexandra were two days into a months-long European vacation when Justin abruptly had to leave. He was urgently trying to sell off his company, which had been struggling after his business partner unexpectedly dropped out. After driving an hour to the nearest city to send an email to a potential buyer, Justin decided that he needed to meet the buyer face-to-face to try to close the deal. He booked a flight back to the US the next day.

Then he broke the news to his wife. As you might imagine, she didn't take it well.

"I was pissed," Alexandra shared honestly. "The decision was made without consulting me. I didn't understand what the urgency was. Why can't it happen tomorrow? Why can't it be next week? I was completely blindsided." Even worse, she was suddenly left alone in an unfamiliar country, responsible for moving all their luggage from one lodging to another until Justin was able to return.

Justin readily admitted, "I could have been better about talking about it. I was not making good decisions. I was under so much pressure I just wanted to get things done."

More likely than not, you have been blindsided by your entrepreneur in some way over the years. I've lost track of the number of last-minute, unexpected business trips Ned has taken over the years. I know several couples that have made cross-country or international moves with only one or two days' notice.

Given the dramatic twists and turns of the start-up journey, it's inevitable that there will be surprises—and probably mostly unpleasant ones—along the way. But the negative impact of those surprises can easily be mitigated by ongoing and intentional communication between the two of you.

Communication is the oldest topic in the marital survival handbook, and any book or seminar on maintaining a successful relationship is going to discuss it. But it's a skill that takes a lifetime to master, in large part because we all bring a lot of baggage into our communication styles.

In her book *Making Marriage Beautiful: Lifelong Love, Joy, and Intimacy Start with You*, pastor Dorothy Greco writes that we can't underestimate the influence of our families of origin in shaping our attitudes and behaviors as adults. Early on in her marriage, after multiple arguments with her husband over the proper way to host a dinner party, Greco realized that "our family cultures had so deeply shaped our preferences, biases, and beliefs that we reflexively judged anything different as wrong."[1] This extended to their communication styles as well. She describes her husband's family's communication style as "operatic": loud, passionate, and dramatic, with little quiet in between proclamations. Greco's own family tended to speak at a more measured pace, with plenty of space for question-asking and reflection.

Each of us has grown up accustomed to a particular way of talking and listening and being—and it's probable that your significant other grew up with a dissimilar way of talking and listening and being. We each respond differently to certain tones or words or body language. Oftentimes, those responses aren't entirely under our control. They've been deeply ingrained in us since childhood and may reside in the more subconscious areas of our brain.

Our communication preferences are also inextricably intertwined with fundamental aspects of our personality. Relationship expert and research psychologist Ty Tashiro explained to me that entrepreneurs "are a little more allergic to being told what to do." (Remember how the majority of them are motivated by the desire not to work for someone else?) "They can have this reflexive reaction that's unpleasant," even if their spouse comes to them with a perfectly reasonable request. One way to counteract this reflexive response, suggests Tashiro, is to invite your entrepreneur into a collaborative problem-solving process instead. "You can say something like, 'I need you to work with me on this' or 'Can we problem-solve this together?' If you make it a collaborative thing and you're married to a good person, nine times out of ten they'll work on it with you."

Growing in awareness of our mate's communication biases and trigger points, as well as our own, can be invaluable for couples as they try to share with one another in a meaningful way. Another thing to be aware of? Neither of you is going to be at your communicative best when the intensity dial of your start-up experience approaches ten, as Justin found when he was fixated on urgently trying to sell his company.

Psychiatrist Mark Goulston, who previously worked as an FBI hostage negotiator, writes that productive communication is especially difficult for individuals who are stressed, angry, or fearful. When people are consumed by these feelings, their amygdala, the lower part of the brain that acts more by instinct than reason, holds sway over their rational brain. "If you're talking to a boss, a customer, a spouse, or a child whose lower midbrain or midbrain is in control, you're talking to a cornered snake or, at best, a hysterical rabbit," Goulston explains.[2]

Given the overwhelming pressure that entrepreneurs and their partners often labor under, it's expected that we would each have our moments as cornered snakes and hysterical rabbits. I have lashed out at Ned many a time when he told me about yet another business trip or late-night conference call. My anger was rarely about that specific event but was instead rooted in Ned's repeated failures to give me advance notice about things that directly affected me. Feeling like I was the last to know about such decisions—after Ned's business partners and board members and distributors had already been consulted—really hurt, and I wanted Ned to viscerally experience my pain.

Ned has also occasionally lost it, taking small critiques I've made and becoming disproportionately defensive about his roles as husband and father in our family.

At our best, Ned and I are levelheaded people who can have rational, empathetic discussions about complex subjects and decisions. But in the crucible of start-up life, those old reptilian claws and snapping jaws emerge more easily. Developing strong, healthy communication patterns that we can rely on even when we're stressed can help us all become a little more evolved.

If communication is an ongoing challenge in your relationship and you're not quite sure how to improve it, a simple and practical place to start is talking through your basic schedule and day-to-day responsibilities. This is pretty much mandatory for all entrepreneurial couples, given the ever-shifting landscape of activities and schedules that a growing business requires, and how that affects the running of your household.

It turns out that simply agreeing on who is doing what on a daily basis actually matters quite a bit. In fact, the distribution of chores between a couple can make or break a relationship. One Pew Research Center study found that married couples rated the sharing of household chores as the third most important factor of a successful marriage, behind only faithfulness and a happy sexual relationship.[3] Why? According to a team of UCLA researchers, "More than constituting a series of simple instrumental tasks, household work represents a complex set of interpersonal exchanges that enable family members to achieve (or fail to achieve) solidarity and cohesiveness."[4]

In addition, psychologists have consistently found that a couple's ability to coordinate logistics says a lot about their ability to collaborate in other, weightier spheres in their lives. A couple that regularly disagrees about household chores will bring that tension into other topics of discussion.[5] If you and your partner have trouble agreeing on who should do the dishes and when, chances are that you won't have much luck deciding where you should live or how much money to invest in a business.

Fortunately, we have access to plenty of digital tools to help us coordinate our daily responsibilities. (That said, if you and your beloved prefer old-fashioned wall calendars, by all means use them.) Many couples have told me how they absolutely depend on shared online calendars and to-do lists to keep them on the same page. They use these documents to coordinate chores, childcare responsibilities, social events, work meetings, business trips, date nights, birthdays and anniversaries, and more. The effort the two of you put into keeping your calendar and to-do list updated and relevant will help you to respect one another's time, coordinate your shared responsibilities, and keep the household running smoothly.

Each couple needs to determine what division of labor works for their particular circumstances. If your beloved is an entrepreneur, it's very likely that you will be taking on the lion's share of household chores and childcare. If you are both working on the business, it may make more sense to outsource the cooking, cleaning, and after-school pickups to someone else. The most important factor is clarity: a mutual understanding of who is doing what, and when.

If you're like me, the prospect of having such a carefully scheduled existence doesn't sound particularly appealing. Having to write down everything from "take out the trash" to "watch movie with kids" and "date night" on your calendar seems to take all the zest and spontaneity out of life. But keep in mind that you and your significant other simply don't have as much brain capacity to remember all the big and little things in life. Having agreed-upon systems in place and allowing your computers and smartphones to do the work of remembering everyday tasks can free up your mental bandwidth for more important matters. Hopefully, you will then actually remember to take out the trash and watch a movie with your kids.

Coordinating your schedules could also save your marriage from a lot of conflict. I can't even count the number of arguments Ned and I have had when he scheduled a work event that interfered with a personal commitment. The resulting scheduling conflict was often hard to resolve, logistically and emotionally, as it reflected far more complicated issues in our relationship. *Whose calendar item is more important than the other's?* we would have to ask. *Who gets to decide? Does this set precedent for the next time we have two conflicting events?*

That kind of disagreement never had any winners, and I would much rather avoid needing to have that argument to begin with. Now, Ned and I can each see one another's calendars and we each do our best to work around the other's schedule. We have been clear with each other about the things on our calendars that cannot be touched or moved. And if something absolutely needs to be scheduled but it would overlap with something else, we check in with each other and decide together what would work best.

But having good communication in a relationship does so much more than keep you and your mate on task. When you communicate proactively and consistently with one another, you are actually transmitting respect and care for one another. *You are important enough that I want you to know what I know. I care enough about your opinion that I want to know what you think.* A 2017 study of 162 couples found that just having one pleasant, positive conversation with each other helped both partners feel more connected and less lonely. They even fell asleep faster that day.[6]

"Every couple needs a daily time when they can look into each other's eyes, talk, and listen as they share life with each other. This kind of quality time spent daily is one of the most fundamental exercises a couple can do to enhance intimacy in a marriage relationship," writes Dr. Gary Chapman in *Now You're Speaking My Language: Honest Communication and Deeper Intimacy for a Stronger Marriage.*[7]

Even if your entrepreneur is traveling frequently, it's still important to try to check in with one another on a daily basis. Video chats are a great way to gaze into one another's eyes from afar. And if that's not possible, then use whatever means are at your disposal, whether it be a phone call, texting, or something else.

Of course, that brings up the questions of what to talk about and how to talk about it—which can be harder than it sounds. For me, one of the more bizarre aspects of being in a relationship with an entrepreneur is that the two of us are oftentimes simultaneously living very different realities. While your entrepreneur is happily pursuing his dreams, you may feel like you have put all your dreams on hold. While he's invigorated, you're exhausted and resentful. While she is being intellectually challenged and stimulated, you're stuck at home with the kids or working a job you don't like to pay the bills.

Each of these is a distinct reality from the other. The important thing to remember is that they are equally real.

But the end result may be that you and your spouse are experiencing entirely different perspectives, emotions, and thoughts, perhaps even more so than the average non-entrepreneurial couple.

As Dr. Chapman writes, "As humans, we are each unique. That means that the thoughts and feelings that we experience will inevitably be different. When a husband expects his wife to agree with his thoughts and she expects him to agree with hers, they will be forever frustrated. We must first of all accept our humanity and allow each other the freedom to think and feel differently."[8]

Though I'm sure we all know this to be true, it bears saying: Effective communication in marriage is not about winning an argument, assigning blame, or proving who is right. It is about our ability to share openly and respectfully; to listen to one another attentively and graciously; to commit to increasing our understanding of one another; and to provide input and feedback that is for the betterment of our partner and our family.

That starts with letting go of our own ego. That doesn't mean you should stop advocating for yourself—as the spouse of an entrepreneur, you absolutely *need* to advocate for yourself!—but it does mean accepting that you're not always right and that you can't control everything. It also means recognizing that your partner's thoughts, emotions, and ideas are as valid as your own, and should be treated accordingly.

This is far from simple. Swallowing our pride can often feel like swallowing the bitterest pill. Twelve years into my marriage, I still want to choke each time I need to apologize or concede a point to Ned. But my willingness to do so makes it easier for Ned to offer me the same level of respect and care, and it makes our relationship healthier. (It does get easier over time. I used to want to vomit, so that choking feeling is a significant improvement for me.)

Fortunately, some simple adjustments in perspective and practice can shift you and your entrepreneur toward what psychotherapist David Richo calls "cooperative love."[9]

Liz and Cameron Grace, whom you met in chapter 8, told me that one of the most helpful things they learned about communication is the power of "both/and." Even as co-preneurs running the same business, they found that their individual experiences of the same reality could be distinctly different. But that didn't mean that one of their perspectives was truer than the other. "Both perspectives can coexist," they explained to me. "You can hold those feelings at the same time. Both are validated."

The both/and approach is helpful even when considering the multifaceted perspectives of a single individual. I have many conflicting feelings about Ned's entrepreneurial ambitions. I love d.light and how driven Ned is, but I hate how much stress the business brings into our lives. In turn, I know that Ned deeply loves me and our son—more than anything else in the world—but he will still prioritize traveling and working long hours for the sake of the business. One is not mutually exclusive of the other.

When you and your partner are able to accept the existence and validity of multiple emotions and perspectives, you can let go of the need to figure out who is right and instead move toward understanding and finding any necessary solutions.

In his aptly titled *How to Be an Adult in Relationships: The Five Keys to Mindful Loving*, Dr. Richo describes a three-step process for working through conflicts or challenges: addressing, processing, and resolving. Addressing means that you and your mate commit to "bring up all your concerns rather than covering them up or disregarding them. . . . This includes what gnaws at you from within or what you keep feeling but fail to mention." Processing means to talk through what happened and its implications. Richo suggests that we "say what happened as you saw it; express what you felt then and what you feel now; explore what is left to be resolved and followed up." Finally, resolving means developing agreements on what needs to change or what could be done differently.[10]

If you want a more specific template for how to bring up hard topics with your spouse, business adviser Jim Warner encourages his clients to use the following step-by-step process:

1. List the facts of the situation, which can be verified by both parties. "You said you'd be home at five, but you're home at seven," or "You said you'd help with putting the kids to bed, but you didn't, and the same thing happened last week."

2. Explain your opinion or story about this, to help contextualize why this is important to you. "I feel like you're putting your business ahead of me and breaking commitments that you've made to me."

3. Describe your feelings about the situation. "I feel angry and hurt about this."

4. Name your part in creating this dynamic. "I've seen this pattern
   of making commitments and breaking them in the last three
   months, and I haven't said anything about it. In my silence, I've
   become complicit in this behavior."
5. Name your big want in specific, actionable terms. "I want to
   get this off my chest so it won't bother me anymore, and I want
   to have a sit-down so we can make agreements in a clean fashion and count on the other to deliver. If you need to break an
   agreement, try to give advance notice so I'm not wondering
   where you are."

I can say from far too much personal experience that communicating hurt and frustration to your spouse in snappy, sarcastic
one-liners or through a flood of tears isn't particularly effective.
When I've done this, Ned has never quite known what to do, and
we both ended up feeling worse. But when I've approached him
with a clear articulation of what is bothering me, why it matters to
me, and what both of us could do to make it better, he is far better
equipped to respond in a meaningful way—assuming he is willing
to listen, of course.

Which brings us to the other, equally important part of the
equation: listening well to each other. Warner believes that
active, reflective listening is a mandatory skill for every couple.
Your goal—at all times, but especially during a conflict or difficult conversation—is to be fully engaged and to hear what your
partner is saying without becoming reactionary or defensive. You
want to be able to reflect back to her what you heard, so she knows
that you understand.

When your mate is feeling emotional, it's particularly important
not to offer solutions or rationalizations, but simply to allow him

to be heard. And if he is opening up about a challenge related to the business, it's important to resist the temptation to react emotionally in response. Ty Tashiro explains, "If your partner is experiencing something hard, the natural reaction is to freak out with them. It's empathic, or what clinical psychologists call *expressed emotion*." But by adding more emotion to the pressure cooker, you are increasing your entrepreneur's stress and pushing him toward overload. Instead, Tashiro recommends, "If you take out expressed emotion from the situation, that will ultimately help them get to where they want to go."

In previous chapters, we've covered many of the topics that you and your significant other should strive to communicate to one another, including expectations and agreements, priorities, responsibilities, and needs. If you feel stuck in any of these areas, consider approaching it again through Richo's or Warner's recommended process. In these high-stakes conversations, more often than not we probably get stuck at the beginning of the conversation, when each partner comes to the table with a very different list of desires. The more you and your entrepreneur can practice talking through tough decisions, giving constructive feedback, and listening reflectively, the easier it will be to find common ground or to compromise.

While you and your entrepreneur could probably discuss dozens of challenges from sunup to sundown, I hope you will also set aside time to communicate simply to nourish your relationship and to keep yourselves connected to one another. You don't even need to invest much time to do this effectively—you just need to invest that time well.

One simple but meaningful practice that Ned and I have used since our darkest days in China is something called the Daily

Examen. A spiritual practice developed by Saint Ignatius Loyola in the sixteenth century, the Examen provides a way for us to reflect on our day with gratitude and mindfulness. There are several steps to the practice, but Ned and I use a simplified, one-step version. Once a day or once a week, we share with one another our *consolations* and *desolations*, or the recent experiences that invigorated us and those that drained us. Another way of thinking about this would be to simply share your highs and lows with one another.

While extraordinarily uncomplicated, it's actually quite a powerful exercise. When we were in China, doing this practice every day gave Ned and me significant insight into one another's lives. Most immediately, we learned what had happened and how the other person felt about it; over time, we came to better understand the other person's values, hopes, fears, and needs.

In addition, this practice helped me develop a greater sense of contentment and gratitude—no small feat when I was living in a foreign country, mired in loneliness and depression, and feeling like I had given up everything that mattered to me to help my husband's struggling business stay afloat. Each day, I was challenged to find something that had fed my soul. The more I could name things I was grateful for, the more I became aware of the positive things in my life. The challenges still existed, but I began to see my existence—and especially my existence with my high-risk-loving, entrepreneurial husband—as something more than just awful. And when I moved beyond pitying myself, I was in turn better equipped to have productive conversations with Ned about how we could find better balance in our lives.

You and your beloved may have an entirely different way that you like to check in with each other regularly—and that's perfectly fine. What matters is not exactly what you do, but that you do it faithfully and with the honest desire to deepen your relationship. And, as with many other things in life, the more you practice communicating in healthy ways with each other, the better you'll get at it and the more it will benefit you as a couple.

In the next chapter, we'll go over one key topic that you and your entrepreneur will definitely want to talk about: setting boundaries, which can help anchor you through the surging tidal waves that seem to knock every new business about.

11

Setting Boundaries

A columnist for Inc.com once made the claim that entrepreneurs love their work so much that it must be considered fun and relaxing for them. "No need to ever tell an entrepreneur to slow down or take time off," he wrote. "It's like trying to teach a pig to sing. It just wastes your time and annoys the pig."[1]

My first response, I'll admit, was to try to prove him wrong by searching on the Internet for a singing pig—a *joyfully* singing pig, to be specific. I found a surprising number of YouTube videos that claimed to feature singing pigs. But when I watched the pigs "sing," they were really just snorting. Their snorts were loud, sometimes rhythmic, and perhaps even joyful, but any human would be hard-pressed to categorize it as singing. (Obviously, this didn't stop several humans from doing just that.)

I was disappointed—until I remembered this: No one's well-being is affected by a pig's singing ability, or lack thereof. Its mates will not care; its piglets will not care; and the pig itself will certainly not care.

In sharp contrast, an entrepreneur's unwillingness to slow down or take time off can have serious ramifications—for him and those closest to him. It doesn't matter how much he loves his work or how much he gets energized from it. We were not designed to be creatures that never rest or never take the time to connect with our loved ones, just as pigs were not designed to sing *The Barber of Seville*.

Many entrepreneurs seem to have a come-to-Jesus moment when this reality finally hits them. (And for those who haven't had this moment, it's likely coming soon.) Brad Feld, an entrepreneur-turned-venture capitalist, and his wife, Amy, wrote about a weekend that was supposed to be a relaxing getaway with friends. After Brad worked through the entire first day, including through dinner at a nice restaurant, Amy confronted him. "I'm done," she said. "Not with the week. But with living this way. You aren't even a good roommate anymore. I love you, but I just don't want to live this way. I'm done."[2] That conversation was "the nadir of [their] marriage"—and the turning point for how Brad lived his life.[3]

Ned and I had a similar moment, catalyzed by the birth of our son and culminating in a very telling Excel spreadsheet.

When our son was born in 2012, just eight months after we moved back to the US from Hong Kong, he brought us much joy—and the beginning of a prolonged argument about Ned's travels. Before we became parents, I didn't like the amount Ned traveled; after we entered parenthood, I hated it with a passion. His trips, which often took place with no more than one week's notice, now meant proportionally more work, more stress, and less sleep for me. I had to wrestle with all the terrifying questions that haunt new parents—Is my baby eating enough? Is he sick? Is he still breathing?—but I spent far more time pondering these questions alone than I would have wanted.

We both agreed that Ned's frequent business trips were not ideal. But he maintained that he couldn't travel any less, and I argued that I would lose my mind if he continued traveling at the same rate. We couldn't even agree on how much Ned traveled. He contended he was gone only 25 percent of the time; I argued that it was closer to 40 percent.

We spent so much time bickering over this that Ned finally sat down and created a detailed Excel spreadsheet tracking every day, including every half day, that he had traveled in the past twelve months. It turns out he was traveling 33 percent of the time, exactly in between our estimates.

Ned has always been a numbers guy, so seeing in black and white that he was spending one-third of the time away from his wife and baby gave him the kick in the pants he needed to fix specific limits on his travel. At long last, we were setting a boundary that had remained fuzzy for the better part of six years. Part of the problem, I'll admit, was that we had never been particularly skilled at setting boundaries in our marriage as a whole.

According to renowned psychologists Henry Cloud and John Townsend, a boundary "denotes the beginning and end of something," like a property line. In marriage, having healthy boundaries allows us to know who owns what in the relationship. The delineation allows us to see how we are each responsible for our own feelings, attitudes, and behaviors—and clarifies what we can and cannot change.[4]

As much as we may wish otherwise, all the cajoling or raging or reasoning in the world cannot force another person, not even your soul mate, to change. I could not get Ned to adjust the amount he traveled unless he also wanted to. Nor could I pressure him into being more proactive in his trip planning or more empathetic toward my situation when we argued about it.

I'll be the first to admit that the idea that I can't change or control my spouse is a little alarming. Does this mean we're stuck with our significant others' habits, quirks, and neuroses, even if they're harmful to the relationship? Definitely not, claim Cloud and Townsend. Knowing the boundaries in your relationship should be empowering. "We are not at the mercy of our spouse's behavior or problems," they write. "Each spouse can act both to avoid being a victim of the other spouse's problems and, better yet, *to change the marriage relationship itself.*"[5] Appropriate boundaries can break harmful patterns of codependence, support our development as individuals, and help us each understand what we can do to improve the relationship. This is true regardless of how willing your partner is to respect your limits or establish her own.

Of course, setting boundaries works best when both partners take responsibility for what is within their emotional and behavioral domains. Ned had to own that his frequent and spontaneously scheduled trips were encumbering our family connections. He also had to acknowledge the challenges that continued when he was home, since he was often too exhausted or jet-lagged to help out. When I struggled with resentment, I should have examined where those feelings came from and how I could address them in a productive way. I also needed to better communicate how his travels strained my already frazzled new-mom nerves, and what specifically he could do to help alleviate that stress. And I had to do a better job of asking for help, even if that meant paying more for childcare or being more indebted to gracious friends.

For us, having healthy boundaries in our *relationship* was inextricably linked with having healthy boundaries with the *business*. Recognizing the first allowed us to more successfully implement the second. The more deeply Ned and I each understood what we had to own, the closer we moved as a couple toward real solutions when his work life encroached into our family life.

Cloud and Townsend call such couples *boundary lovers*. Among other traits, they take ownership of their own problems and feelings, are open to feedback and change, and recognize that their spouses are separate individuals with separate experiences.[6] I would add that boundary-loving couples probably also have a high degree of trust in the relationship, and believe that each wants what is best for the other person and the relationship as a whole.

Do you and your partner have a clear sense of boundaries in your relationship? Do you know where your responsibility ends and your significant other's begins? If you're not sure, perhaps the two of you should take some time to consider the following questions. These are not easy questions to answer, so I recommend looking at them when you have the mental and physical space to review them as objectively as possible. (Put another way, don't try to answer these questions right after having an argument with your partner.)

1. What attitudes, emotions, behaviors, and consequences am I experiencing because of my significant other's business and its impact on our lives? (Examples: resentment, losing my temper with the kids more, disappearing savings, lackluster social life)

2. Objectively speaking, which of these attitudes, emotions, behaviors, and consequences do I need to own? In other words, which of these do I have some measure of control over? (Examples: resentment is my own emotional response; losing my temper with the kids is because I'm projecting my resentment onto them; we never set a limit on how much my significant other could invest in the business; I haven't been scheduling social engagements)

3. Which of these attitudes, emotions, behaviors, and consequences do I want to change? If you're not ready to change a long list of things, that's okay. Pick one or two—perhaps those most negatively affecting you—to start with.

4. What are specific and practical things I can do to change them? (Examples: examine the sources of my resentment, both internal and external, and try to address those; use breathing techniques when I get frustrated with my kids; talk to my partner about setting a ceiling on the burn rate of our savings; schedule a night out with friends at least once a month)

As you can see from the examples, your response to that last question will likely include actions you can take independently of your significant other, as well as something to the effect of "explain to my partner what I'm struggling with, what I'm going to do about it, and what he can do to help."

Though I can't control how Ned will respond when I ask him to do something, I certainly have the power to make the request and to explain why it's important to me. I've found that my doing so significantly helps motivate him to make changes. When Ned knows that something he's doing is creating hardship for me *and* he knows I'm doing everything I can to mitigate those effects, he is much more likely to want to partner with me to find a better way—which, in the start-up world, almost always involves setting better boundaries between work and family life.

If your entrepreneur needs a little extra motivation to set boundaries, you can also gently remind her of the harm she may be doing to herself if she never takes a break. Yes, launching a business will probably require more than forty hours a week. But studies have consistently shown that working nonstop actually *reduces* productivity in the short term and increases burnout in the long run.[7]

Those who keep answering phone calls and writing emails after the typical workday report "worse sleep, higher levels of burnout, and more health-related absences from work."[8] Believe me, you don't want to burn out. It's a terrible thing to experience. The threat of burnout alone should be reason enough to pursue setting limits on work.

If you and your spouse work together, you should feel even more empowered to set boundaries. To be frank, you probably need them more than anyone. One big challenge for co-preneurs is the complete enmeshment of the relationship with the business. Therapist Chris Bruno has seen this often. "Everything they're doing in the relationship with one another is for the business. The marriage has been put on the back burner," he explained. "When they finally realize they don't want to just be business partners, there's no love left." It's essential, then, to invest in your relationship outside of the company.

One of the most common pieces of advice that Ned gives to fellow entrepreneurs is *It's a marathon, not a sprint.* While it may not feel that way in the height of start-up madness, your significant other should remember that no one benefits—not even the company—if he works himself into a zombielike state. Taking breaks, doing something just for fun, and resting are common-sense practices. They will keep him sane, healthy, and productive.

But taking time off work probably isn't going to happen unless your entrepreneur sets some clear boundaries. As a starting point, let me suggest some areas in which you may want to set boundaries, based on the categories I've seen entrepreneurial couples wrestle with most frequently: time, physical space, finances, and business relationships. As you look at this list, don't forget that *you* also need to set and honor boundaries—whether you work, are a stay-at-home parent, or fall somewhere in between.

Setting Boundaries with Time

- When you will normally end the workday/come home from work
- When you won't be checking email
- When you won't be taking phone calls
- When you can be fully present to your partner each week
- When you can be fully present to your children each week
- How often you will travel in a month/quarter
- The maximum length of a business trip
- How far in advance you will notify your partner of an upcoming trip
- When you will take time off (with no work at all)
- Which holidays and special occasions you will prioritize

Setting Boundaries with Physical Space

- Which parts of the house will be used for work
- Which parts of the house won't be used for work
- Which parts of the house will remain screen-free at all times
- How much storage is available, if any, for business-related supplies
- What other places will remain work-free (friends' and relatives' homes, the beach, at restaurants, etc.)
- What part of the house, if any, will be available for colleagues and business partners to use
- Whether you will host visiting business partners in your home for meals or overnight stays

Setting Boundaries with Finances

- Your monthly household budget
- How much personal money will be invested in the business
- How much debt you will take on for the business

- Whether you will cash out other investments to support the business (retirement accounts, college savings accounts, etc.), and if so, how much
- How much in business expenses can be charged to a personal credit card each month
- The minimum monthly income needed for the family
- How long you can go with no or limited income from your significant other

Setting Boundaries with Business Relationships

- How much you will socialize with business colleagues and partners outside of work, and in what way
- How much your family will socialize with business colleagues and partners, and in what way
- Which family events or parties that colleagues will be invited to
- What limits you will set with colleagues of the opposite/same sex

If some of the above items remind you of the agreements we discussed in chapter 9, they should. Ideally, your agreements should encapsulate many of these boundaries. And, as with agreements, you should probably revisit your established boundaries on a regular basis to make sure they are still meeting your needs as a couple.

Hopefully the above list resonates with your experience and seems fairly reasonable. But if it looks daunting, as if every aspect of your life were going to be boxed in by an endless array of restrictions, let me assure you that your boundaries don't have to be massive in number or size. They just need to be clear, strategically applied, and as firm as possible.

As I write this chapter, these are the primary boundaries that Ned is adhering to:

- Keep business trips to one week or less.
- Limit business trips to one or two each month.
- Arrange trips so they overlap with as few weekend days as possible.
- Be home for major holidays and celebrations, including birthdays and our anniversary.
- Limit late-night business calls to three nights a week.
- Have one date night a week. (No phones allowed.)
- Have dinner together as a family at least four nights a week. (No phones allowed.)
- Help with our son's bedtime routine on most nights.
- Aside from offline e-readers, no screens allowed in our bedroom at any time.
- Make time for attending church and at least one family activity each weekend. (No phones allowed.)
- If the family needs to attend a company function or host a colleague in our home, provide at least one week's notice. (I have veto power if I don't want to participate.)

When you count them, there actually aren't that many boundaries on Ned's work. He still has quite a bit of freedom to travel and work on weekends or in the evenings after our son goes to bed. He even has flexibility with several of the boundaries, since extenuating circumstances might necessitate more travel or late-night conference calls. Overall, though, these boundaries are the rule of thumb we live by. And having just a few times each week that are work-free and reserved for family has made all the difference for us.

Of course, establishing boundaries for time and physical space is one thing. Creating mental boundaries can be another challenge altogether. Many professionals I know (including those who aren't entrepreneurs) continue thinking, worrying, and problem-solving about work long after their computers have been shut down. When something has been consuming you or your beloved all day, it's not easy to simply pack it away into a mental box. We've probably all seen that glassy-eyed look that means our mate is physically present but mentally buried in her hard drive.

Occupational psychologists have consistently found that detaching from work after hours and on weekends is critical for daily recovery, improved job performance, and overall well-being.[9] But detaching is particularly challenging when tasks are left unfinished—and, in the life of an entrepreneur, there are always unfinished tasks.[10] The secret to preventing these unfinished tasks from encroaching upon personal time is to bring as much closure as possible to each workday.[11] If an incomplete email or phone call is going to hang over your significant other for the rest of the night, encourage him to go ahead and spend a few minutes doing it. With larger tasks that can't be finished, suggest that he write down a brief plan for how he will complete this task.[12] With those concerns out of your entrepreneur's head, he can hopefully be more present, and the time you spend together can be richer.

According to Dr. John Gottman, you don't need that much time together to nurture a relationship. He argues that couples can maintain a strong relationship by spending just six hours together each week through intentional partings, reunions, end-of-day debriefings, appreciation, affection, and a weekly date. He calls this the *Magic Six Hours*.[13] Research on children says the same: it's not quantity of time but quality that matters when it comes to bonding with your children.[14] Even though Ned spends significantly less time with our son than I do, the time they have together is so focused that their connection is as strong as our mother-son bond.

We can probably all agree that investing a few hours a week in your most important relationships, regardless of whether your company is coasting or hobbling, makes a lot of sense. Just talk to any businessperson in his or her twilight years who has always put career first. The most common theme you'll hear from them is regret—deep, sorrowful regret. Bronnie Ware, a longtime palliative nurse from Australia, wrote about the top five regrets that she heard her dying patients share. The two most common regrets? *I wish I'd had the courage to live a life true to myself, not the life others expected of me* and *I wish I hadn't worked so hard.*[15] (The latter regret was particularly common among men.)[16]

The conversation about work-life balance has been happening in corporate America for years, but the reality is that many of us don't actually believe in it. A global study of supervisors, managers, and executives found that half of them believed that "men who are highly committed to their personal/family lives cannot be highly committed to their work." An even higher percentage thought this of women.[17] Those who don't like feeling pressured to be on call for work all the time still expect their colleagues to be available 24/7.[18]

Thankfully, some in the start-up world are looking seriously at this and trying to find different ways to work.

When Eric Kim cofounded Goodwater Capital after working in venture capital for seven years, he and his business partner wanted to remake the investor-entrepreneur relationship. While most venture capitalists focus only on professional performance, Goodwater Capital takes a more holistic approach. "We want our entrepreneurs to be holistically empowered," Kim explained. "We want them to be great leaders *and* great spouses." For investees with families, Kim and his colleagues see a close relationship between the personal and professional: for someone to be the best entrepreneur and manager he can be, he also needs to be the best spouse and parent he can be.

Kim's team has direct conversations with entrepreneurs about their personal lives and the importance of balancing work and family. And they model this in practical terms. "We don't do email between five thirty and eight thirty each night," he told me. "That's family time." In other words, if the investor isn't going to be sending emails during a certain time period each night, then entrepreneurs will hopefully feel freer to focus that same time at home instead of work.

Andy Kuper, founder and CEO of LeapFrog Investments, a private equity firm headquartered in London, makes a point of meeting with his investees and saying to them, "I've sat in your chair. Tell me about your challenges, and maybe I can be helpful." He makes sure to discuss far more than valuation and leverage, but to also cover "the human struggle" of building a company and how that impacts their personal lives and families. Kuper models the prioritization of family in his own life: he has based himself near relatives in Sydney, Australia, which allows his wife to pursue her own career as a human rights lawyer and his children to see their grandparents regularly.

But even if an investment firm isn't explicitly family-friendly, it's still possible to incorporate some boundaries into the working relationship. "Every savvy investor knows that an unhappy founder is an unproductive founder," explained investor Bill Reichert. "Whenever I'm interviewing a founder or new executive, family life will inevitably come up." Once he understands an entrepreneur's family circumstances, Reichert can work with him or her to develop reasonable expectations for work.

Investors want their entrepreneurs to succeed. If the founder's personal life falls apart because of the business, it doesn't do the investors any good either. Not all will be as supportive as the investors mentioned above, but more investors than you'd expect are open to the conversation.

Regardless of where investors stand, though, your entrepreneur has more power in pursuing work-life balance than she may realize. She can set the tone for the company's work culture. She can model a way of working that is not health destroying, relationship harming, or generally crazy making. You may remember that one of the top reasons people give for starting a new business is to have more say over their lives. Creating a workplace culture in which boundary-setting is possible is one of the most meaningful ways entrepreneurs can exert that control.

Katy Yeager is a senior consultant with Accretive Solutions, a consulting firm that has valued work-life balance since its inception in 1989. Back then, a certified accountant named Leslie Murdock was troubled by the many women he saw leaving the accounting industry because they couldn't maintain the requisite long hours after having children. He decided to start a consulting firm that explicitly esteemed work-life balance for these professionals—who were talented, experienced, and motivated, but just needed a little more flexibility in their schedules. When Katy joined Accretive in its early days, all fifteen employees had part-time schedules that they themselves set around family and personal priorities.

I asked her what impact such an office culture had on her and her colleagues. "It made me more efficient," she told me. "I had to finish everything by 3 p.m. each day so I could be with my kids. I was very motivated and dedicated. And so were my colleagues." She believes this has been a substantial competitive advantage for

the firm over the years. Their employees are happier and more efficient; worker turnover is much lower than the industry average.

Today Accretive Solutions has over seven hundred employees (both men and women) across the country and continues to
prioritize work-life balance in its culture.[19] According to Katy,
there have been two key ingredients to maintaining their family-
friendly values. "Most of the responsibility is on the employee,"
she explained. "They have to be okay saying no. They have to ask
for help if they need it. They have to be okay leaving the office."
But this is only possible when the leadership explicitly models and
supports boundary-setting. If an employee chooses not to work on
a project that requires more hours than she wants to put in, a manager doesn't ask questions but instead assigns another project that
fits within her limitations. "You shouldn't ding people or make
them feel bad for leaving the office early," Katy told me. "If someone has to go to a kid's soccer game or a doctor's appointment,
they should go. Those are the important things in life."

As I spoke with Katy, I was struck by how this flexible, collaborative workplace culture, which has benefited hundreds of
families, can all be traced back to the visionary leadership of one
individual nearly thirty years ago. His business has flourished, and
so have its employees.

Just imagine: *that* could be part of your entrepreneur's legacy as
well.

If your significant other has business partners, he will need their
help to develop this kind of organizational culture. The two of you
could develop the clearest, most reasonable boundaries between
work and family, but if his peers do not respect those boundaries, he will be hard-pressed to honor them himself. Hopefully
your mate feels empowered to inform his business partners about

the limits that you as a couple have set, and to ask them to respect those limits. It could be a natural opening for a discussion about the kind of work-life balance the company culture could support.

After all, having a healthy work culture supports the long-term success of the organization, especially as it grows. As reported by journalist Brigid Schulte in the book *Overwhelmed: Work, Love, and Play When No One Has the Time*, "a raft of new research is demonstrating that better work gets done when workers have more control over and predictability about their time and workflow, and when managers focus on the mission of the job rather than the time in the chair and recognize that workers are more engaged, productive, and innovative when they have full lives at home and are refreshed with time off."[20] The goal in setting boundaries is not to get less done, but to work smarter and more efficiently.

But even if your significant other doesn't have the support of her colleagues or her company culture, she can still maintain *some* boundaries. And by doing so, she may give others permission to do the same. The effort you and your spouse put into boundary-setting might actually create a way forward for her colleagues and business partners to lead more sane and balanced lives. If your entrepreneur is driven to create meaningful change in our society, then modeling how to live the start-up life and still have time for family is certainly a worthy cause for him or her to pursue.

But what if your significant other *isn't* willing to set boundaries? Perhaps you have asked him—lovingly, clearly, and persistently—to respect your limits and set his own, but to no avail. Don't despair. There's plenty you can do to make your own life manageable while nudging your partner toward better work-life balance. A good place to start is to nurture the intimacy in your relationship.

12

Staying Intimate

Here's one fact we can all agree on: our entrepreneurs sure are fascinating individuals. "Entrepreneurs are set apart from others in business by their novelty seeking. They're fantastic because they're interesting, fun, spontaneous," psychology professor and author Ty Tashiro explained to me. And being in a relationship with an entrepreneur comes with its own brand of excitement. "There's rarely a dull moment with them. They're likely to be curious about you and the relationship. They'll give you an intense focus, which can feel really good at the start of a relationship."

These are all great qualities, Tashiro went on, in someone you're *dating*. When you're in a long-term, committed relationship with a novelty-seeking entrepreneur, the very qualities that drew you to him will likely threaten the satisfaction and stability of both partners in the relationship over time.

According to Tashiro, the impulsiveness, curiosity, openness to new experiences, low constraints, and tendency to fantasize that help entrepreneurs succeed in business also place them at an 8 to 10 percent higher risk of addiction, infidelity, and divorce than the general population. Not a colossal difference, but not insignificant either, considering that the percentage of those who have admitted to being unfaithful to their partners hovers around 20 percent for men and women.[1]

Recent research has found that our evolutionary tendencies, our personalities, and even the makeup of our genes can be linked to our tendency to cheat. One study of 7,400 Finnish twins and their siblings found that 40 percent of promiscuous behavior in women could be attributed to variants in the vasopressin receptor gene, which strongly affects social behavior like trust and empathy. For men, the link between evolutionary urges to stray and the desire to procreate ever-larger numbers of mini-mes has already been well documented.[2]

So, the fact that entrepreneurs have a tendency to get bored and to look for something different and new absolutely matters when we're discussing long-term faithfulness. And it doesn't help that, nowadays, it is easier than ever to start up a flirtation (or more) through online chats, texts, video calls, trips to other places, or other means.

But before you start despairing that your relationship is doomed, it's important to remember this: Our entrepreneurs may be a little more vulnerable to the temptations of infidelity, but their fates are by no means sealed. You and your mate still have very important roles to play in maintaining a healthy, dynamic, and deep connection, which could inspire both of you to remain fully (and happily) committed to one another.

Consider what executive coach Jocelyn Kung sees happening when entrepreneurs cheat. To her, their infidelity is the behavioral indicator of long-term resentment. "The entrepreneur may feel lonely or not understood. They may lose respect for their spouses, whom they've known for a long time," she told me. "It can be easy to flip into seeking short-term gratification." Spouses of entrepreneurs could easily fall into the same trap. With everything that may cause entrepreneurs and their significant others to struggle in their relationship—financial stress, uncertainty, lack of communication, and more—plus the fact that founders often travel and work long hours, it's not hard to see why entrepreneurial partners may also look for a little extra fun, romance, and affirmation on the side.

Social science research findings support this. In the general population, some of the most consistent factors linked with infidelity are, unsurprisingly, related to the state of the relationship. A team of researchers at the University of Denver found that low relationship satisfaction, negative communication, lower dedication, and a partner's previous infidelity, among other factors, significantly predicted a future affair.[3] Other studies have found that sexual dissatisfaction can play a role, but that usually comes in tandem with emotional dissatisfaction.[4]

Maintaining a strong level of intimacy in your relationship, then, is fundamental to remaining committed to one another and staving off the risk of someone wandering. It's something we should prioritize, even when there's a needy, demanding business venture regularly coming between you.

Since this is among the dicier topics covered in this book (is anyone else sweating like I am?), I want to clarify a couple of things first. To begin with, when I talk about intimacy, I'm not just talking about sex. Sex is vital to the health of a marriage, but it is only one element of intimacy. When married couples in a psychological study were asked to define what intimacy meant to them, they listed the following categories in order of importance: affection, expressiveness, sexuality, commitment, compatibility, autonomy from parents, minimal conflict, and healthy self-identity.[5]

Intimacy involves afternoon walks and late-night talks, cuddling on the couch and sharing deeply. It is acts of service, light touches, shared looks, or companionable silence. Intimacy takes many forms other than sex. (Never fear, though, as we will get to sex later in this chapter.)

Secondly, by emphasizing the importance of intimacy, I don't mean to suggest that your beloved entrepreneur should be your be-all and end-all. Internationally renowned psychotherapist and author Esther Perel claims that, in the US in particular, we have remade the definition of intimacy to be "into-me-see." We expect our significant other to see all our needs and to, on his or her own, meet all those needs. According to Perel, we say, "You need to be my best friend, co-parent, and intellectual equal. . . . One person needs to give me what a whole village used to."[6]

In reality, healthy intimacy in a romantic relationship is best experienced in the context of a larger community. You can expect your beloved to provide a unique level of companionship and closeness, but it is also important to cultivate friendships to meet your other relational and social needs. (We'll discuss this more in the next two chapters.)

All that said, intimacy is still essential to your relationship. Feeling some measure of nearness to and affection for your partner makes everything easier, including managing the unpredictable start-up journey. It will be easier for you to choose to stay and endure and work through and improve when you feel deeply connected to your mate.

Now, let's review all the various factors that are probably getting in the way of your feeling intimately bonded with your significant other: You spend very little time together. You're occupying different worlds most of the time and have little overlap in your daily experience. You're both exhausted. You don't have enough hours in the day to manage your work, household, and children. You're stressed and worried about finances and your future. You may feel resentful of one another. As a result, the last thing you're interested in is hanging out or getting frisky with your entrepreneur. It may take all your energy just to be civil to him.

That's okay, as the small kindnesses you do for your entrepreneur can actually do quite a bit to build a foundation of intimacy. In his bestseller *Love, Sex and Staying Warm: Creating a Vital Relationship*, marriage-family therapist Neil Rosenthal explains, "You can be feeling rather hurt or withdrawn or miffed and still do positive gestures of goodwill—with the desire to communicate that you value your partner's happiness—and that you are making daily efforts to nurture your relationship and to help the two of you to feel closer to each other. What you are shooting for is to soften the atmosphere of tension and distance—with emotionally generous behaviors that are intended to rekindle the feelings of greater warmth and love. Your partner may not reciprocate, and certainly not immediately, but be patient and continue to reach out anyway."[7]

Just as one partner needs to be the first to apologize after an argument, it is often the case that one of you needs to take the initiative to build intimacy. It can start with simple but intentional acts, such as asking your entrepreneur how her day was or cooking her favorite dish or giving her hand a squeeze. Whether or not your significant other responds, your acts are still doing something. If nothing else, they are softening your heart toward your beloved entrepreneur and closing the emotional gap between you.

Intentionally drawing near to my husband even when he's not

seeking intimacy with me is, to use a very unromantic term, an act of discipline for me. I'm strengthening my giving and for-giving muscles. As a result, my emotional connection to Ned is strengthened, leading to a deeper sense of intimacy that is increas-ingly buffered against the wild ups and downs of the start-up jour-ney. Relationship expert Michele Weiner Davis puts it this way: ". . . there is a reciprocal relationship between what you do, think, and feel and your body chemistry. Since your mind and body are inextricably interconnected, a change in your actions can alter how you think, feel, and act."[8] In other words, small acts can lead to real emotional movement in a relationship.

When Ned has been experiencing some of his most stress-ful seasons with d.light, he often acts like he's in a personal fog, unseeing of anything but what his business needs. I could revamp his entire wardrobe or whip up a cookies-and-cream ice cream cake (his favorite dessert) from scratch, and he probably wouldn't notice. Or, more accurately, he wouldn't have the energy or brain space to give me any indication that he noticed.

Sometimes, after Ned emerges from his fog, I can't help but ask, "Did you notice that I put our son to bed every night this week? Or that I did the dishes for you? Or that I gave you plenty of time and space to work without complaining about it?" Nearly every time, his answer has been: "Yes, and I really appreciate it."

For years, the give-and-take of affection in our relationship didn't feel particularly equal. I felt like I was always the one ini-tiating, asking for more time and more attention, trying to reach out to Ned even when he didn't have the bandwidth to recipro-cate. But, as our relationship has matured and we've learned how to prioritize our marriage, the dynamic has become more bal-anced. These days, when it is my turn to be in a fog—when I have a conference to attend or a big deadline to meet—Ned does small acts of service for me without my asking. He takes on more of the housework or watches our son or helps run errands. I see what he's doing for me, even when I don't say I do, and it grows my affection for my spouse. (Of course, it would be ideal if Ned and I not only noticed what the other does for us but also made a point to regularly express our gratitude for these gifts.)

Something else that can make a big difference in a relationship: small investments of time. In the last chapter, I explained how couples need only a few hours a week to stay connected. A quick but intentional check-in can do much more for your bond than an hour of small talk. A short walk could connect you more than watching a three-hour movie together. And the effects can last for days: studies have shown that one high-quality relational experience can have a positive impact on a couple for one to two weeks.[9] This is a perfect example of an effective relational strategy that provides *leverage* and *value-add*—two terms that every entrepreneur is familiar with.

Justin and Alexandra, the couple who had the interrupted European vacation in chapter 10, ended up enduring quite a bit in their first two years of marriage, including the sale of one business and the start of another, a dozen moves, a major health scare, the death of a close friend, and the impending arrival of their first baby. As they told me their story, listing one hardship after another, they kept mentioning these walks that they would take together almost every day. When they had a difficult decision to make, they would walk together and discuss it. When they had a disagreement or misunderstanding, they would walk and talk through it. When one felt deeply hurt by the other, they would walk. When one was feeling particularly stressed or depressed, they would walk.

This seemingly inconsequential act of togetherness has anchored Justin and Alexandra through incredibly intense, uncertain, and even frightening times. It has remained a foothold of intimacy when so many other circumstances in their lives were pulling them apart.

For the couple that works together on the same venture, such moments of intimacy can happen fairly naturally. You're around each other all the time; you have plenty to talk about; and you have an abundance of opportunities to do things for one another. Many co-preneurs I've met genuinely enjoy collaborating with one another. "We get to spend all day together for very long hours," said Will Smelko, whose company develops organic, vegetarian supplements, of his experience working with partner Erica Bryers. "I really don't know if I could survive the alternative right now, which might be only seeing each other half an hour a day and then passing out."

There's also the added benefit of getting to see your mate thrive in his or her role. I'm sure I'm not the only one who finds my spouse particularly sexy when I see him in his element, kicking ass and taking names like there's no tomorrow.

But co-preneurs also have an extra challenge: they're around each other so much that they risk staying in work mode all the time. Over time, the love and intimacy in the relationship fizzle. "They have created a business and have lost any sense of the marriage," explains therapist Chris Bruno.

Erica saw this happen with her own parents. They ran multiple businesses together, to the point where they became friends more than romantic partners. Fortunately, Erica's experience working with Will has been the opposite so far. "When Will and I started working together, the relationship became more exciting," she told me. "There were all these new challenges and adventures we were having together."

While a relationship may be nurtured by that sense of adventure in the beginning, the long-term task for co-preneurs is to remember that they are life partners first and business partners second. Setting firm boundaries between the work life and home life can certainly help, especially when you set aside time to be together without talking about work. But the reality is that you can't fully separate these two aspects of your identities. Pretending that you're not spouses at work or pretending you're not also colleagues at home just isn't realistic. A happy medium instead might be to find meaningful ways of nurturing your relationship throughout the workday and at home.

When Ned and I worked together in China, we spent every minute of every day together. Our dinner conversations and even our pillow talk often centered on to-do lists and work issues. But then, just as I would start to worry that we were becoming a little too collegial, Ned would do something to remind me that I was more to him than an employee. He would give me a conspiratorial wink in the middle of a meeting or squeeze my shoulder as he walked by my desk. Occasionally he would ask me, in a serious voice, to come into his office. Then, when I closed the door behind me, he would give me a sunny smile and say, "Hey, I just wanted to see how you're doing." I loved these little stolen moments with Ned. They reminded me that, even when we were surrounded by other people and giving all we had to this company, he and I shared a particular bond.

Other entrepreneurs might find it helpful to inject a bit of professionalism into how they interact with their significant others. Janica Alvarez, who runs a women's health technology company, admits that she can sometimes talk to her husband, Jeff, without much of a filter. But in their workspace, where she is CEO and he is CTO, she is very conscientious of how she addresses him. "I can't talk to him like my husband or treat him like my husband," she explained. "I need to treat him like other employees." For Janica, that means speaking to him with more respect in the office than she would if they were, say, just lounging around on the couch at home. She is intentionally interacting with her husband at work in such a way as to maintain and strengthen her personal connection with him.

But there's something else that co-preneurs need: space away from each other. Nicki Boyd of Portola Valley, California, worked with her then-fiancé, now-husband, for a couple of years on an educational technology start-up. "We lost some of the romantic element because we were spending so much time together," she told me. "We thought it might be healthy if we spent some time apart as well." When the two of them took time to pursue their own interests and eventually began working at separate companies, the intimacy in their relationship was revived.

Wait a minute, you may be wondering. *Haven't we been discussing how all the time entrepreneurs and their significant others spend away from each other can cause strain in a relationship?* Yes, it can. But when it comes to sex, it turns out that time apart and well-developed individual identities are among the most important ingredients for a healthy sex life. According to many sex therapists, desire is cultivated through excitement and distance.

This is how Esther Perel explains it in her internationally bestselling book, *Mating in Captivity: Unlocking Erotic Intelligence*: "Love enjoys knowing everything about you; desire needs mystery. Love likes to shrink the distance that exists between me and you, while desire is energized by it. . . . It thrives on the mysterious, the novel, and the unexpected. Love is about having; desire is about wanting."[10]

If Perel is right, then you and your beloved entrepreneur may actually have a significant advantage in the erotic department.

Unlike your friends who have regular schedules and conventional life trajectories, you've signed up for a much wilder ride, full of uncertainty and unexpected events. Your mate probably isn't at your beck and call most of the time. He can easily fit the mold of the elusive, mysterious, and unavailable object of your desire.

Of course, that alone doesn't mean that you and your significant other are having a raucous time in the bedroom. If one or both of you is struggling with fatigue, stress, or depression—as many entrepreneurs and their spouses are—then you're not going to be particularly interested in making love. If your relationship itself is struggling, then you're not going to get much action either. Addressing these challenges separately will help your sense of connectedness. But I wouldn't recommend waiting for everything else in your relationship to be resolved before turning your attention to maintaining—or, if need be, increasing—the level of desire between you and your mate. There are definitely things you can do now to facilitate greater physical intimacy.

Michele Weiner Davis encourages partners to practice being giving to one another sexually, meeting your partner's needs and wants in the bedroom rather than focusing on what you want. "Real giving is when you give to your spouse not what *you* want or need but that which *your spouse* wants and needs," she writes. "Plus—and this part is really important—you don't really have to fully understand why your spouse feels the way s/he does. . . . Love is contagious. When you give genuinely and consistently, your spouse will reciprocate."[11]

Perel has similar advice, especially for the entrepreneur in the relationship. "Entrepreneurs must learn to straddle the commitment, the passion, and the focus they bring to the personal and the professional dimensions of life," she said in a 2014 interview. "It always amazes me how much energy and attention they invest in their startup, and how often they bring the leftovers home. Treat your partners as well as you treat your customers, I say. You will do better at work if your home life is stronger and your business will benefit from the resilience of your relationship."[12] I don't think it would be a stretch to claim that Perel's reference to "home life" includes a healthy and engaging sex life.

Leanor Ortega Till, whom you met in chapter 3, found a surprising connection between her bedroom activities and her husband Stephen's performance in his screen-printing business. She's careful never to use sex as a reward or a punishment, but she does believe it can be an expression of affirmation. Through the ways she chooses to be intimate with her husband, she communicates to him: "I believe in you, and I'm going to be generous."

"When I show him I believe in him, I have seen a direct connection with his success in the business," Leanor told me. "His ability to connect with me is a nutrient. The more I can bolster him and give him support in the bedroom, the more I see his confidence and his ability to be an awesome boss grow." Stephen's increasing confidence and success, in turn, make him more attractive in Leanor's eyes—thus perpetuating a positive feedback loop of intimacy and achievement.

When I first heard Leanor's story, I thought it was a cute anecdote about a creative way she supported her husband. It turns out that there is scientific evidence to back her up.

A few years ago, two separate teams of researchers, one at the University of Maryland and the other at Konkuk University in Seoul, conducted studies on rats and mice, respectively.[13] The Maryland researchers found that middle-aged rats that were allowed to have intercourse had an increased number of new neurons generated in their brain, improving cognitive function.[14] In

Seoul, the "sexually experienced mice," as the scientists called them, performed better on memory and learning exercises than their chronically stressed counterparts. The sexual activity also helped counteract some of the negative impacts that stress could have on memory and learning.[15] (In contrast, pornography seems to detract from humans' ability to multitask.)[16]

If you'd rather not think of yourself as comparable to a middle-aged rat or a sexually experienced mouse, there's plenty of (less brain-invasive) research on humans demonstrating the link between sexual activity and markers of well-being and success. Across the medical and psychological fields, sexual activity has been linked to improved physical and mental health, as well as healthier lifestyles (better diet, more exercise) and higher self-esteem and confidence.[17]

One 2013 study from the Institute for the Study of Labor in Germany, which examined a large dataset of working-aged adults in Greece, found that higher rates of sexual activity were linked with higher wages, regardless of education level, industry, or occupation. Specifically, individuals who had sex four or more times a week earned 5 percent more in wages than those who didn't; those who weren't having any intercourse made 3.2 percent less than their sexually active peers.[18]

Regular sexual intercourse, it turns out, is good for your marriage but also good for your respective professional careers. That fact alone may be enough to motivate your entrepreneur to stop working at a decent hour so the two of you can get intimate. And it provides further evidence that you play an integral role in supporting your mate's start-up efforts.

So, go on, have a little more fun with each other. Share secret looks and extra touches and long walks. Prioritize time in the bedroom and practice being generous to each other while you're making love. You'll both likely end up feeling better and doing better, in the workplace and at home.

But even if you and your mate have the most sizzling of relationships, it's important to remember that you can't only look to one another to meet your needs. In the next section we'll discuss the role that a robust self-identity and reliable community have in sustaining you through the many curveballs that start-up life will probably throw your way.

PART IV

BUILDING A TEAM

13

Investing in Yourself

As you may have already guessed, I'm a verbal processor. I need to articulate what is going on in words—either verbally or in writing—for me to fully understand what I'm experiencing and how it's impacting me. So, when Ned and my depressed, worn-down self moved from Shenzhen to Hong Kong in early 2010, one of the first things I started doing was writing.

Following the morning pages routine that artist Julia Cameron recommends in her classic *The Artist's Way: A Spiritual Path to Higher Creativity*, I faithfully journaled, without filters or editing, every single morning. I wrote pages and pages of complaints, questions, and reflections about the depression and anxiety that continued to burden me. My stream-of-consciousness ramblings were regularly punctuated with age-old philosophical questions like *Who am I?* and *What is my purpose in life?* I allowed myself to express a wide range of emotions through my words: anger, fear, confusion, despair, frustration, and, eventually, a tiny sliver of hope over how I could learn and grow from this experience.

That writing led me to see a therapist who helped me sort through the most painful elements of my time living in Shenzhen. I then became interested in documenting the previous year and a half, to make sure I gleaned everything I could from that experience. That, in turn, pushed me to find other writers who could encourage me, advise me, and provide me with helpful feedback on my writing.

Soon I was taking long walks along the edge of Hong Kong's iconic Victoria Harbor, watching the ferries and junk boats as I pondered what I should do next in my life. I took writing classes and photography classes. I had coffee with various expatriates working in different industries. I meditated and did yoga. For perhaps the first time in my life, I allowed myself to explore a wide range of options, both personal and professional, of what my future could look like. And for the first time since we had moved overseas, the bulk of my energy and effort was focused on my own needs and desires and dreams, not Ned's.

For his part, Ned loved what I was doing. He missed working with me at d.light, but he felt content knowing that I was doing activities that made me healthier and more balanced. When I applied for a nonprofit job in Hong Kong in hopes of going back to what I already knew, he encouraged me to look past my familiar horizons. He told me not to worry about the money or time I felt like I was frittering away. "I would rather you take your time to find what you are meant to do instead of jumping into something because you feel like you need to work," he said. In short, he was giving me permission to take the best, most freeing aspect of the entrepreneurial life—having enough hope and confidence in myself and my dreams to pursue them—and apply it to myself.

I had done a little bit of this back in 2006, the first time I burned out. But it had been far too easy to slip back into my old habits of trying to keep up with Ned's busy schedule or waiting around for him to come home. Codependency was, unfortunately, my default mode. But now, that pattern of behavior had been blown up to bits by my fiercely independent husband. I had a hard-earned clarity that I couldn't build my life around him, and it would be foolhardy for me to continue trying.

Entrepreneurial couples certainly aren't the only ones who struggle with codependency and overattachment. Psychologists use terms like *symbiotic*, *merged*, or *fused* to describe such relationships.[1] Social scientists and relationship experts seem to have all different ways of defining exactly what this means and what behaviors it leads to, but in general they agree that fusion shouldn't be the ultimate goal of your relationship.

Dr. Robert Firestone, a longtime clinical psychologist who specializes in negative thought processes and their consequences, coined the term *fantasy bond* to refer to any relationship in which we are not present to the actual state of the relationship but are instead enamored of the idealized version of that bond. According to Firestone, these "fantasies" are often based on shortcomings in the caregiving relationships we had in childhood, causing us to compensate by trying to merge with others in our adult relationships. "Most people are afraid of leading separate, independent lives and therefore cling to family ties and fantasies of love, which offer the illusion and false promise of connection," Firestone explains. ". . . They give up a free existence and the intimacy and closeness that is part of a genuinely loving relationship in a desperate attempt to find fusion with another person."[2]

Psychotherapist David Richo sagely writes, "A relationship cannot be expected to fulfill all our needs; it only shows them to us and makes a modest contribution to their fulfillment."[3] Unsurprisingly, it is a tall order to ask your partner to be the solution to all your childhood and familial pain, or to counteract every personal insecurity or deficiency you may have. Even more so when that partner has absolutely no interest in playing such a role.

Almost every entrepreneur I know falls on the other end of the spectrum of dependence—that of not wanting to feel much dependence at all. They are itching for independence and freedom, to be their own person doing their own thing. They don't want demanding bosses or overly needy significant others. They are deep in the throes of *individuation*, or differentiating themselves as individuals apart from others or society.

If this sounds like your spouse, then your own individuation may actually be imperative for your well-being. Trying to build your life around someone who has no desire to be pinned down, controlled, or beholden to another will only set you up for a world of hurt. I know this from personal experience—and so, unfortunately, do many other entrepreneurs' spouses.

A woman I'll call Zoe told me how she was always informing her entrepreneur husband how lonely she was. She constantly asked him to take her out or to do something romantic for her. Retired and at home alone during the day, she wanted him to come home during his workday to take her to lunch, or to leave work early and spend the afternoon with her at the beach.

Year after year, he failed to respond to her entreaties. Once, when she called him at work to tell him how lonely she was, he recommended that she get a dog. "It's a very lonely existence, being married to someone who works 24/7," she told me. "There's no time for play and romance."

When I asked her if there was anything she would have done differently in her twenty-five-year marriage, Zoe instantly replied,

"I stopped working ten years ago, but I should've stayed working." She had given up her job in hopes of spending more time with her husband; instead, she just ended up feeling even more lonely and isolated without her colleagues and work responsibilities.

A few years ago, Zoe's husband finally retired. She has now gotten her wish of having a readily available spouse—but it hasn't quite turned out the way she expected. He now has *too* much time on his hands to keep her company. "I went from being alone to having a shadow," she said. "I went from total autonomy to no autonomy." Today she laments how the two of them have only lived in extremes. They have never been able to find a happy medium, that middle-ground balance between togetherness and individuality.

I have experienced the consequences, up close and personal, of failing to invest in myself or in other relationships. Fortunately, I was fairly young (thirty) when I hit that wall, allowing me plenty of time to hit the reset button. Coming to the place of recognizing that Ned could only meet a small number of my needs—an even smaller number than the typical nine-to-five working spouse could address, it seemed—was a long and painful process for me. But I can say with certainty that this has been one of the best, most healthy things ever to happen to me.

How can you evaluate whether or not you have fallen into the pattern of trying to fuse with your entrepreneur? Dr. Firestone tells us that "perhaps the most significant sign that a fantasy bond has been formed is when one or both partners give up vital areas of personal interest, their unique points of view and opinions, their individuality, to become a unit, a whole. The attempt to find security in an illusion of merging with another leads to an insidious and progressive loss of identity in each person."[4] I would add that this loss of identity could happen rather quickly when one partner is an entrepreneur. Your beloved's dreams are already larger than life, and the effort required to pursue those dreams can be all-consuming. Even the most self-possessed spouse could get swallowed up by the supernova of this kind of existence.

If you are bending over backward to accommodate your entrepreneur's unpredictable schedule; if you are regularly putting your hobbies, social life, and other activities on hold until your entrepreneur has the time to do them with you; if you don't have any strong interests or desires outside of supporting your partner; if you have trouble advocating for yourself or giving a contradictory opinion in the relationship, then you may very well be overly dependent on your significant other. I would venture to guess that this kind of arrangement isn't working out well for you, and you are being regularly hurt by the imbalanced nature of your relationship.

The good news is that no matter how old you are or where you are in your career or life stage, it's never too late to try to create a healthier relationship dynamic. One Silicon Valley therapist assured me that having a busy entrepreneur as a mate could actually be a great opportunity. "Having an absent partner is not the worst thing in the world," she told me. "It can be a blessing too. You can come to the point where you can say, 'I've really learned to love my alone time.' "

That's what happened to a woman I'll call Hope. When she first married her husband, Gregory, she would wait for him to come home for dinner every night. But he would often work until midnight, come home to sleep for a few hours, and then begin work again at six the next morning. He traveled 50 percent of the time. Whenever he had a bit of free time, he would fill it with other activities that interested him.

"That was when I learned I needed to have my own identity outside of my marriage," Hope told me. "I wanted fulfillment in my husband, but my husband can't be the one who fulfills everything for me." Hope learned how to do things on her own that she enjoyed but her husband hated, like attending the opera. She became active in her faith community. She traveled for her own career. She would even give herself extra treats when Gregory was away on business, like eating cereal and wine for dinner and allowing the dishes to pile up in the sink.

Though I'm sure Hope would have preferred to spend a little more time with her husband in the early days of their marriage, she also made the most of her time alone. She stretched herself and tried new things, and can now actually look back on that early season with gratitude. When she and her husband moved to Europe for two years because of his work, she took that well-developed sense of individuality with her, building her own social circles and activities in a foreign country. Having a less available partner broke the inertia of their preexisting relationship patterns and forced her to do things she otherwise might not have tried.

To be clear, living as two individuated partners isn't the same as living parallel lives. I am not advocating for you and your beloved to go your separate ways in life and just meet up occasionally to give each other a high five. Your entrepreneur is still one of the most important, if not the most important person in your life. It is reasonable and healthy to expect him to make an effort to meet some of your needs and to be available to you some of the time. Even while Hope was developing her own friendships and interests, she still spoke up when things weren't working for her and asked Gregory to make specific changes for the sake of their relationship. Investing in yourself is simply part of the equation of a robust marriage in the start-up journey and must work in tandem with staying connected to one another.

If you have been flirting with codependency for a while, I'm sorry to say that moving to a place of healthy individuation isn't going to be a particularly straightforward process. It may involve confronting some unpleasant emotions like disappointment, frustration, and anger, aimed at both yourself and your beloved. It may push you to see your entrepreneur in a new light, as a person with limits and deficiencies who is still worthy of your love. It will involve trying new things and placing yourself in unfamiliar environments that feel strange and risky.

Like many deep changes that we want to make within ourselves, this one starts with small steps. For me, I started by journaling, pouring all my feelings out on a page and asking hard questions of myself without any clear sense of where they would lead me. Then I gradually started asking those questions of others, followed by trying out activities I could do on my own. The more I connected with other people and tried new things, the easier it became. I felt a growing sense of courage and vitality that I hadn't experienced in years.

And in the funny way things work out in our human existence, if you take these risks, it is more likely than not that you will find yourself on an adventure you never would have imagined. In fact, I can draw almost a straight line from those days of loneliness, sadness, and desperation in Hong Kong to this book that you hold in your hands. These words would not exist if I had remained on the same path of codependency and safety that I trudged on for the first five years of my marriage. Only when I acknowledged that what I had been doing wasn't working, and that Ned wasn't going to fix it for me, could new and unexpected opportunities open up to me. (We'll talk much more about how this can happen for you in chapter 18.)

Individuation is also helpful when you have two entrepreneurs in the family. Neal Thornhill and Bridget Sampson of Chatsworth, California, each runs their own business. Neal has an insurance claims business and Bridget a consulting firm. After being married for twenty-three years and raising two kids together, Neal told me one of the most valuable lessons he had learned was that "the less you expect from the other person, the better it is." He and Bridget like to compare their emotional well-being to a gas tank. "You've got to fill yourself up 90 percent. Then your partner can top you off with 10 percent," Neal explained. "If you expect your partner to fill up most of your tank, you're going to be running on empty."

That's not to say that Bridget and Neal don't ask each other for support when necessary. But when it comes to emotional fulfillment, the two of them have a realistic picture of what the other can provide, and so they nurture their spirits through other activities. Bridget, for example, does yoga six times a week and meditates every day. She voraciously reads spiritual books and regularly attends spiritual training programs. Such activities have helped keep her centered and grounded, and have kept their marriage well balanced. "That's probably the biggest thing that has helped us remain happy through our marriage," she told me.

Fortunately, there are many sources that you can draw that 90 percent of emotional well-being from. Here are just a few of the paths you could pursue to cultivate your own sense of identity:

- Arts and culture: Visit a museum or attend a dance performance or listen to your favorite album. Experience an old favorite or try something completely new. Simply being exposed to art and music can release chemicals in your brain that elevate your mood and act as natural painkillers.[5]
- Career: If you already have a career you enjoy, great. If you don't have a career and don't feel the need for one, that's also great. But if you are somewhere in between and aren't content with your professional life, do something about it. Brainstorm

what you'd like to do next. Talk to a career counselor or personal coach. See what new skills you could learn. Update your résumé and search for opportunities that excite you. Conduct informational interviews with individuals whose careers or jobs interest you.

▪ Creative pursuits: Whether or not you have artistic talent, just engaging in a creative activity can improve your well-being. Practicing creativity has been linked with increased happiness and reduced anxiety.[6] I know people who have tried activities as varied as ceramics, flower arranging, graphic design, poetry, and improv theater, and every one of them has been glad they took the risk to do so.

▪ Community activities: Unless you prefer the life of a hermit (and no judgment if you do), spending time with other people who share similar interests is one of the easiest ways to expand your social circles. Join an activity, like a class or outdoor adventure or faith group, and get ready to mingle with some like-minded people.

▪ Community service: Doing something for others is a meaningful and positive act in and of itself, of course, but it will also help you. Those who volunteer tend to have lower rates of depression and improved brain functions. And the more someone volunteers, the greater the health benefits.[7] I've found that serving others is also the perfect antidote to self-pity and helps fuel that sense of purpose we all need.

▪ Continuous learning: Learn a new skill or study a topic you don't know much about through a class with a community center, college, business association, or other organization. Or, if you're feeling particularly passionate about something, go back to school as a full- or part-time student.

- Health and fitness: One of the simplest, most effective defenses against depression and anxiety is exercise. Even if it's taking a brisk walk, the resulting release of endorphins will energize you and lift your spirits. Eating healthy, if you don't already, will also help give you a greater sense of vitality. If you need help in this area, you could ask a nutritionist or a personal trainer to develop a program for you.

- Hobbies: Having favorite pastimes taps into the same benefits of creativity and rest. Engaging in a hobby can improve your mood and your outlook on life. It can also help increase your sense of focus and concentration, which can benefit other areas of your life.[8]

- Recreation: Do something purely for fun. Go to the beach, watch a movie, or read the latest bestselling novel. It's good for you to spend time without worrying about being productive or doing anything particularly meaningful.

- Relationships: Get back in touch with old friends. Hang out with a relative. Make new friends through one of the above activities. Having other nurturing relationships that offer support and encouragement is one of the most critical components of being individuated. You no longer require one person to meet all your needs if you have a small community of people you can call on for companionship. (Just keep in mind that you should still respect any boundaries that you and your spouse have set, in order to avoid unnecessary temptations.)

- Solitary time: Do something just for yourself and with yourself, like journaling, taking a walk, meditating, or having a cup of coffee. Enjoy the quiet and the opportunity to sit with your own thoughts. It can be uncomfortable at first, but growing in mindfulness, self-awareness, and self-acceptance is advocated by experts across various fields. Learning to enjoy your own company can actually be remarkably freeing.

- Spirituality: No matter your preferred approach to spirituality or faith, the notion that there is a Higher Power in the universe and a higher purpose for each of us is extraordinarily helpful for maintaining a healthy perspective. Psychologists have found that spiritual practices and beliefs can help individuals cope with stressful situations and can encourage personal growth.[9]
- Therapy: I have had therapists walk me through grief, burnout, depression, and anxiety. If you are able to find a therapist whom you are comfortable with, and who can both affirm and challenge you, he or she could be one of your best allies in discovering more about yourself and what you need to be healthy and content.
- Travel: Not everyone has wanderlust, but if you do, traveling to new places is a great way to create an exciting new chapter in your life story. You are essentially guaranteed novelty and adventure and learning. Similar to community service, going into a different environment or cultural context can activate new perspectives on your own life circumstances.

I have tried every single category on this list throughout my marriage. Being with an entrepreneur has prompted me to be much more creative in how I spend my time and what activities I pursue in order to build a meaningful life for myself. Ned is very much a part of that meaningful life, but he can't be the sole foundation—and we were healthier and happier after we accepted that reality.

You don't need to try the entire smorgasbord of options like I did; even picking one or two of these to focus on could be a great start. Just keep in mind that not every unfamiliar and challenging experience you try is going to transform your life; sometimes you may even take a few steps backward in the process. The class about the history of genocide that I took definitely worsened my depression rather than helped it. The cross-stitching I pursued fed into my perfectionistic tendencies and added more items to my to-do list. A community service activity I participated in exhausted my already meager emotional reserves.

But despite falling flat on my face on numerous occasions, I have no regrets about stretching myself in so many different ways. Some of my dearest friendships have come out of risks that I took to reach out to someone I didn't know or to try something unfamiliar. The soul nourishment I have received from these relationships and activities far outweighs any failures or embarrassments I may have experienced along the way. And the greater balance that Ned and I have in our relationship, as separate individuals with our own unique interests and activities, has been its own priceless reward.

It's possible that, for some of you, the above list may be nothing but fodder for frustration. Perhaps you and your entrepreneur are on an extremely tight budget and you can't afford to travel or see a therapist, no matter how much you'd like to. Perhaps you have to work multiple jobs to support your entrepreneur's venture and you don't have time for taking a nap or picking up a new hobby. Perhaps you have young children, elderly parents, or a family member with special needs who requires constant care and attention, leaving very little energy for you to invest in yourself.

Your entrepreneur may be able to help alleviate some of these burdens, but in all likelihood, his or her efforts alone won't be enough. That's why asking for help—and being able to receive it—will be one of your most useful practices for surviving the start-up life.

14

Asking for Help

When Ned was in business school, one of his classmates was a young woman named Jessica Jackley, who had just recently cofounded a new kind of microlending platform called Kiva. Kiva has gone on to become one of the most celebrated nonprofits in recent years, providing $964 million in small loans to budding entrepreneurs in the world's emerging markets as of April 2017.[1]

If you were to meet Jessica in person, you would likely be impressed by her energy and enthusiasm, her passion and thoughtfulness. She is married to religious studies scholar and television host Reza Aslan and has three adorable children. In many ways, she is exactly the kind of woman that makes you think, *There's someone who has it together.*

But when I asked Jessica for her thoughts on how to balance marriage, family, and entrepreneurship, the first anecdote she shared with me involved a personal SOS signal that she and Reza developed after the birth of their twin sons. If Reza was out and

Jessica really needed him, she would call his cell phone, hang up, and then call again.

When the twins were only a few months old, both Jessica and one of her sons became very sick. Like most new parents, she was terrified and didn't know what to do. So she sent out the Bat signal, calling Reza, hanging up, then calling again.

It just so happened that Reza was beginning a guest lecture at a nearby university. But when his wife called the second time, he paused his talk and answered the phone—in front of the entire class. Even more astonishing, after Jessica explained why she had called, Reza excused himself, walked out of the classroom, and headed straight home.

I couldn't help feeling impressed when Jessica told me this story. I was impressed by her willingness to ask for help when she needed it, and by Reza's willingness to respond immediately—even if it meant breaking a longstanding professional commitment.

Ned and I don't have any kind of comparable story to share, in large part because I have never been good at asking for help. There are elements in my cultural background that discourage this, but I think the bulk of the problem stems from my own desire to be seen as a competent, high-achieving person. *I should be able to handle this*, I have told myself over and over again. *Everyone else seems to handle work and busyness and kids just fine, so I should be able to as well.*

If you have ever wondered at your own relative incompetence, know this: the idea that there are all these other people who are managing their lives on their own with nary a problem is an illusion. Dig a little further under the surface, and you'll find that everyone who has found a way to juggle careers, health, kids, and personal activities has had a small army of people who have offered practical support and taken on some share of the responsibility.

Those that haven't had such help ended up paying a high cost in terms of their well-being.

In the previous chapter, we discussed the importance of developing your sense of individuality in your relationship, to ensure that your needs and desires aren't swallowed up by your beloved's dream. Becoming individuated, however, is a far cry from trying to manage everything on your own. Unfortunately, many of us try to do so anyway—and find plenty of reasons to justify why.

Cheng-Ling Chen, whom we met in chapter 4, raised her two young children mostly on her own as her husband, Andy, focused on his start-up. Knowing that he wasn't available to lend much practical support, Andy had encouraged his wife to get some help after the birth of their first child. But Cheng-Ling resisted his suggestion. "I'm the one who said, 'I don't need help. I don't deserve help. I'm not working. My mom did it,' " she told me. "Our life didn't fit the model that I knew." Her parents were not entrepreneurs; her mother was a stay-at-home parent. Her family background and expectations of herself got in the way of her asking for help, even when she was desperate for it.

I had a similar experience shortly after our son was born. Ned would travel for two to three weeks at a time. My mom and my mother-in-law would pop over occasionally to help out for a few hours, but for the vast majority of the time I was by myself with a little human, so exhausted that I could barely see straight. Ned kept encouraging me to think of other options, like hiring a nanny or putting our son in daycare. But I could hear all those voices from parenting circles that warn against letting someone else care for your child. Maybe my son and I wouldn't be able to bond properly as a result. Maybe he would develop attachment issues. Maybe I would mess up his social development for the rest of his life.

I had fears aplenty. But if I was honest with myself, I also had a lot of pride. I didn't want to admit that I couldn't handle parenting on my own, especially when I wasn't even working a regular job.

But the exhaustion got the better of me and I eventually relented. We hired a part-time nanny when our son turned four months old. She was incredibly sweet with him, and I often walked in on the two of them sharing smiles and giggles. Contrary to my worry that my son would lose the ability to bond, I saw how fortunate he was to be able to bond with another adult who cared for him. And since I was able to engage in more activities for myself with that extra help—exercise, recreation, socializing, writing—I was becoming a healthier version of myself, who was then equipped to be a better mom.

Unless you come from a long line of ancestral entrepreneurs, you probably have preconceived notions about what you should or should not be able to do as a spouse and parent that are built around a more stable lifestyle, just like Cheng-Ling and I did. Perhaps your parents never ordered takeout or never hired someone to clean the house. Maybe one parent stayed home with you until you started attending school full-time. Or perhaps both of your parents were able to hold full-time jobs and raise you and keep your house spotless.

Let's pause a moment to remember the reality that you are living in: Your spouse, the person you are most likely to call upon for help, is often unavailable to you physically and emotionally. You are managing high levels of stress and uncertainty, which come in sudden, uncontrollable, and intense bursts. Many of the needs you thought a partner would meet—companionship, shared responsibility, co-parenting, emotional support, and more—aren't actually being fully met. You often find yourself operating like a single parent or just a single person, managing an entire family's worth of responsibilities on your own. There's a reason why entrepreneurs' spouses are sometimes called *start-up widows*.

Hopefully that reminder blows up any preestablished ideas you have of what you should be able to handle or how your household should operate. The truth is that you cannot survive the start-up life on your own. There is no shame in this admission. I like to think of it as a simple statement of fact, applicable to all humans who find themselves journeying through life with an entrepreneur.

Just like your beloved needs investors and business partners and employees and customers to make her business thrive, you need a team of supporters to help *you* thrive. You need people in your life who can act as mentors, advisers, and confidants. You need folks who can provide logistical support to manage the extra share of household management and childcare that you are responsible for. You may need work colleagues who have more margin and flexibility to step in and offer assistance when you're overstretched. And last but certainly not least, you need to be empowered to ask your mate to step up—no matter how crazy busy or stressed out he is—when you need him to provide more support to you.

I once spoke with an entrepreneur who, by her own admission, had trouble focusing on a single venture. Even while she was in the middle of one business idea, she would get distracted by the next shiny object. She tended to jump from venture to venture without wholeheartedly pursuing any of them. Her husband, in turn, worked two full-time jobs to support the family and to fund her various ideas.

She knew her husband was frustrated by her inability to commit to a business, but she didn't realize how much it was affecting him until the day she saw a sticky note on his computer at home. "Help is not coming. Get back to work," the note read. The entrepreneur interpreted the note for me: "If it's going to happen, he's going to do it. He feels like, every time we make progress, I will make a choice that gets us further behind."

Whenever I think of that note, I feel a little twist in my gut. Those few words communicate such loneliness and despair and exhaustion, as well as a husband's desire to keep doing right by his family—but without anyone to help him along the way. I know I have sometimes felt that way, and it's a pretty awful place to be. Yet this is certainly not the way it needs to be. No matter who you are, where you live, or what resources you have access to, there are others who can help.

But the first step toward getting help is to acknowledge that you need help and are worthy of receiving it. That can be extraordinarily difficult for many of us, even when we know that our need is normal and rational. Musician Amanda Palmer, who successfully funded the largest music project on Kickstarter and has regularly relied on others to house and feed her, gave a TED Talk in 2013 entitled "The Art of Asking." In her memoir of the same name, she describes how huge numbers of people responded to her talk, causing her to realize that "*everybody* struggles with asking." But it isn't the act of asking that stops most of us in our tracks. Instead "it's what lies beneath: the fear of being vulnerable, the fear of rejection, the fear of looking needy or weak. The fear of being seen as a burdensome member of the community instead of a productive one."[2]

Personally, I have found this narrative of being "a burdensome member of the community" to have extra potency when I compare myself to the entrepreneur in my family. There is Ned, taking the reins of his life, building an organization from scratch, and changing the world, all in one fell swoop. If anyone deserves people to rally to his side, it's him. In comparison, I seem much less valuable to society. What am I doing to change the world? Why should I be deserving of help?

In the book *Mayday! Asking for Help in Times of Need*, longtime executive coach M. Nora Klaver explains that, despite being social creatures who have always been dependent on community support, we have come to see asking for help as a sign of weakness, shame, and vulnerability.[3] Americans in particular seem to be susceptible to the belief that we can and should do everything on our own. In contrast, the actual truths that we need to embrace are that "we deserve, we are cared for, we are blessed. When we accept these truths, our perception changes. We see what we had been missing all along: that asking for help is a declaration of self-worth, a bold belief in the connection of all things, and another blessing in a long line of blessings."[4]

This sense of worthiness is an especially important and meaningful affirmation for entrepreneurs' spouses. When we occupy an existence in which we are constantly competing with a business for our beloved's affections, having someone come alongside to say, "I see you and how you're struggling. I care for you enough to do what I can to assist you and hold you up" provides much-needed nourishment to our thin, tired souls.

There *is* vulnerability in asking for help, in admitting that we can't do it on our own. But, according to author and shame expert Brené Brown, that's a far cry from weakness. "*Vulnerability sounds like truth and feels like courage,*" she writes. "Truth and courage aren't always comfortable, but they're never weakness."[5]

Asking for help is an act of courage. It is an affirmation of self-worth. And it is one of the most powerful ways in which we can connect with others. "Through the very act of asking people, I connected with them," says Amanda Palmer in her TED Talk. "And when you connect with them, people want to help you."[6] It's a lovely self-perpetuating cycle. The more you ask for help, the more connected you are to others; the more connected you are to others, the more you are able to ask for help and receive it.

In short, having the courage to admit our own needs and then to ask for and receive help can contribute richly to our own personal growth and sense of community. It is anything but shameful. "Help cuts about as close to the bone of what it means to be human as any subject I can think of," observes writer and former Episcopal priest Garret Keizer.[7]

Perhaps you're in a place where you're ready to ask for help but you're just not sure *what* you should be asking for or *when* you should ask for it. One exercise that could help is an honest assessment of what you are responsible for—whether it be at work, at home, or elsewhere—and whether that activity energizes you or drains you. Taken by itself, without any consideration for what else is going on, does that particular undertaking result in a positive, negative, or neutral outcome for you, emotionally and physically? Another way to think about it is: If you did not *have* to do this activity, would you still choose to do it? Or would you discard it as soon as you could?

You could create a list that looks something like this:

Responsibility	Net Outcome for Me (Strongly negative, Negative, Neutral, Positive, Strongly positive)
Make meals for the family	Negative
Drive kids to and from school	Positive
Pay utility bills	Negative
Grocery shopping	Strongly negative
Household chores	Neutral
Manage project X	Strongly positive
Lead team Y	Positive
Do presentation for Z	Negative
Coach soccer team	Neutral
Put kids to bed	Strongly positive

This kind of list could provide much-needed clarity on what tasks are taking the most energy out of you, and which responsibilities are soul-nourishing or neutral. The areas in your life that make you feel the most physically exhausted or emotionally drained are probably a good place to start asking for assistance from others. Focusing on these tasks will give you the most bang for your buck, in terms of increased energy levels and contentment.

Of course, I'm not advocating that you happily shirk all your responsibilities if you find there are things that don't energize you. You're still going to need to care for your kids and complete your duties at work. But if you can figure out how to alleviate the pressure from those tasks—perhaps having a sitter come help with your least favorite routine with the kids or asking to reconfigure your job responsibilities—you might find yourself feeling a little less overstretched.

Recognizing when you actually are overstretched can be its own challenge. It has taken me years to recognize the cues my body gives me when I am trying to do too much. Now, I am very familiar with the progression of physiological and emotional warning signs: My sleep usually gets affected first; I need more time to fall asleep and may wake up more frequently in the middle of the night. That is usually followed by a lot of tension in my body, as evidenced by clenched muscles and a racing heart. Then I tend to become more cranky in general and more short-tempered with Ned and our son. Whenever any of these signs begin to manifest themselves, I know that I need to adjust how much I'm juggling—and I need to do it fairly soon. I usually have only a week or two to get assistance or to simply do less before the exhaustion and stress take a greater toll on me.

In an ideal world, we would all be so well plugged into a support network that we wouldn't ever get to the point of feeling overcommitted. But given the unpredictability of your beloved's venture, how much you're taking on—and your physical and emotional capacity to handle it—will probably fluctuate quite a bit. So, even if you have a team of family and friends who regularly step in to offer assistance, knowing your own warning signs of burnout is essential for ensuring that you stay healthy and well balanced through the most stressful seasons in a business life cycle.

One co-preneur couple I spoke with used a more quantitative strategy for assessing when they needed others to step in. They assigned a dollar figure to the value of their time, valuing it at $500 an hour. With this assumption, deciding when and how to leverage assistance became a simple math equation. If it cost them less than $500 an hour to have someone else file their taxes or fix the plumbing or watch the kids, then it made sense to have someone else to do it. Time, after all, is often an entrepreneur's most valuable resource.

Now, what forms could this assistance come in? These days we have access to many easy methods to streamline your tasks, such as making use of delivery and automatic payment services for buying groceries and paying bills, respectively. We have gadgets and gizmos that can help us do everything from vacuuming to maintaining a household budget. I would encourage you to use as many of these services and technologies as you have access to.

If you're in a financially comfortable place, you could also pay professionals to take care of the duties that drain you the most, whether it be household chores, cooking meals, or childcare needs. You could hire a personal assistant or concierge or a chauffeur for you or your children. You and your entrepreneur can discuss which of these services would most ease your mind without breaking the bank.

If, however, you and your entrepreneur are facing an uncertain financial outlook, hiring help may not be a possibility for you. Ned and I managed to scrape together enough money to hire a part-time nanny, and have put our son in daycare since he turned one, but we've had to rely on the goodwill of others for almost everything else.

There are still plenty of ways you can draw upon the time and expertise of those around you. And, I would argue, such forms of assistance and the interdependence they generate will likely foster richer relationships with others.

If you are fortunate to have relatives nearby that you actually like and trust, family is often the first place that many of us look to for assistance. I have found family to be especially helpful around childcare and carpooling needs, as well as meals and helping with emergencies. One entrepreneur told me how she, her husband, her mom, and her in-laws took turns taking care of her two children when they were young. All five adults worked full-time but they were fortunate enough to have flexible job schedules. So they devised a schedule that provided twenty-four-hour care for the kids, passing them off from adult to adult as they were available. She admitted that it got a little complicated at times to figure out the scheduling, but they were able to make it work without needing to rely on a nanny or childcare provider.

I have spoken with more than one entrepreneur who moved their spouse and kids close to extended family just so they could make use of this kind of support. More often than not, this meant that the entrepreneur had to telecommute or set up shop in a less ideal market, but it was a concession they were willing to make in order to make sure their family was well cared for.

If you're not living near family, you may need to get a little more creative in how you ask others to support you. This could actually be a really positive thing, pushing you to find new ways to manage your household and to broaden your support network. Friends, neighbors, and colleagues are all possibilities. Maybe you've made some new acquaintances in a class you're taking or a community group you've joined, as we discussed in the previous chapter. Places of worship are another great place to find support. These days, meeting friends online is also a real possibility. Some of my most treasured friendships have grown out of Facebook groups or Twitter exchanges. (The downside being that most of these online friends probably won't be geographically close to you, so they may only be able to provide emotional support.)

If you have a specific need in mind, and you are willing to ask someone for it, you're already 90 percent of the way there. Now you just need to make the ask—and trust that most people will respond positively. That's what entrepreneur Jaynée Howe, whose company creates educational apps for children, has found. She encourages others, women in particular, "to get comfortable asking for what you need. People can't read your mind. You'd be surprised how many people are thrilled that you're asking for help."

Perhaps all this talk about asking others for help has you worried about turning into a mooch. Another very viable option is to exchange services with others. You could swap playdates with another parent. You could take turns driving the kids, shopping for groceries, or cooking meals for each other. You could share a nanny or a personal assistant. You could also just commit to checking in with each other once a week or so, to see how you're doing. I have a number of friends who have tried this and have been rewarded with deeper friendships for themselves and their families.

In addition, there are absolutely going to be times when the person you most need help from is your mate—like Jessica and Reza's experience at the beginning of the chapter. I often have the hardest time asking Ned for help because I am so intimately acquainted with the work that I would be pulling him away from. In some ways, it's even worse because the mission of d.light is so meaningful. I can't help but think about all the people in developing countries who are gaining access to electricity because of Ned—and how can I, a privileged person with plenty of electricity and resources, compare to that? One entrepreneur I interviewed actually groaned in sympathy when he heard about Ned's business. "The triple bottom line," he moaned, referring to the outcomes of profit, social impact, and environmental impact that social enterprises like d.light often aim to have. "You can justify almost any personal sacrifice when you're doing that kind of business."

But this is what I have come to learn over the years: such comparisons are never helpful, because it's like trying to choose between eating and sleeping. They are both vital. Whether your entrepreneur is developing life-saving medical devices or providing safe drinking water to rural communities or promoting interethnic dialogue, you are still a priority in your entrepreneur's life. Your needs still matter and deserve to be voiced aloud.

That said, the responsibility to know your needs and to form them into specific, achievable requests for your significant other is yours. Her responsibility is to listen well and to respond to the best of her ability.

The shared responsibility in this kind of give-and-take is something that therapist Chris Bruno encourages all couples to have. Especially when things get really bad—such as one or both of you being on the verge of burnout—it's important to have agreements about raising red flags. "It will only be raised when things are really bad," Bruno explains. "And there will be a commitment from both of us to really look at this." As the two of you consider solutions, Bruno recommends that you try to think as long-term as possible, to see the more far-reaching consequences of what you choose to do today, and to act accordingly.

More often than not those solutions, I believe, will include calling upon a community of supporters to walk along this journey with you. This entrepreneurial adventure is a lot more manageable and a lot less lonely when there are others who can help carry burdens for you. But they may not know that you need them unless you speak up.

In other cases, it may be your entrepreneur who needs *your* help in the business. We'll look next at when it makes sense to join the venture and in what capacity, and how to keep romance in the relationship when most of your waking hours are spent as colleagues.

Getting Involved—or Not

When Ned was running his children's music business after college, he had the brilliant idea of promising his customers that every Christmas CD would come with a personalized letter from Santa that was hand signed.

Ned has many talents, but neat handwriting is not one of them. So, for weeks, I would go to his place after work each night and join the assembly line of family members and friends processing the orders. I signed *Santa* on thousands of letters until my hand cramped up. I occasionally added flourishes, like curls or hearts or stars, to the signature, just to keep it interesting.

Ned did not approve. "You're making Santa's signature way too feminine," he told me, as if he knew what the handwriting of a magical man who lived in the company of elves and flying reindeer should look like. I raised my eyebrows at him—I'm doing all this for free and you're asking me to do *what*?—and he wisely backed off.

Years later, Ned and his d.light cofounders asked me to solder some circuit boards to help them meet a next-day deadline to deliver twenty prototypes to South Asia. I had never soldered a circuit board in my entire life. But it was all hands on deck, significant others included. Even then we didn't finish until well into the middle of the night. (Later on, I heard that the electrical engineer had to redo every circuit board that I had soldered, confirming my lifelong suspicion that I do not have an engineering bone in my body.)

Chances are that you've also helped out with your entrepreneur's business at some point, whether you were keen to do so or not. Perhaps you've attached labels and shipped products; maybe you've printed receipts and tracked orders; or you've written press releases and designed advertisements.

In the beginning phases of a new company, there is always too much to do, and never enough free labor to do it. As a result, significant others are often called upon to be involved in some way with the business, even if they are not officially business partners. In small businesses, I've found that mates often fill roles that are heavily administrative or require a high degree of trust, such as scheduling client appointments or bookkeeping. Big-dream entrepreneurs can sometimes struggle with the details of running a business, and they look to their (hopefully) more organized counterparts to step in and offer support.

That's what happened to Leah Everson of Minneapolis, Minnesota, when her mechanic husband, Tim, opened an auto shop out of their garage. Since Tim was not particularly business minded, she volunteered to help with the books. "I was helping with invoices, making sure sales were logged, all while trying to find an accountant to help us," she told me. Leah may be detail oriented, but she's not a bookkeeper by training. As a result, she struggled with the unfamiliar tasks. "It was harder than I expected and took more time. We did a lot of things wrong in the process."

Their business relationship led to quite a bit of conflict. Tim would keep all the receipts from parts he had purchased in a single stack. But Leah couldn't tell which receipt went with which customer, so she was constantly asking Tim to give her the information she needed. "I felt like I was always nagging him, asking questions while he was trying to work," she explained. "There were lots of interruptions for both of us. We didn't have a good flow." After a while, they learned that they didn't have to be as detailed in their record keeping as they thought. Today Leah realizes that "our conflict came out of trying to work out details we didn't understand."

They eventually figured out the ins and outs of tracking expenses and revenue, and reporting taxes, but the irregular revenue stream and their many arguments took a big toll on their relationship. Six months after the start of the business, one of their fights escalated until Leah said she was done. "I still don't know if I was fired or I quit," she explained with a laugh. They eventually agreed that Tim would take on the more day-to-day accounting operations, while Leah would step in once a quarter to make sure the books were balanced and to help file that quarter's taxes.

As the Eversons found, there are some real risks to working together, especially if you are both still learning how to run a business and manage your household through the uncertainty of the start-up existence. If neither one of you is entirely certain what you're getting into and you're both figuring things out as you go, it's likely that you will experience a high degree of stress and anxiety—and end up taking it out on each other. For couples in this situation, doing what you can to strengthen your relationship through building trust, maintaining communication, and other strategies can go a long way in ensuring that permanent damage isn't done to your relationship through business-related conflict.

Tensions can also arise when your entrepreneur asks you to take on tasks that don't match your skill set or interests. Jenny Rae Armstrong, whom you met in chapter 9, took on many administrative responsibilities for her husband Aaron's music and real estate businesses—but she quickly discovered that she wasn't the administrative type. "When I've helped him, it seldom turned out well," she told me. She helped Aaron's businesses register as limited liability companies, and assisted with filing, developing marketing copy, and other administrative tasks. She became increasingly unhappy in the role, and working together seemed to increase the conflict between them. "I didn't want to be his secretary," Jenny explained. "Like many visionary entrepreneurs, Aaron had a specific vision for the business and had a hard time letting go. He wanted to control everything." Eventually Jenny began saying no when her husband asked for help, a decision he respected, and that ultimately ended up strengthening their marriage.

There are, of course, plenty of couples who work together in a business and enjoy it. The extra level of partnership actually enhances their relationship. The reason these couples make it work seems to boil down to the issue of control that Jenny mentioned. Can the partner who is the entrepreneur fully trust her spouse to fulfill his responsibilities in the way he sees fit? Or, if both partners are company founders, can each commit to allowing the other to be fully empowered in his or her area of responsibility? Significant others who feel respected and empowered, and who are given roles that match well with their interests and skills, tend to be able to stick with the business longer. Those who aren't allowed to fully own their job, or for whom there is a mismatch between their duties and their interests, typically end up moving on in a few months.

Unfortunately, most couples don't know how they'll respond to one another in such a situation until they try it. Before Jake and Hillary Denham experienced their "winter from hell" described in chapter 3, they endured another reckoning of sorts when Jake asked Hillary to join his carpet cleaning company as a business partner. They both thought it would be great—until it actually happened. "We didn't accomplish anything for six weeks. We fought for six straight weeks," Jake told me. He and Hillary couldn't make any decisions because they kept questioning one another. Neither was clear about who was responsible for what. They both wanted to control everything in the business. Finally, their conflict led to a pivotal moment, at which point they realized, according to Jake, that "either we need to get a divorce so we can work together, or we need to stop working together to stay married."

Looking back now, Hillary found that insight to be surprisingly liberating. "The conversation took the pressure off me to force our business relationship to work," she said. "I had put the business relationship and the marriage together. I thought that if the business didn't work, the marriage wouldn't work either." Once they were able to decouple their personal relationship from their business relationship, the stakes were lowered just enough for them to let go, draw dividing lines between their responsibilities, and trust the other partner to fulfill his or her duties. As a result, both their marriage and their business flourished.

Working together, even if it's with the best of intentions and the most hopeful of expectations, will likely create additional tension in your relationship. There are that many more things, on top of the day-to-day management of your household and family, that the two of you could disagree about. Your respective schedules may become more unwieldy and unpredictable, making it harder to figure out the logistics of chores and childcare and social events. Your financial outlook as a family will probably be less stable. You will be hit with the challenges and failures of the business at the same time, such that neither of you has the wherewithal to support the other. It's a lot harder for one of you to conduct a rescue or to pull the emergency brake when you're both on the roller-coaster ride.

If you and your significant other already wrestle over control and decision-making in other areas of your life, you may want to approach the idea of working together with an abundance of caution. If your relationship is already plagued by conflict or you already have trouble collaborating with, trusting, or listening to one another, it would be wise to ask if your marriage can weather additional stress. Some couples can handle it and actually use it to reinforce their bond. Others can't. The two of you, along with the help of trusted confidants and mentors, will need to decide for yourselves whether it makes sense for you to work together on this particular business at this specific moment in time.

That being said, if you have confidence in the resiliency of your relationship and are genuinely interested in supporting your beloved's venture, there is plenty to be gained from the experience. "Finding a shared mission as a couple is essential to a vibrant marriage," write authors John and Stasi Eldredge in their book *Love & War: Finding the Marriage You've Dreamed Of.* "It might be the very thing to rescue a floundering couple, and it will surely take you both to a whole new level of companionship regardless of where you are now."[1] And what better mission to drive your relationship than building an organization that you both care about?

Lauren Schneidewind, whom you met in chapter 1, cofounded a

product design and technology consulting firm with her husband, Daniel Rice, about a year after they married. The two of them have certainly experienced a deeper link with one another because of their shared work. "We have similar long-term goals, and that goes hand in hand with marriage," Lauren explained. Daniel added, "Our personal finances and business finances are so tightly connected that our fates are truly tied together. It makes it easier to know if you're going in the same direction."

This is the kind of synergy I was hoping for when I started working full-time for d.light. Up until we moved to China, I had been content to assist Ned's business on an ad hoc basis, leaving a clear demarcation between his career and mine. He was the entrepreneur; I was the nonprofit professional. The separation was practical as much as it was emotionally fortifying. I could bring in a steady income, albeit a pathetically small one, and I could retain something that was wholly mine, untouched by the ever-increasing reach of d.light.

But when we relocated to China, my only realistic career options in Shenzhen were to: 1) find work with a manufacturing or shipping company or 2) teach English to the locals. Neither appealed to me in the slightest, a fact that made Ned strangely excited. "You should work for d.light," he encouraged me. "We really need the help. You could make a big difference. And it'd be fun to work together." He made it sound so easy.

I didn't believe him, because he had a tendency to make everything sound easy. In this case, though, he was actually right.

Despite my many concerns about having my husband as my boss, working with Ned was one of my favorite parts of our otherwise challenging time in China. Ned and I were partners in the fullest sense of the word, relying on each other in every aspect of our lives. We underwent what felt like an accelerated marriage track, learning far more about each other and how we could best support one another in two years than many couples do in ten. We experienced a deep level of bonding that has remained with us ever since, and for which I am deeply grateful.

The secret to our successful working relationship was that Ned never really acted the part of my boss. He treated me more like a peer, giving me free rein to make decisions and manage tasks in the areas I was responsible for. He regularly demonstrated to me and those around me that he respected me as a professional and he trusted me entirely to do what was best for the company.

It helped that the business culture around us reinforced this idea. In China, it's actually so common for husbands and wives to run businesses together that there is a term in Mandarin for "boss's wife": *laobanyang*. For our Chinese colleagues, the label held far more weight than any job title. Being the laobanyang garnered me instant respect and authority as the assumed second in command. Everyone on the team came to me for guidance if Ned was unavailable.

I loved sharing a meaningful, world-changing passion with my husband. I loved putting everything we had as a family into the same mission. I loved the opportunity to see my spouse in a different light—as a problem-solver, innovator, and leader. My respect and admiration for Ned grew considerably as a result, and I'm pretty sure he would say the same about me.

But, in the end, the start-up life was too intense for me. The emotional turmoil of constantly skirting disaster, the exhaustion of working fourteen-hour days, and the stress of trying to do a job that I wasn't experienced enough to do wore me down until I had nothing left to give. I loved working with Ned, but I did not love the start-up life. For my own health and that of our marriage, I had to leave.

I have never returned to working for d.light full-time since we left China. Now that we have a young child, I don't think it would even be possible for both Ned and me to keep up with the demands of the company. I am still involved, stepping in occasionally to help with a project or to provide guidance to a new employee taking on some of my old responsibilities. However, my most prominent role in d.light today is simply as supporter-in-chief, providing affirmation, encouragement, and advice whenever Ned needs it. The balance we've found allows me to contribute to Ned's business in ways that feel meaningful while still allowing for a healthy separation between his life and mine.

For a couple to be able to work together long-term, I believe both partners have to feel strongly about the business, about doing it together, and about living an unconventional, unpredictable life. Without all of these elements in place, one or both partners will eventually become discontent or burn out.

Jeff and Gail Wall of Freeport, Maine, have been working together on their concert promotion and music festival business for several years. Their partnership has been far from easy, especially as they've had to navigate the unusual hours required in the music business along with taking care of their three kids. But when I asked Gail how her marriage has been impacted by the business, she provided a long list of benefits and lessons learned: "We have more time that we're together. We've had to work harder to relate to and communicate with each other. We have to spend time to work through stuff that we didn't have to before. You have to make it work for the job, but you also have to live together." The depth of understanding that Jeff and Gail now have of themselves and their relationship, as well as the challenges that they have endured together, gives their marriage an extra measure of resiliency that I'm sure will serve them well for years to come.

Even better, they've been able to involve their children as they have gotten older. All three children have worked alongside their parents in various jobs, like selling water bottles, preparing catered food, and even being responsible for the musical artists. "That's been a really positive thing for our kids," Gail told me. "They've seen how hard you have to work. It's been valuable for them to be part of it and to be entrepreneurial themselves." Their oldest daughter has already expressed interest in being an entrepreneur and is planning to major in business in college.

Nate and Vanessa Quigley, whom you met in chapter 2, also intentionally involved their seven children in their photo-book-printing company. Even before they launched the business, they asked their kids for help. "We brainstormed with the kids," Vanessa explained. "They got so excited about being involved and learning how to start a local business." Another tangible benefit to involving the kids? They understand more clearly why their parents have to work so hard and they recognize the benefits, such as an unusually flexible work schedule, that an entrepreneurial career can provide. They see what is possible. "I hope my girls can see that I can be a stay-at-home mom and work," Vanessa reflected. "I want them to pursue their professional dreams."

Turning the business into a true family affair could help align your family's values and priorities, and leverage the business as a meaningful teaching tool for your children. Having an entrepreneurial parent, after all, is one of the strongest determinants of someone becoming an entrepreneur herself. Kids with at least one entrepreneurial parent are 60 percent more likely to become entrepreneurs themselves—with the role modeling they see having a stronger effect than any biological commonality.[2]

Jake Wellrich[3] of Seattle, Washington, grew up in a household in which both his parents ran a home-building and development

company. "The whole notion of someone running their own business was part of the household my sisters and I grew up in," he told
me. "That whole notion of business ownership—we thought this
was common." As a result, Jake and his sisters have started multiple companies throughout their professional careers.

Working together with your spouse can be a gloriously rich experience. But it also makes your marriage far more complex. When
both of you are working on the same business, the issues that every
couple wrestles with—such as power, communication, conflict resolution, and boundaries—seem to come center stage with greater
urgency and higher stakes. If you're not able to work through these
issues together, not only will your relationship suffer, but so could
the business and everyone it touches, including employees, business partners, and customers. That's why co-preneurial couples,
more than any other type of couple I've interviewed, tend to have
particularly detailed and formal agreements on how they interact
with one another. Some specific strategies I've heard include:

- "I am the majority shareholder with 51 percent; my spouse has
  49 percent. This helps us make decisions for the business when
  we can't reach a consensus. The marriage is equal but the business can't be."
- "We don't discuss work issues when we're in our pajamas. We
  interact as colleagues only when we're in our work clothes."
- "We have a meeting every Sunday night to do a detailed review
  of our schedules for the upcoming week."
- "When we finish our work for the day, we come out of our home
  offices, physically close the doors, and focus on just being spouses."
- "If we want to take a vacation, we set a budget, scope out our
  to-do lists to prepare for it, and make sure we're organizing our
  lives to make it happen."

- "If I have a work question for my spouse, I will email him about it, even if he's sitting just a few feet away from me."
- "I take care of the business side, my spouse does the technology side. We give each other full authority in those areas and don't interfere at all with one another's work."
- "We regularly do big outings with our daughter for the distraction and to practice doing normal family stuff."
- "When we have fights, we have to be able to forgive one another wholeheartedly and give each other a clean slate."
- "We do one weeklong getaway each year as a retreat to reconnect with each other."

As fastidious as some of these agreements may sound, having such practices in communication, decision-making, and boundary-setting can significantly help a couple navigate through the stickiness of being both spouses and colleagues. Even then, there is no magic formula to ensure that a couple will work together well. Some amount of trial and error is unavoidable in learning how to be business partners—or in discovering that the two of you just aren't meant to be professional colleagues. No wonder, then, that Lauren Schneidewind feels that "starting a business with my significant other is the best and worst decision I've ever made."

If you are seriously considering jumping on board with your beloved's business, it may help for you to explore some key areas together to determine whether the benefits outweigh the risks. Here are some questions you can ask one another to get the conversation started:

1. Finances: Is our financial situation stable enough to have both of us working for a start-up? Will we both receive salaries? If so, how will we establish what is fair and reasonable

compensation? If we are not receiving salaries, can we agree on how much of the business's revenue will go to the family and how much will be reinvested?

2. Job responsibilities: Do the tasks in question align with your personality, interests, and skills? Is this job one that you can at least tolerate, if not enjoy? Can you accomplish the required tasks in the amount of time you actually have to dedicate to the work? Are you truly the best person to do this job, or are there alternative options that should be explored?

3. Empowerment and respect: Is there a clear division of labor? Can your spouse trust you to do your job without micromanaging you? Can you treat one another respectfully at work, especially in front of employees and customers?

4. Decision-making power: How will you make business decisions? Will you share authority equally, or will one person have the authority to make the final call?

5. Giving and receiving feedback: How will you give one another feedback on your job performance? What specifically will you give feedback on? What do each of you need to be able to receive that feedback well?

6. Children: If you have younger children, do you have the childcare resources necessary to allow both of you to work for the business? If you have older children, can you manage the logistics of their activities along with the company's needs? Can you agree on how you'd like to involve your children in the business, if at all?

7. Boundaries: What kind of boundaries can you both agree to? How will you hold one another accountable to these boundaries? What will you do to remind one another that you are spouses first and colleagues second?

There are no right or wrong answers in this conversation. You are simply exploring if working together is prudent and beneficial for your family and the business. As an added bonus, just having this discussion will give you some idea of how you and your mate work together. If you can successfully come to an agreement in the above areas, that bodes well for your ability to make decisions as professional partners. But if any of the above questions becomes a wrestling match over control and power, then you may want to seek additional counsel or wait a little longer before joining the company. Your relationship, after all, should come first—no matter what is happening with the venture.

That's one of the greatest challenges that entrepreneurs and their spouses face: how to stay committed to one another in the long term through the unpredictable journey of building a business. We'll explore this more in the next section of the book.

PART V

SCALING UP

16

Establishing Goals and
Deadlines

One of the most disconcerting feelings I have experienced as an entrepreneur's spouse is not knowing what my life will look like next month, let alone next year. Where will we be living? Will Ned be around? Will he receive a paycheck? Will I have time to work or to see friends? It's unsettling, and not a little bit anxiety inducing, to ask questions without knowing when, or in what form, the answers to these questions will come. It's particularly difficult when you are not in control of discovering those answers; they are, instead, entirely dependent upon the fickle, unpredictable business that has taken up residence in your life.

The start-up life, as we've already established, is chock-full of uncertainty and turbulence. One marriage-family therapist I spoke with went so far as to say that couples "collect uncertainty" on the entrepreneurial journey. For the most part, that can't be avoided. But you and your beloved entrepreneur can certainly draw some lines in your future path, setting clear milestones that will instigate important conversations about how the company is impacting your family, and how you will decide what to do next.

Having a shared set of goals and deadlines that you both develop and keep an eye on will provide some much-needed structure around your chaotic lives, and could help you feel more empowered in shaping your destiny as a family. These markers will also help you determine two of the most critical decisions in the start-up journey: when to go all in with the company, and when it makes sense to walk away.

As I've interviewed therapists, executive coaches, and entrepreneurs themselves, I have frequently heard comparisons between managing a business and managing a family. It turns out that many of the tools that we know are necessary for a successful business—budgets, strategic plans, communication systems, mission statements—are also exceedingly helpful within the context of the family. But we often forget this, preferring instead to fly by the seat of our pants when it comes to our personal lives, figuring things out as they come up and dragging our significant others and children along the way.

If some major pieces in your life, such as your home and your job, are set in place, this relaxed approach to personal planning could work just fine. Who knows? It might even add a bit of spice and spontaneity into your family life.

But for you and your entrepreneur, life is likely overflowing with spice and spontaneity. More likely, you're in need of some measure of structure, answers, and clarity. Just as goals and deadlines help keep a business on track by focusing on priorities and providing concrete measurements of progress, so they can assist the two of you in figuring out whether you as a couple are doing what you need to do to get where you want to be. This involves evaluating the impact that the company is having on your lives, the sustainability of your current pace and quality of life, as well as how this interplays with other personal goals, like having kids or buying a house.

To be clear, when I talk about goals in this chapter, I'm not referring to your ultimate wish list of nice-to-haves, which probably includes things like an around-the-world vacation or an extra million dollars in retirement savings. You're welcome to keep such a list, but far more helpful in the entrepreneurial journey are concrete goals with within-sight deadlines that provide a roadmap for where you are headed as a couple. They could be short-term goals ("We will earn $5,000 in revenue this month") or longer-term deadlines around nonnegotiable priorities ("We will begin trying to conceive a baby within three years").

Another way to think about effective goal-setting is with the oft-cited mnemonic acronym S.M.A.R.T. First coined by consultant George T. Doran in 1981, the acronym has been around for more than thirty-five years and remains exceedingly useful for businesses and individuals alike. The word that each letter stands for has evolved over the years, but the most commonly cited are Specific, Measurable, Achievable, Relevant, and Time-bound.[1] When the goals we establish meet the S.M.A.R.T. criteria, it's easier to objectively determine what progress has been made on the goal.

There are three categories of goals that you and your beloved may want to consider establishing together: 1) business goals; 2) quality-of-life goals; and 3) business entry and exit goals.

The first category, business goals, is the most straightforward but not without its emotional baggage. While many spouses I've met are genuinely interested in their entrepreneurs' businesses, there are also plenty who don't want to know anything about the widget or platform or network that their mates are building. Given all the ways the start-up is intruding into your life, I completely understand the desire to shut out any additional information and focus on what you need to do to survive. But no matter how hard you try to push away thoughts of the company, what's happening within it will continue to impact your life in very real ways.

If you are able to track, even on a very high level, where your beloved's start-up is headed, you will be better equipped to anticipate how the company's trajectory will affect your family. You will be better positioned to have a voice in major business decisions that will directly impact you, especially when it comes to issues related to finances and time.

A simple way to begin this conversation is to ask your entrepreneur to share her business plan with you. What are her milestones? What is she trying to achieve in three months or six months with regards to production or sales or revenue? If she doesn't yet have a business plan, you could offer to help her brainstorm goals or targets.

Some business goals and deadlines that I have found helpful to know include:

- The business should be able to secure funding by _____. This funding will sustain operations for _____ months/years.
- The company will begin generating revenue by _____.
- The company's next major product/service/offering will launch in _____.
- The company will have _____ customers, or _____ in monthly revenue, by _____.
- The business will hire _____ people in the next _____ months.
- The business will become profitable by _____.
- The stretch goal for the company is that it will achieve _____ by _____.
- The ideal exit plan for the business is _____, by _____.

Though incredibly important, this isn't always an easy conversation to have with your beloved entrepreneur. He is likely already feeling a lot of pressure from customers or investors, and the idea of fielding pointed questions of what and when and how much from his significant other may feel like a bit too much. If done right, however, this discussion could actually bolster your partnership and alignment as a couple.

P.J. Simmons of Atlanta, Georgia, married his wife, Ashley, in early 2016. Almost immediately, she began to ask him a lot of questions about his business, which provides resources for faith-based entrepreneurs. She wanted to know about his plans, his long-term strategy, his markers for success and failure. And he couldn't help but get defensive.

"As a visionary and as someone starting a business, it's easy to wonder about someone else's motivations," P.J. told me. "I thought, 'You're asking these questions because you don't trust me. You don't think I can do it.' " But Ashley persisted, explaining to him clearly and gently why she wanted to know this information and how that would help her better partner with him. "She helped me realize that she's not coming with ulterior motives. She wants to be involved. She wants to champion me and cheer me on. She wants to be in the know when things go south, so she knows how she can properly encourage me and lift me up."

What I love about Ashley's approach to a potentially delicate situation is her emphasis on partnership. She is not trying to put P.J. on the spot by asking him to defend his business plan or to prove his competency. She is instead asking him to give her information that will allow her to know how and when to support him. As a result, she is more prepared to collaborate with him in decision-making about the business.

It's important to remember that a company's goals can change, and often do. Rather than giving your mate a hard time about these shifting goals and timelines, I'd suggest taking the posture of simply wanting to be informed when it happens. That way you can keep up with whatever your entrepreneur is wrestling with and what he or she may need from you.

Another benefit to knowing more about the company's key milestones? You will have more context to inform your shared goal-setting around quality of life. Unless you are particularly fond of minimalist, nomadic living, you will likely have trouble sustaining the compromises in quality of life that a start-up, especially an early-stage start-up, typically requires. It is absolutely reasonable to want to know when you can stop using your savings to pay for regular monthly expenses or when you'll be able to spend an entire weekend together as a family.

The mistake that many entrepreneurs' significant others, including myself, often make is that we demand an improvement in our quality of life without naming what specific shape or form those improvements should take. "I just need you to be around more," I have told Ned on many occasions. Or, "I need more stability and certainty." Even the most understanding spouse is going to have trouble knowing exactly how he or she is supposed to help make this happen.

That is the power of goal-setting, especially when we attempt to establish goals that are specific, measurable, achievable, relevant, and time-bound. Goal-setting forces us to sift through our needs and wants, discovering both what is most important to us and what is actually possible. In fact, just the act of writing down our goals can move us closer to achieving them. According to communications expert Henriette Anne Klauser, "writing it down says you believe it's attainable."[2] She contends that it doesn't matter what medium we use to write it down; once we do, though, the goal becomes more clear and tangible, and you will naturally begin aligning your actions and decisions toward achieving those goals.[3]

Justin and Alexandra, the couple who had a dramatic first two years of marriage full of business transitions and moves, told me that they have now gotten into the habit of writing down *everything*. They schedule dates as if they were meetings and regularly make agreements with one another. Every agreement, from how much paternity leave Justin will take off to what Alexandra needs to pursue her professional passions, is meticulously discussed and revised until both of them are comfortable with it. Then they sign the document and upload it to Google Docs, to be revisited regularly in the future.

"It's crazy and formal, but it clears up those expectations, especially if you don't remember what you agree to, or if you're not on the same page but you think you are," Alexandra explained. "It's more businesslike, but it takes the hard conversation and the fight off the table."

In case you're wondering if there are overlaps between establishing goals and the making of agreements discussed in chapter 9, the answer is yes. But goals are different in that they don't name what you commit to doing now; they name what you are working toward, or where you want to be at a particular moment in the future. Rather than relying on your entrepreneur's vague promise that things will get better, the two of you can create a concrete plan that will actually allow you to *make* things better. Having this clarity—and the hope that it provides—will enable you to hang on through the choppy ride you may currently be on.

The quality-of-life goals that you and your entrepreneur set should center on the priorities that you have established as a couple and a family. Some of the most common categories will probably be related to health, finances, family planning, and professional pursuits.

Here are some examples of goals about quality of life, as impacted by the start-up, that the two of you may want to write down and agree to:

- We will stop investing personal money in the business after _____ months.
- Your entrepreneur expects to begin collecting a salary of $____ when _____. This salary can be increased to $____ when _____.
- Once the product is released, your entrepreneur will take off _____ days for vacation.
- We will live in a smaller home and pay $____ in rent for _____ months/years. At that point we will move to a larger place that is no more than $____ in rent.
- When our household salary reaches $_____, we will both sign up for a gym membership.
- When the baby is ____ months old, we will hire a nanny so I can work or pursue other interests.

Aside from focusing your attention toward a milestone, articulating these goals helps you and your entrepreneur in a few other ways. For starters, you can both see, in black and white, how the new venture is directly impacting your relationship, your family, and your future plans. It can be surprisingly hard to name these specific impacts when you're full of resentment or exhaustion.

In addition, you have established a clear marker of when it's okay to initiate a conversation or raise a flag. "We said this would happen by this time, but it hasn't happened," you could say to your entrepreneur. "Can we talk about why we're not reaching this goal? Is there a way we can change course? Do we need to reset our expectations around this goal?"

These are the kinds of conversations that all entrepreneurial couples should be having, but the truth is that they rarely happen organically. Agreed-upon goals give you a structure for what those conversations need to be about and when they need to happen. And, as Alexandra says above, because the commitment was previously agreed upon by both of you, these kinds of discussions are less likely to devolve into conflict. You can instead focus your energy on working together to problem-solve.

Finally, having these shared quality-of-life goals helps to emphasize your shared priorities. They remind you that you're on the same team, working toward the same things, even when your day-to-day existences can feel disparate and at odds with one another. This sense of close partnership is especially important when entering into conversations about what may be the most sensitive of discussion topics for entrepreneurs: when to launch a business, and when to walk away from it or close it down.

If you and your mate are able to set goals around starting or walking away from a business, you will be able to have some influence over a process that could otherwise seem random and disempowering. As a couple, you can preemptively set limits to protect the financial and personal well-being of your family, thus minimizing risk for any long-term damage. And you can move forward, whether it be launching a company or closing one down, with more wisdom and clarity in your plans.

When Jenny Silva of San Francisco, California, wanted to start a company that helped facilitate summer camp sign-ups for parents with kids, her husband at the time was uncomfortable with dipping into their savings to start the business. Instead Jenny used the severance from her last position and got a part-time job. These two

Start, Love, Repeat

sources of funding covered all the expenses of starting up the business for at least six months. That gave Jenny a clear target for when her business needed to at least be breaking even, and it helped her spouse feel more comfortable with the risk she was taking.

Jordan Raynor of Tampa, Florida, was running a crowdfunding site for government projects when he decided to start his own consulting agency in 2014. He and his wife, Kara, were expecting a daughter, so he wanted something that would allow him more flexibility in his schedule. But he wanted to launch his venture with as much financial certainty for his family as possible.

"Nothing Jordan did required a huge investment from us. We didn't have to do anything that would financially ruin us," Kara told me. "When he did the consultancy, he stacked his clients ahead of time." By the time Jordan made the leap to starting his business, he had enough clients lined up so that his income remained virtually unchanged.

Here are some examples of goals that you and your entrepreneur could set to determine when it makes sense for him or her to go all in with the business. The majority of them have to do with finances, which is one of the greatest causes of strain and stress for entrepreneurial couples but can be easily quantified.

- When we are able to save $_____ or _____ months' worth of expenses
- When our baby is six months old and we hire a nanny or put him in daycare for _____ hours a week
- When I attain a monthly salary of $_____
- When we can lower our monthly spending to $_____
- When I have completed my graduate school program
- When you have lined up _____ number of customers or $_____ in purchase orders

- When we have paid off our school loans and credit card bills
- When you have raised $_____ in investment from angel investors or venture capitalists
- When you are able to pay yourself a minimum salary of $_____

Setting these kinds of parameters around the launch of your entrepreneur's business isn't meant to stifle her dreams, but to allow her to enter into the venture more deliberately and wisely. Many companies have been started by founders who were working full-time jobs or had other commitments. They were then in a position to wait out some of the growing pains that all new businesses experience, devoting themselves fully when the venture was more sustainable or at an inflection point of major growth.

Just remember that launching a new venture could be a long process, and so the goals that you and your mate set will likely need to be revisited and revised over the course of months, if not years. Jenny Silva and her then-husband ran into trouble when her business hit the six-month mark and it wasn't breaking even yet. She saw how much the business had grown and the great potential it had; he couldn't see past her lack of an income. Jenny ultimately found another job and passed off the camp sign-up business to her cofounder. But this lack of alignment in goals and priorities played a significant role in Jenny and her husband's eventual divorce.

Even more emotionally fraught than setting goals around starting a business is establishing deadlines for when to step back from it. One spouse told me how, when she gave birth to her first child, she finally understood what it was like for her husband to start a company. "It's just like having a baby," she said. "It's something deep inside of them. It's their creation." Bringing up the possibility of your entrepreneur stepping away from his or her baby, even if it's partially or temporarily, will likely be a sensitive conversation.

But if the venture is struggling, or if your relationship and family are buckling under the weight of trying to support the company, this is an essential conversation to have.

Because P.J. and Ashley Simmons had been so intentional about discussing P.J.'s business goals earlier on, they had laid a strong communication framework by the time they needed to make some tough decisions about their financial future. "If the business isn't bringing in this amount of money by this time, then this is when I begin putting feelers out there for something else," P.J. explained. "I'm not quitting but I am doing something else to supplement the income." He stuck by that commitment when his company wasn't able to meet those revenue targets. Fortunately, he was able to make the most of the situation by finding a part-time job that complemented the mission of his own company. This job built up his skill set and allowed him to continue working on his business during off-hours.

Depending on the type of venture that your entrepreneur has, she may not have to close it down even if it isn't taking off. Perhaps she could simply scale back her hours for a while, or she could put it on the back burner while she does something else. Perhaps he could sell off the company or its assets, or license a product or program. There are multiple directions he could go to keep the business going. The more clearly the two of you define the goals that the company and your family are working toward, the easier it will be to determine what he should do next.

Some ideas for goals to set that would trigger your entrepreneur stepping away from the business include:

- If $____ in investment is not raised by _____
- If the business is not able to bring in $____ in revenue by _____

- If the business is not able to break even by _____
- If we have spent $_____ in personal savings on the company but it is still not sustainable
- If there are fewer than _____ customers

I'll be honest: talking about your entrepreneur stepping back from his business, even if it's just temporarily or partially, is really, really difficult. Ned and I have been doing the start-up thing for more than a decade, and we still haven't figured out how to have this particular conversation well. Perhaps it's because all entrepreneurs tend to be optimistic that the next big break for the company is just around the corner. But if you jointly set a specific deadline and that big break doesn't come by then, you have a viable opening to begin this tough but necessary discussion.

Knowing that you are talking to your mate about possibly abandoning or neglecting his or her treasured creation, you'll want to approach this conversation with as much sensitivity and gentleness as possible. It's a delicate dance of asking and listening and respecting. It may take weeks or months or even years, but as long as the two of you are continuing to talk and move forward in the same direction, you're still doing fine.

Gregory and Hope, whom you met in chapter 13, were really struggling in 2008. Gregory had been trying to raise a certain amount of funding for his financial start-up for two and a half years. But then the economy tanked, and Hope couldn't see how Gregory's venture could find any investment or gain any traction under those circumstances. Eventually, Hope, who was working two jobs to pay their bills, told her husband that she had had enough. "I'm tired and exhausted," she told him. "You're not getting closer to your fund-raising goal. I think you need to get another job."

Gregory told her that he needed time to think about it. Hope intentionally gave him plenty of space, checking in with him only once a month. Three months later, he agreed to shut down the company. "Once the decision was made, I didn't bring it up again," Hope explained. "I just tried to be very understanding of his big loss. I knew he needed to mourn."

Gregory ended up joining a start-up as one of the earliest employees. He was then given the opportunity to open up a new office in Europe, gaining valuable entrepreneurial experience within a more stable context. Gregory stayed in the job for five years before he struck out on his own again. By agreement with Hope, he had a certain amount of savings, strong cofounders, and an already developed product when he left his job to launch his next company. They had learned what they needed to enter a new business with minimal collateral damage to their relationship and finances.

While the idea of setting goals together and sticking to them may sound strange or unnecessarily formal, the practice actually provides some extraordinary benefits. You and your entrepreneur will have plenty of opportunity to practice communication and trust—and the entire process could actually bring you closer together. Establishing goals is also one critical component in pacing yourselves over the entrepreneurial journey that you may find yourself traversing for the next few decades. And, as we'll see in the next chapter, every little thing you can do to help sustain one another on this long and tiring road can make a big difference.

17

Sustaining the Entrepreneurial Life Together

S ticking by your entrepreneur through a couple years of craziness is one thing; staying by his side for decade after unpredictable decade requires another level of fortitude altogether. It also
requires an extra measure of patience and wisdom, something I
am still very much trying to learn. It is no longer a sprint to survive, but a slow, steady study in perseverance and commitment.

In the waning days of 2014, I dubbed the upcoming year as "the
year of the family." Ned had been working on d.light for more
than eight years, and it seemed like we were finally emerging from
the start-up phase. The company had hired other experienced
executives, and Ned's scope of responsibilities was becoming more
manageable. He was traveling less, was home for dinner more, and
generally seemed less stressed. Our corporate child had finally

grown up and was functioning with some independence. I was looking forward to some hard-earned peace and stability.

Then 2015 arrived. Within days, it became clear that d.light had hit a really rough patch. Ned was suddenly instated as CEO, and I had to bid an abrupt farewell to my dreams of normalcy. We would be lucky if we could set aside one Saturday a month for family time.

Even though we were past the point at which the average start-up becomes an established firm, we suddenly found ourselves in the most exhausting and stressful season of d.light's existence. Ned started traveling frequently again. When he was home, he spent every morning and every night on conference calls with team members and partners in other countries. I could sense the depth of his stress and anxiety in the way he spoke in short bursts or paced around the house at night. We could barely have a coherent conversation together, so distracted was Ned by his new responsibilities. Even when he was home, he was, mentally, a world away.

For all intents and purposes, my husband was gone, sucked back into the start-up vortex I thought we had left long ago.

Meanwhile, I was back in the familiar role of almost-single parent, trying to manage a cranky, tantrumy three-year-old who could not understand why his favorite person in the world was suddenly so unavailable. Once again I had to oversee our household on my own and put my own goals and priorities on hold to give Ned what he needed to resuscitate his baby.

I'm sorry to say that I did not handle this unexpected twist in our collective fates with grace. I was grumpy and resentful and stressed out. But most of all, I was tired. Our past start-up adventures had already stretched me further than I wanted to go, and now I was being asked to sacrifice even more. I wanted *out* of the start-up life. But, unless I was ready to walk away from my marriage—which I wasn't—getting out didn't seem like an option for me.

Here's the thing about entrepreneurs: most of them never really stop being entrepreneurs. One twentysomething entrepreneur I spoke with kept emphasizing how he wanted to be successful enough to retire early. When I pressed him on what retirement meant to him, he admitted that he simply wanted the time, financial resources, and flexibility to build an even bigger business than what he is currently able to do. "Retirement means doing what I want to do," he told me. And what he wants to do more than anything else is to start yet another company.

Far from being simply a career, being an entrepreneur is more of a lifestyle choice, one that our significant others will choose for as long as their minds and bodies allow them to. (Ned has assured me that we will soon have the technology to reverse the consequences of aging, thus allowing him to be an entrepreneur for centuries, if not longer. God help me.)

Committing to being with an entrepreneur, then, could very well mean signing up for a lifetime of uncertainty, unpredictability, and risk. So how can this kind of life together be sustained for the long run?

Ned has a business school classmate who runs one-hundred-mile ultramarathons on a regular basis. As if running such a ridiculously long distance isn't enough, he tends to sign up for races that take place in extreme weather conditions or across punishing terrain, like the Sahara desert or the Colorado Rockies. I read this guy's Facebook updates with a combination of admiration, respect, and more than a little horror.

Marriage is its own kind of marathon, hopefully one of the longest commitments you will make in your life. Marriage to an entrepreneur, far from being your run-of-the-mill race through paved city streets in temperate climate, is more like a Sahara desert ultramarathon.

I have never enjoyed long-distance running; going one and a half miles in middle school was far enough for me. But there are plenty of good lessons to be drawn from the practice of endurance running—beginning with the fact that no one can run a marathon without proper planning, training, and pacing.

If you've read up to this point in the book, you hopefully have some ideas for how you and your beloved entrepreneur can plan for the ups, downs, and one-eighties of the start-up journey. You can, for example, create financial budgets and stick to them. You can establish your priorities and organize your lives around them. You can recruit a team of people to help you along the way.

The training comes through many of the practices we have already discussed, especially around setting boundaries; investing intentionally in your relationship through time, affirmation, and addressing tensions; and establishing healthy individual identities. These practices will strengthen your relationship muscles, eventually becoming habits that make you consistently healthier and happier.

But, in order to retain a robust relationship through more than one venture, through successes and failures and everything in between, you and your mate must learn how to pace yourselves. According to training specialist and author Matt Fitzgerald, a successful marathon runner "must have a solid sense of the fastest pace he or she can sustain through the full race distance and the ability to make appropriate adjustments to pace along the way based on how he or she feels."[1]

Most entrepreneurs will probably chafe at the idea of pacing. In the highly competitive start-up landscape, many founders act based on fear—fear of not moving fast enough, fear of being squashed by the competition, fear of missing out on their big break. They can't stop, can't rest, can't slow down because to do so could result in the death of their idea. (In chapter 19, we'll talk more about failure and why it doesn't have to be the frightening specter that we make it out to be.)

But if we look again at Fitzgerald's words above, the role of pacing is not to slow you down. It is to help you go further. Pacing teaches us to expend our energy with a long-term view, in hopes that our accomplishments will be greater and more lasting than the results of a short sprint. And, although many of us don't like to think about this, we need to make allowances for how our bodies age over time. If your beloved entrepreneur started his first company when he was twenty-three, chances are that he's not going to be able to operate at the same pace when he starts his next company at thirty or thirty-five or forty. Nor should he try to.

To be clear, I'm not saying that you should pester your mate to spend minimal time on her business, building it leisurely and with little effort. Pacing oneself doesn't mean being ineffectual or not working hard. Your significant other will still have to pour huge amounts of time and energy into her venture. She will experience times of particular intensity that require long hours and frequent trips. But such intensive times should be occasional seasons, not a way of life. Your entrepreneur should not pour so much into her business that she has completely emptied herself while she still has decades of life before her.

Despite our assumptions that 24/7 devotion is the best strategy for a new company, social scientists have found that hard work is not the best determinant of success. Nor is IQ or privilege. The commonality that academically and professionally successful individuals share is actually *grit*. According to psychological

researcher Angela Lee Duckworth, "Grit is passion and perseverance for very long-term goals. Grit is having stamina. Grit is
sticking with your future, day in day out, not just for the week, not
just for the month, but for years. And working really hard to make
that future a reality."[2] Hard work is extraordinarily important, of
course, but so are perseverance and stamina.

Even if you weren't born with entrepreneurial DNA, you can
just as easily forget how to pace yourself. After years of seeing
how hard and how long Ned works, my perspective of what is normal and healthy has been skewed. I am more likely to push myself
as well, picking up the slack at home or dedicating more hours to
work. Or I may feel the need to prove my capabilities as a spouse,
parent, or professional by refusing to ask for help.

If you are planning to stay with your entrepreneur for the long
run, you need to pace yourself as much as he does.

The possible consequences of either of you *not* slowing down
are deadly serious. It's not your livelihood but your life that is at
stake, from your physical and mental health to the relationships
and activities that sustain you. Without proper pacing, you open
yourself up to depression, exhaustion, and illness. The longevity
of your marriage or your ability to stay present in your children's
lives may be seriously compromised. Unfortunately, most of us
(myself included) don't learn this lesson until we extend ourselves
to the limit and then hit bottom—hard.

Amanda Slavin of Las Vegas, Nevada, operated at a completely
unsustainable pace in her twenties. She worked fifteen-hour days,
while also exploring other career opportunities on the side. When
she started her marketing and events company, she traveled constantly, couch-surfing wherever she went to save money. She
would go out for drinks or to socialize and network every spare

moment she had. Sleep was not a priority. Unsurprisingly, she got very little of it.

And then, at the tender age of twenty-five, Amanda had what she calls "an early-life crisis." She wasn't healthy, she realized. She wanted a family one day, and her current lifestyle wasn't doing anything to lay the groundwork for that. As a result, she began making significant changes in her life, reordering her schedule so she could travel less and sleep more, making arrangements to sleep in actual beds instead of on strangers' couches. She also implemented changes at work, more clearly defining and narrowing the scope of her own role.

More than five years after she had that original epiphany, Amanda now sleeps eight to ten hours a night. She regularly goes to the gym, meditates, and does acupuncture. Over the next two years, she plans to hire and train other leaders to take on most of her business's daily operations. "Then I can be an ancillary support for the company," she told me. "I want to be able to work from home. I'm altering my role but I'm not leaving." With each of these choices, Amanda is making additional space for her relationship with her boyfriend and the kids that she hopes will come one day.

Business adviser Jim Warner would say that Amanda is absolutely on the right track. The secret to enduring such a "high-octane career," as Warner calls it, is to delegate responsibilities and empower others. The entrepreneur needs to know exactly what he is good at and be willing to delegate everything else to those with greater capacity or capability. This requires making excellent hires, including those who are more experienced or more skilled or who bring a particular area of expertise that he doesn't have. It also means letting go and learning to trust other people to nurture his start-up baby.

This ability to share the burden of responsibility with others is directly related to the health of your marriage. "Entrepreneurs have to delegate and empower," Warner explained, "or else they will be divorced a few times or have a numb marriage." A numb marriage is one that is flat and polite, and involves going through the motions more than any kind of genuine affection or partnership.

Delegating isn't easy for most entrepreneurs, who become accustomed to doing everything for themselves and jumping on every opportunity that comes their way. It's part of the reality of pursuing a nonconsensus, unconventional idea. Your entrepreneur needs to chart her own path. Without knowing what that path is, she will try every open door, window, and doggie door that comes her way.

I get it. Sometimes that's necessary. But there is the real risk that your entrepreneur could become addicted to this kind of behavior.

Warner says entrepreneurs have a tendency to be "opportunity junkies." "Those who have grown up in a scarcity type of environment are wired to never go back to that place, and they will take advantage of every opportunity they have," he told me. With about 22 percent of entrepreneurs coming from upper-lower-class backgrounds, the fear of scarcity is not an insignificant force among business founders.[3] But even those who grew up with plenty are susceptible to becoming addicted to the thrill of chasing the next potential big break.

This is where accountability really comes in handy. From Warner's perspective, such accountability shouldn't come from the significant other but from a more objective third party, like a mentor, coach, or trusted friend. This should be someone who can "watch the entrepreneur's back, and can say, 'You're not going to do this because it will harm your family and personal well-being.' "

Warner goes so far as to ask some of his clients to treat him like a sponsor, in the Alcoholics Anonymous tradition. If ever they feel the urge to chase after a new opportunity, they have to call Warner first. Only if he gives his blessing can they pursue it.

I think most of us would squirm at the idea of giving another person this kind of veto power over our career decisions. But the reality is that we—entrepreneurs and non-entrepreneurs alike— sometimes have a hard time evaluating what is truly worth our time and energy. We can't see how a choice we make will hurt ourselves or those we love. That's why the outside, more objective perspective of a wise and trusted individual, who has likely seen these patterns in the behaviors of others, is so valuable.

The ability to say no and to delegate can make a significant difference in how your life, your family life in particular, looks. Neal Thornhill, whom you met in chapter 13, decided to truly pri- oritize his family several years ago. He started with reducing his own workload at his insurance claims company. "I decided that I wanted to make the company run on its own," he explained. "That became my focus. I learned systems to put in place and make it happen." As a result, Neal is no longer deeply involved in the day-to-day operations of the business. He now has lots of free time to be with his family and to pursue another passion of his: search- and-rescue service. As an added benefit, his business is more suc- cessful than it's ever been.

Perhaps your entrepreneur isn't a work or opportunity junkie. Perhaps his justification for lack of pacing is the greater mission of his work, such that he tends to consider his own health and well- being a lower priority.

When Ned and his cofounders first started d.light, they were extremely frugal with the funding they had received. In many ways, I think this was a wise and correct approach. But they were frugal to the point at which they sacrificed their own health. This is why we stayed in motels in rural India that cost a few dollars a night but were so dirty and dilapidated that I broke down sobbing after a couple of nights there. Ned would buy the very cheapest plane tickets he could find, following exhausting itineraries of red-eyes and multiple stopovers. He even occasionally put himself in situations that didn't seem entirely safe, arriving in a developing country he had never been to before in the middle of the night, without anyone to meet him, and walking to his hotel while dragging his luggage behind him.

In those early days of d.light, the rationale was that every dollar spent on an unnecessary luxury was a dollar that wasn't being spent on improving the lives of off-grid families. It was a rationale that Ned and I both had trouble disputing. We even carried this way of thinking to China, skimping on our own comfort—compromising on our housing, our transport, and any help from others. We didn't think taking care of ourselves was nearly as important as the work we were doing.

Entrepreneurs who are driven by a social mission seem to be particularly susceptible to this way of thinking. So many people in the world are suffering, we tell ourselves. How can I prioritize my own comfort and well-being over theirs? Shouldn't I be willing to sacrifice for the good of others?

I have found this way of thinking to be unhelpful at best, and paralyzing at worst. If you and your beloved are pursuing the entrepreneurial path, you are likely already making sacrifices. There is no need to kill yourselves in the process. In fact, pushing yourselves too far too fast will, in the long run, limit your ability to serve the cause you passionately believe in. The positive impact that your beloved could have over ten, twenty, even thirty years is magnitudes greater than what she could achieve in a short sprint of a few years.

As much as Ned and I can help it, we don't push ourselves to the brink of burnout anymore. Truthfully, we *can't* push ourselves like that anymore. Our bodies experience aches and pains and injuries that we didn't experience as twentysomethings; our ability to push through long days is not what it once was. Fortunately, d.light has more financial resources than those early days, giving us more options. Ned now allows himself to purchase direct flights whenever possible; he even occasionally upgrades to a business-class ticket so he can sleep while making transatlantic journeys. I allow myself to rely more heavily on friends and family, asking others to help watch our son or provide a meal when I feel especially stretched. We have learned to notice and respond to the limitations of our bodies and minds. It is both a kindness to yourself and your loved ones, and a necessity if you would like your start-up journey to last beyond a few years.

If we can pace ourselves well, we can also create margin in our lives for the unexpected—positive or negative. Shortly after Neal put systems and people into place to make his business more self-sustaining, his wife, Bridget, had a major opportunity to grow her consulting business to the next level. That would require Neal to take on the responsibilities of running the household, including being the lead parent for their two children. Fortunately, he now had the time to do so. "I became the primary caretaker for the kids. I drove them everywhere. I was more involved in everything," Neal told me. "It was great." He was able to spend precious time with his kids and help propel his wife's career forward—all because he had created space and time in his own life.

The year 2015 was our own unexpected surprise. Neither Ned

nor I had thought he would take over the company, or that our lives would suddenly become so stressful and demanding. Yet the slightly calmer existence we had led in the couple of years prior gave us the stamina to persevere. Whenever Ned was able to slow down and breathe, we made sure to schedule date nights and fun family activities. Those months were difficult and exhausting, but they were tolerable.

Like anything worthwhile in marriage, pacing doesn't just happen. It requires planning and deliberate choices. Try to put a hard stop on your workdays. Make sure you have at least one day a week in which you're not working. Say no to opportunities that would require you to overstretch yourself. Prioritize rest and comfort and leisure when you can. If you have a little extra space to breathe, use that space to breathe instead of filling it up with new activities. When you go on vacation, make sure it's actually a vacation. If possible, take a few months off in between different start-up ventures.

Each of these small choices can eventually become habits—which will ultimately affect your overall lifestyle and quality of life. Trust me: your future self will thank you for your decision to intentionally pace yourself now. And you may even find that taking care not to burn yourself out can enable you to do far more than you thought you could.

After our disastrous year in 2015, you'd think the last thing I would want to do is consider another international move. But by the end of the year, it became increasingly clear that Ned needed to spend several months in the company's office in Nairobi, Kenya. We knew that we didn't want to be apart for that long, and we obviously didn't want to leave our three-year-old son behind. Therefore, the only feasible options were to move to Kenya as a family, or not go at all.

Ned and I spent hours discussing and debating every aspect of a stay in Kenya: how long we'd be there, schooling arrangements for our son, the kind of support I needed, the type of home and neighborhood we would reside in, Ned's work hours. Now older and as parents, we knew we couldn't afford to make the same mistakes we had made in China. So we deliberately arranged our lives in Kenya in a way that was sustainable, including staying in a nice expatriate neighborhood that was close to Ned's office and hiring both a driver and a house helper. Ned even committed not to travel for the duration of our stay, so we would have more time together as a family in Kenya than we typically did back home.

The remarkable thing is that, for all the challenges of living in another country, the plans and choices we made for our time there turned it into a wonderful experience. We prioritized our marriage, continuing our tradition of weekly date nights even when making childcare arrangements was a little more complicated. We prioritized family, taking our son on local excursions to explore the vast natural beauty of Kenya. We prioritized community, so we intentionally sought out places where we could find like-minded friends. Against all odds, the seven months we spent in Kenya ended up being one of the richest, most balanced seasons in the entirety of our marriage. On top of that, Ned was able to be extraordinarily productive while there, building up new systems and making key hires so that the office could run on its own after we left.

We had learned some valuable lessons and had actually been able to apply our learnings to the benefit of our own health and the health of our family. This willingness to learn and adapt will not only make your entrepreneurial life more satisfying and sustainable, but, as we'll see in the next chapter, it could actually end up being the best part of the entire experience.

18

Growing with Your Entrepreneur

Pastor Timothy Keller writes, "Marriage by its very nature has the 'power of truth'—the power to show you the truth about who you are. . . . Marriage does not so much bring you into confrontation with your spouse as confront you with yourself. Marriage shows you a realistic, unflattering picture of who you are and then takes you by the scruff of the neck and forces you to pay attention to it." If this has you feeling like you want to punch marriage in the snout and demand that it let you go, Keller adds this bit of inspiration: "This may sound discouraging, but it is really the road to liberation."[1]

When I dug a little into the history of the human concept of self-awareness, I found that philosophical writings on this subject go back thousands of years. Ancient Chinese philosopher Lao Tzu, who lived in the sixth and fifth centuries BC and is considered the founder of Taoism, wrote, "He who knows others is wise; he who knows himself is enlightened."[2] Across cultures, societies, and generations, the consensus is that truly understanding ourselves—in all our glory and messiness—provides clarity on our values and goals, and empowers us to pursue them in an authentic and meaningful way. Liberation, indeed.

The challenge is that this particular road to liberation can feel more like a superhighway when you are doing life, day in and day out, with an entrepreneur. What other kind of relationship forces you to confront your deepest fears and issues around money, control, self-worth, time management, codependency, and self-care—all at once?

It's overwhelming, to be sure. I've seen many entrepreneurs' significant others get stuck in that state of feeling deluged by the emotional and psychological chaos that their beloveds have created. As a pessimist, I find it far too easy to dwell on the costs of being married to an ambitious entrepreneur.

Yet that would be only a fraction of the story of how my marriage has impacted me. Far richer and more lasting are the ways in which being married to an entrepreneur has grown me—as an individual, a professional, a spouse, a parent, a friend, and even a global citizen. Consider these lessons that being with Ned has taught me:

- I had my first burnout and "midlife" crisis when I was twenty-six years old, which forced me to confront my addictions to people-pleasing and perfectionism, as well as my poor professional boundaries, early in my career.
- We have moved—sometimes across town, sometimes across the world—almost every year of our marriage. This more nomadic lifestyle has made it very clear what is most important to me and has diminished my attachment to material things.

- The many unpredictable circumstances that Ned and his venture have thrown my way have steadily chipped away at my need to control and plan for everything in my life. I've been forced to learn how to make due in all circumstances, and to seek contentment and gratitude no matter what my life looks like.

- After a concerted effort to have a codependent marriage, I soon learned that I couldn't depend so much on Ned and had to develop my own sense of independence and autonomy. As a result, I have a strong sense of my individual identity and have cultivated my own social circles and activities outside of our relationship.

- I have always hated asking for help, but I had to learn how to after our son was born. Doing so has given me the opportunity to benefit from others' care and generosity, and assured me that I am not alone in this journey.

- Our stays overseas—in mainland China, Hong Kong, and Kenya—have been extraordinarily stretching, pushing me to the limits of my tolerance and courage. Yet I have a much deeper understanding of other cultures and places, and how global systems of business, trade, and politics operate.

In all honesty, each of these areas remains a work in progress for me. But I had made significant strides in each before I reached my mid-thirties. I couldn't imagine this happening if Ned and I had journeyed down a more traditional path that relied on stability, predictability, and security. Being with Ned, and hanging on for dear life through his wild start-up journey, has completely transformed the person I am—and almost entirely for the better.

My growth trajectory has certainly not been a straight line. I have had long seasons of inertia or regression, of anxiety and depression, of frustration at having to deal with the same issues over and over again. It has been extraordinarily painful at times, like a kind of dying as I laid to rest aspects of my character, personality, and ego that I had relied on for over three decades. More than once I have wondered if I would be able to emerge from a particularly difficult season with my soul intact.

Despite the short-term discomfort that this dynamic of deep, enduring personal growth may cause us, it actually represents marriage at its most ideal. In fact, having a partner who will challenge you and push you to grow and mature may be one of the most essential things we should consider when entering into a long-term commitment. Relationship expert Susan Quilliam, known for authoring more than a dozen books on sex, relationships, and parenting, addresses this in her most recent book, *How to Choose a Partner*. "The most important factor is not whether we are currently ecstatic," she explains, "but whether we are currently growing, and whether we trust that we will grow in the future, and whether we believe our partner is growing too."[3] *This* is what makes for a successful relationship—not happiness or passion or financial plenty. And this, in my experience, is what keeps a marriage engaging and compelling for decades.

The good news is that entrepreneurs, by their nature, may be ideal partners in this quest to acknowledge and grow into our most authentic selves. In his nearly three decades of work with entrepreneurs, Silicon Valley executive coach Julien Adler has found entrepreneurs to be among the most adaptable people around. One of their greatest strengths is their ability and willingness to try new things or to approach a problem from multiple perspectives. "That adaptability can be used to great effect in a relationship," he told me. "A lot of the skills and strategies required to build a successful business can also be used to build a dynamic and great relationship."

In other words, the constantly shifting approaches and strategies that Ned successfully applied when d.light first got started—and that drove me crazy with uncertainty—are actually a strength in our family life. He can adapt to how I change over the years and what our family needs from him. He can find new ways to prioritize his personal life even as the needs of his business morph in unexpected ways. He can continue to be a partner who stretches me, in all the best possible ways, no matter how long we have been together.

Just like the old maxim says, "As iron sharpens iron, so one person sharpens another."[4] And, if you'll allow me the extended metaphor, the "irons" our beloved entrepreneurs bring into the relationship always seem particularly hot and ready to strike. The question is: Are you willing to embrace the process of being sharpened, or are you going to fight it or run away from it?

In my second job out of college, I had the privilege of working for a nonprofit that had a core value of "continuous learning." We talked about how everything, whether a success or failure, progress or misstep, was an opportunity to grow. We emphasized the importance of giving and receiving feedback, of not operating out of assumptions and being willing to ask questions. I'll be honest: continuous learning, especially in the intense context of the short-term leadership program we ran, was a messy process. Despite all our best intentions, we would still become frustrated at one another or end up hurting one another. There were tears and raised voices and many, many difficult conversations.

When it comes to our own development, it is normal to resist growth and change. We don't like letting go of the versions of ourselves that are familiar and comfortable; we don't like admitting that we have a lot of room for improvement. And sometimes, we resist this push to change the most when it comes from those closest to us, including our spouse.

Fortunately, those feelings of resistance or anxiety are actually a good sign, as they indicate that something substantial is probably happening within you. According to internationally recognized Enneagram experts Don Richard Riso and Russ Hudson, "The process of growth entails an ongoing cycling among letting go of old blockages, opening up to new possibilities in ourselves, and then encountering deeper levels of blockage. Although we might wish that spiritual growth would be more linear and that it could be accomplished in one or two major breakthroughs, the reality is that it is a process that we must go through many times on many different fronts until our whole psyche is reorganized."[5]

It is perfectly fine to feel anxious, uneasy, or even fearful when we feel like we are being pushed beyond what is comfortable. But the key is to stay with that process rather than withdraw from it, even when you are tempted to stick with the status quo version of yourself. The reality is that, if we are unwilling to deal with our shortcomings today, we will have to deal with them another time. They're not going away until we intentionally make the decision to try to learn and grow and change.

Another essential? Remember to be especially kind to yourself and your mate when you are undergoing a season of personal development. If your experience is anything like mine, it is likely that, just when you think you've got it figured out, you will experience a new challenge, courtesy of your unpredictable entrepreneur. The learning journey doesn't let up. It's exhausting. I have gone through many periods when I didn't particularly like myself, and I have tended to lash out at Ned when I was feeling that way. I have had to learn to forgive myself for not living up to my own standards and to give myself the space to try again.

If we can weather the storms of our spiritual and personal development, we get closer and closer to what Riso and Hudson call our *Essence*, which they define as "what we fundamentally are, our Essential self, the ground of Being in us."[6] Aligning your daily experience with your Essence brings peace, confidence, and an assurance of your place and purpose in the world.

I'm not just talking about transformations in your heart and mind; whatever development you undergo will also have practical implications. The personal growth that you experience through your relationship with an entrepreneur will affect the kind of friend, family member, and colleague you are to others. And it could very well affect your own career path.

For example, it took only two years for Amanda Slavin, whom you met in the last chapter, to infect her boyfriend with the entre-preneurial bug. He went from being a salesman to launching his own company. "Once he started getting around people who were really doing it, he couldn't sit still anymore. He couldn't be in a normal job anymore," Amanda explained.

Erica Bryers, whom you met in chapter 12, ended up taking a big risk after she met and fell in love with Will Smelko. When Will started his supplements company, Erica started helping out when she got off work in the evenings. But there was an extra wrinkle to their relationship. Erica, a native of New Zealand, was living and working in Sydney. Will was in California.

When they made the decision for Erica to officially join the team, it required not only a change in careers for her but also an interna-tional move. She admits that moving to the US was challenging. "In the beginning, it was unsettling," she explained. "I'm very used to my independence. I couldn't drive very well on the other side of the road. I couldn't go out and do stuff on my own." Over time, though, the benefits have far outweighed the costs. She is now able to spend all her time "with the guy I was waiting my whole life for," and she has developed a new community and sense of identity.

I am quite certain that I would never have had the courage to pursue writing if I hadn't learned from the many calculated risks that Ned took. The twenty-six-year-old version of me who married Ned would have been horrified at the idea. Just five years later, it didn't seem so crazy after all.

I've spoken with a number of other spouses who have tried new things and taken unfamiliar risks, in part because being with an entrepreneur makes these kinds of choices seem more accessible. And given the novelty-seeking profile of most company founders, it's likely that your mate will encourage, affirm, and be inordinately excited by such untraditional interests and choices. One woman I met started pursuing photography after her husband founded his business; she now works as a wedding and portrait photographer. Another started a nonprofit to fight human trafficking. Others have moved to new cities or new countries. A surprising number have joined their significant other's venture or started their own businesses.

I love hearing stories like this, about men and women who have been empowered to make the most out of a trying experience. Instead of focusing on the ways in which they have been neglected or felt out of control in their relationship, they have drawn valuable lessons from life with an entrepreneur and used it to open up new opportunities for themselves. This, I believe, is one of the most powerful strategies that an entrepreneur's significant other can employ: Look at everything as a learning opportunity. Apply that lesson in a way to make your own life, and the lives of those around you, better and more meaningful.

Doing this, however, requires a release of expectations that you may have had about how your life would turn out. The more you are holding on to hope that your beloved will settle down and follow a predictable trajectory, or that your family finances will be stable and support a certain quality of life, or that your days and weeks will be predictable and controllable, the more you will have trouble adapting to—and benefiting from—the topsy-turvy start-up life. But if you can embrace the volatility and ride the waves coming your way, you will open yourself up to new possibilities that you may not have imagined before.

Perhaps this is why therapist Chris Bruno told me that the best antidotes for resentment are "curiosity and wonder." When we're feeling resentful and stuck, we only see what we have lost or don't have, rather than what is possible. An emotionally healthier option is to ask ourselves questions like: *What else could be in store for me? What new opportunities are available to me because of this? What have I learned about myself and my spouse that I could apply in the future? What can I do to turn this into a positive experience?*

For example, here are some common challenges that entrepreneurial couples face, and possible opportunities that could come out of those hardships.

Challenge	Opportunity
My significant other is unavailable to me much of the time.	I can reach out to other family members and friends for support and assistance, giving me the chance to grow those relationships.
Our family income is unpredictable and unstable.	We can become very clear on what material things matter most to us, and what things we can do without.
We have had to move multiple times in only a few years.	We can experience life in new places and develop friendships all over the country/world.

My spouse and I keep fighting about her business and how it's affecting our family.	We can learn effective conflict resolution skills and practice reconciling with and forgiving one another.
I am stuck at home with the kids while my significant other gets to work and travel and make his dream come true.	I can explore new activities that I can do at home or with my kids that would be nourishing for me, such as taking online courses or joining a parents' group.

As you can see, the context of a difficult situation can shift dramatically if you are able to focus less on the challenge itself and more on the opportunities available to you. Even the hardest of circumstances will offer some possibility to try something new or to learn something new. But we have to have the willingness to acknowledge those possibilities and the courage to pursue them.

That's not to say that this shift in thinking is going to happen with the flip of a mental switch. It took me at least five years of marriage to Ned before I moved the dial—even a little—on my ability to let go of my expectations and resentment. Twelve years in, I've made some more progress but am still very much working on it. The greatest barrier for me has been my pride. I wanted Ned to know how much he was making me suffer; I wanted to keep tabs on all that I had given up for him so I could use it as leverage against him; I didn't want to admit that his wholehearted pursuit of something other than me could actually be good for me too.

Because Ned has a remarkably strong sense of self-confidence and purpose, my grumblings rarely caused him to change course and didn't even seem to particularly bother him. Over time I realized that my beliefs about how miserable Ned was making me were just as responsible for my own unhappiness, if not more so, than the circumstances themselves. The unpredictable journey my husband had me on was unlike almost anyone else's. There had to be something valuable I could gain along the way, if only I let myself.

Change in life is inevitable. We all know this to be true. Even if you and your mate followed the most predictable of life plans, working steady jobs and settling down and having your 2.5 children, you couldn't escape unexpected events, pleasant or otherwise. A new family moves in next door. One of you gets laid off. One of you gets promoted. A relative passes away. A new law is passed that affects you personally. You have a big health scare. Your house needs major repairs.

How we choose to respond to these changes, as individuals and as a family, is ultimately what determines who we become as a result of that change.

In the start-up journey, those changes will likely come faster and more furiously than is typical. The hope, though, is that the unexpected twists and turns will push you to dig deeper and adapt faster—and nudge your learning and maturation forward at an accelerated pace.

As I've interviewed dozens of entrepreneurs' spouses across the country, I have been deeply impressed with the wisdom they carry. Many of them can speak about their own foibles, and that of their spouse, with humility and humor. They often have a crystal-clear sense of their own strengths and interests, and a well-balanced perspective about everything from material possessions to parenting and dealing with difficult people. As marriage-family therapist Julian Gorodsky explained to me, "A long-term relationship is like sandpaper to the ego." You will be shaped and softened and sculpted by the many adventures that your entrepreneur creates—and you will likely mature significantly because of them.

The shaping goes both ways, of course, but it may very well look different for each partner in the relationship. It's likely that your mate, just by being who she is and undergoing what is necessary to build a business, will push you to change and grow. Unless you are also an entrepreneur, your existence alone may not have that kind of impact on your significant other. You may need to act with more intentionality, providing the affirmation and challenge to encourage your significant other's growth as a partner, friend, co-parent, and more.

This requires great gentleness, thoughtfulness, and care in how you communicate with your beloved. Even under the best of circumstances, not many of us respond well to constructive feedback. Entrepreneurs are often already on a steep learning curve when it comes to running a business and bringing their product or service to market. Though I'm not sure they would admit it, I'd be willing to bet that many are not particularly interested in also thinking about their personal development. They may feel so inept on a day-to-day basis that they're simply not interested in hearing about other ways in which they could grow.

If this is where your partner is at, then a good place to start is to regularly affirm all the things he is doing that make you feel loved and cared for, and to encourage him to do more of that when he can. Another possibility is to help your entrepreneur apply the growth he is experiencing professionally at home. As he learns how to manage a team or to roll out a product or to pitch to investors, you could highlight those skills—such as negotiating or giving and receiving feedback—that could also strengthen your relationship.

We all want to become better versions of ourselves, but some-times we need a little nudge from a loved one to begin taking the first steps forward. That said, it's important to remember that you don't have the power to change others, not even your spouse. You can encourage their growth, but the bulk of your energy should focus on how you yourself can mature. And hopefully the fruits of those efforts will ripple out across your entire family.

For years, Jake Denham, the owner of the carpet cleaning busi-ness who had the winter from hell in chapter 3, had a very negative reaction whenever his wife, Hillary, tried to give him input. "I had listened to Hillary like she was a nagging person who just wanted to tell me what to do. I thought she just wanted to wash the joy out of my life," he admitted. One day, they attended a marriage seminar together, and Jake had a stunning realization: "I've got a filter that I listen to my wife through, and it's my fault. She wants love and connection, but I want control." For Jake, being brutally honest about his own shortcomings has made it easier for him to receive feedback from his wife.

I think the Denhams' relationship is a wonderful picture of how one partner's self-awareness and willingness to learn can positively impact the other's. If you are willing to model for your spouse that you want to learn and grow and mature, there is a decent chance that he will begin responding in kind.

This prioritization of continuous learning is especially import-ant if your beloved's business fails—or if it succeeds on a massive scale. Both circumstances could dramatically change your lives, and not always for the better. But if you're willing to take it in stride, there are some very valuable lessons that your family could glean from both start-up defeat and start-up glory.

EXIT

19

Surviving Failure

Let's start with the good news about a failed start-up: It's unlikely to harm your entrepreneur's future career prospects. Having a business that doesn't make it is remarkably common-place; remember that around 90 percent of new ventures end up failing, and the typical entrepreneur endures 3.8 failures before hitting upon a successful venture.[1]

In many start-up circles, failure is relished and seen as neces-sary. Some investors don't even want to hear pitches from entre-preneurs who haven't been through the demise of a company. Failure means you believed in yourself enough to take risks. Fail-ure means you learned some important lessons. Failure means you are better equipped—and statistically more likely—to be success-ful the next time you start something.

I know plenty of entrepreneurs whose companies no longer exist, and yet they are doing just fine professionally. They still get invited to speak at conferences and are regularly offered wonderful professional opportunities. Their failure, it turns out, was just a stepping-stone to the next great thing they did.

Now for the bad news: As your beloved is watching the organization she has poured her heart, soul, and countless hours into die a torturous death, nothing I have said above will feel true. She will feel frustrated, humiliated, and small. She may think she's a professional pariah. She may wonder if her life is over.

Sadly, far too many entrepreneurs buy into this belief. Some high-profile entrepreneurs who have taken their own lives in recent years include Austen Heinz, founder of Cambrian Genomics; Ilya Zhitomirskiy, cofounder of social media platform Diaspora; and Jody Sherman, who founded Ecomom. All three companies were struggling and teetering on the edge of failure when these founders committed suicide.[2]

And it's not a challenge that is unique to Silicon Valley or the US. In 2016, *Entrepreneur India* published an article about the risk of suicide among Indian entrepreneurs.[3] In a culture that doesn't celebrate risk-taking and failure as much as American culture does, struggling entrepreneurs can become overwhelmed with shame and isolation.

Walking with your entrepreneur through the demise of a company is a serious, potentially life-and-death matter. If your significant other is one of the nearly one-third of entrepreneurs who struggle with depression (regardless of business success or failure), you'll need to be even more aware of what he is experiencing and the kind of support he may need.

But even if your mate is emotionally resilient, the loss of a business can be incredibly painful and will likely incur real costs in your lives. When Jerlyn Hollars first married her husband, Dennis, twenty years ago, he was embarking on his first company. A successful, well-regarded astrophysicist with a few dozen patents to his name, Dennis had developed a way to transmit information via light waves at the height of the dot-com boom. Just as the company was ready to go public, the dot-com bust at the turn of the century hit. After three years of effort and quite a bit of personal investment, Dennis had to walk away with nothing.

His next company didn't fare any better, collapsing once again just as it was about to go public. Dennis promptly moved on to another idea, developing solar panels that could be integrated into replaceable roof tiles. He and his business partner received some initial funding and had several other foreign investors interested in supporting them. But then Solyndra, the California-based solar-cell manufacturer that had received a $535 million loan from the US Department of Energy, filed for bankruptcy in August 2011.[4] The sudden collapse of one of the darlings of the solar industry made international news—and spooked foreign investors away from the American solar industry. Dennis's company had no choice but to fold.

He and Jerlyn had refinanced their home with an interest-only mortgage to help fund the solar business. They ended up investing one million dollars of their personal money into the company— none of which they got back. Unfortunately, there was more bad news to come. "Almost immediately Dennis started talking about having to sell the home and move away," Jerlyn told me. They could no longer afford to pay the mortgage on their home in the Silicon Valley neighborhood that Jerlyn had grown up in, and instead had to move inland to a more affordable community in central California.

I spoke to Jerlyn more than five years after this happened, but the wounds were still fresh. "I'm still not over it. I miss my family and friends. I spent my whole life there," she told me. She used to live one and a half miles from her daughter and grandchildren, and would regularly walk over to see them. Now she lives more than a two-hour drive away, and sees them only about once a month. She and Dennis are spending their retirement years in a community that is unfamiliar and far from what they envisioned. "It broke up my family. There's a price to pay, and it's a heavy price."

Frankly, these are the kinds of stories you rarely hear in start-up circles, and I'm grateful for people like Jerlyn who are willing to share their experiences. For all the talk among investors and entrepreneurs about how great it can be to fail, few are willing to publicly address the very real and heavy costs of failure— psychological, relational, and financial.

Dennis's experience is unusual in the amount of bad luck and unfortunate timing he seemed to have hit over and over again. In most cases, you will see the failure of a business coming for months. You may get warning signs when the goals and deadlines your entrepreneur sets (as discussed in chapter 16) are missed and clearly won't be achieved anytime soon. Or it may simply be that the financial numbers don't add up, and high expenditures, lack of revenue, or some combination of the two is bleeding the company dry.

It is extraordinarily painful for a founder to watch her precious venture dying a slow, drawn-out death. On the upside, the slow descent gives your family time to prepare for the worst. (Also, keep in mind that the worst may not come. I have been convinced that d.light would expire at several points in its existence, and somehow it managed to pull through each time.)

If the business is funded by outside investors, then how or when the company ends may be a decision that is out of your entrepreneur's hands. But if your beloved is among the majority of entrepreneurs who self-fund or have friends and family fund their companies, the decision to pull the plug may be up to him—and I firmly believe it should involve you as well.

One of the most challenging decisions to make as a business struggles is whether additional capital should be injected, and where that capital might come from. Don't forget that shutting down a company incurs its own costs, such as severances for laid-off employees, fees for broken lease agreements, or final tax filings. So it's wise not to wait until the company's bank account is down to zero before deciding to close it.

In the waning days of a business, the same financial principles that we discussed in chapter 7 still hold true. As much as is possible, it's best to avoid taking on significant debt or wiping out savings accounts and retirement funds. You and your significant other should decide where you will draw the financial line—how much risk or debt or loss you are willing to take on before calling it quits—and commit to honoring that agreement.

That being said, when your partner's company is on the verge of cardiac arrest, it will be much harder for him to be clear-eyed about what he should and should not do to try to save it. In the bestselling book *Sway: The Irresistible Pull of Irrational Behavior*, organizational expert Ori Brafman and his psychologist brother Rom Brafman discuss two powerful forces that cause otherwise smart, rational people to stay the course even when it's clear they shouldn't: commitment and aversion to loss. When we are highly committed to something—and the level of commitment grows the more time and resources we put into it—the Brafman brothers write that "it's difficult to let go even when things clearly aren't working."[5] Similarly, with aversion to loss, "the more meaningful a potential loss is, the more loss averse we become. In other words, the more there is on the line, the easier it is to get swept into an irrational decision."[6]

Remember that long list of things from chapter 3 that an entrepreneur puts on the line when he starts a business? Entrepreneurs have commitment in spades, which is what they need to pursue their dreams to begin with. But this overhyped sense of commitment could get them into trouble if the company is heading south. And they may feel like the possible losses, such as financial capital, intellectual property, reputation, and professional opportunity are too great to be tolerated. I have heard far too many stories of entrepreneurs who kept trying to inject life into a doomed venture, to the great detriment of themselves and their families. Even when it's the right thing to do, letting go of a dying company is terribly difficult.

That's where you—and perhaps a financial adviser or trusted mentors and friends—will need to step in. You may need to walk your partner through the reality of the state of the company and help her see that continuing down the same path will only make things worse, not better. Gently remind her of whatever thresholds the two of you may have set, such as a certain amount of cash reserve or below-target sales orders, that would automatically trigger the shutdown of the business. No matter how wonderful a business, it's not worth sacrificing your family's financial future for it. In the heat of the moment, your entrepreneur may need a little help remembering this.

Once the decision has been made to shut down a company, your significant other will need to begin the bitter journey of accepting this loss and moving on from it. Every entrepreneur experiences loss differently. Some may bounce back fairly quickly, eager to move on to the next opportunity; others may sink into a deep depression. The majority will probably fall somewhere in the middle.

Grieving such a momentous loss is normal, and your mate should be allowed time and space to process this. (And, if he is open to it, engaging the services of a therapist or coach at this time wouldn't be a bad idea.) You might have cause for concern, though, if your entrepreneur exhibits signs of chronic depression, such as prolonged changes in appetite, sleep, and energy level, or remains stuck in the grieving process for a long time.

In his book *Failing Forward: Turning Mistakes into Stepping Stones for Success*, leadership expert John Maxwell cites five warning signs that someone is not moving past a disappointment, challenge, or failure:

1. Comparison: I have it so much worse than other people.
2. Rationalization: I have good reason to wallow in what happened.
3. Isolation: I don't need or want anyone involved in my life.
4. Regret: I can't stop thinking about what I did wrong.
5. Bitterness: I really got screwed over.[7]

You may notice that all five of these stem from an individual's outlook or perspective. There are many things—far too many things—in the start-up world that are out of our control, but how we perceive and respond to the circumstances around us is one thing we *can* control. And it is through cultivating a healthy attitude and seeking the necessary help that our beloved entrepreneurs can process and move on from a failed business in a productive way.

We can try to will ourselves to be more optimistic or content with what has happened to us, and there are plenty of books and resources that encourage that. But I think there is a far deeper character trait that will benefit our significant others. In all the stories of entrepreneurs I've read and heard, those who are best equipped to handle the demise of a business seem to have one characteristic in common: they are able to separate their ventures from their personal identities. "Failure is simply feedback," explains executive coach Julien Adler. "It's like saying make a right here or make a left here."

Here is what all entrepreneurs need to understand, not just with their heads but deep in their hearts and guts: Just because a company is struggling or has failed, it does not mean its founder is a failure. It does not mean he no longer is a person of worth. It does not mean he has lost everything. He has only lost a portion of what matters in his life. In fact, *your* existence is evidence of the fact that your entrepreneur still has plenty going for him.

Even if an entrepreneur hasn't experienced the failure of a company, he will likely become intimately acquainted with failure through the start-up process. Perhaps he wasn't able to secure a big investor; perhaps he lost a vital customer; perhaps his product has a major design flaw. If your entrepreneur is able to own these mistakes without internalizing them or allowing them to define who he is, he will be better positioned to recover from and even capitalize upon these challenges.

In an interview with *Inc.*, entrepreneur Mark Woeppel described how his management consulting business was hit hard in 2009, at the height of the global depression. He was eventually able to turn around the business, but during that dark season he learned some profound lessons that have remained with him. "I used to be like, 'My work is me.' Then you fail. And you find out that your kids still love you. Your wife still loves you. Your dog still loves you."[8]

In the start-up world, many people often express admiration for entrepreneurs who lay it all on the line for their companies. But entrepreneurs who choose to tie up everything—including their identity, self-worth, financial future, and personal lives—with their businesses risk turning into one-dimensional creatures. Every aspect of their well-being is dependent upon a venture that is unpredictable and hugely impacted by circumstances outside of their control. Instead of the limitless potential, vision, and freedom that being an entrepreneur can bring, having such an all-or-nothing attitude actually places vast limitations on who your beloved is and who she could become.

In contrast, the entrepreneur who can separate her identity and value from her business is able to act with more freedom and less fear. Without the risk of losing themselves in the business, they can pursue it with more audacity and make decisions in a more clear-eyed manner. Investing in their personal life and their family actually makes them *better* entrepreneurs.

Martin and Cindy Arroyo started an organic food store and delivery service in Saratoga, California, in early 2015. They love their business and believe passionately in educating people about the importance of purchasing organic and locally grown food, but they both told me they would be willing to walk away from the store tomorrow if they had to. Part of it is the strategic way in which they started the business. They built it up slowly, such that they have never had to take out a loan or invest personal money. From day one, their venture has been cash-flow positive. (They managed to eke out a profit of $1 in their first week of operations.) As a result, the Arroyos are under no pressure to earn a certain amount of money before they move on.

Even more important is how they view their business: as just one step in a lifetime's worth of opportunities. "There's this fear that a lot of people have: If I'm not doing this, what do I do next? What *can* I do next?" Cindy said. She admitted that this fear used to weigh her down, but it has lessened over time. Her optimistic, ideas-driven husband has helped her learn that "there's no shortage of what we could do next."

Julien Adler agrees. "Very few entrepreneurs are one-trick

ponies," he explained. "They don't just have one idea. The skills they have used to get to that point can be used anywhere. When you know both sides of it, you understand better how you can be successful."

Another contributing factor to the Arroyos' healthy outlook, I believe, is that they are able to reinforce this attitude in one another. If one of them begins to go down the rabbit trail of turning the company into something more than what it is, the other can help pull him or her back. Hopefully, the same dynamic could work for your relationship, whether you are both entrepreneurs or only one of you is. The more you can remind your significant other that he has far more going for him than the ups and downs of the business, the easier it will be for him to hold on to that as truth. There will be plenty of voices telling your entrepreneur that his business, and nothing else, needs to be his life. As his spouse, you are best positioned to counter those voices by offering affirmation and encouragement in other areas of his life.

But if your significant other isn't yet able to root her identity in more than her business, how can she begin to make that shift? This is a major alteration in perspective, involving adjustments in behavior and habits and thought patterns. It will take practice and time, and the exact process will look different for every individual. Many of the strategies that we discussed earlier in the book—such as setting boundaries, maintaining communication, establishing goals and deadlines, and asking for help—are good for your relationship but are also good for the soul of your entrepreneur.

When he consistently draws a perimeter around his business and invests time and energy in your marriage, his health, his hobbies, and his friendships, he is building up other aspects of his life that are foundational to his character and well-being. He is broadening his perspective on what matters most in his life, both now and for many years to come. He is also strengthening his support network and his safety net. If things go badly—and for every entrepreneur, things will almost always go badly at some point—he has other people and activities to fall back on to help restore his confidence and sense of optimism. You, your children, and other loved ones will be the best reminder that he still has a lot to be thankful for.

Adler also suggests that spouses play the critical role of reframing for their entrepreneurs. When your mate says something negative or limiting, such as "I'm such a failure" or "I can't do it," your responsibility is to check her on that—kindly and gently, but checking all the same. You could simply say, "Let's cancel that" or "Let's rephrase that." Once she hears that enough, she will become aware of her own negative thought patterns, which sets the stage for her to make concrete changes in perspective and behavior.

Aside from simply surviving failure, your entrepreneur can also gain quite a bit from a company's demise. Mistakes and failures—not successes—are the very best training ground for learning and maturing. "Success leads to the greatest failure, which is pride," writes David Brooks in *The Road to Character*. "Failure leads to the greatest success, which is humility and learning."[9]

Much of the learning will be practical. Starting a business is a remarkably complex process, so the number of skills your entrepreneur can learn from the experience is almost limitless. Depending on the nature of the business, she may be simultaneously learning about creating and executing plans, managing cash and inventory, sales and marketing, supervising employees, establishing contracts, building up partnerships, and much more. No matter what your significant other does next, whether it be starting a new venture or joining an existing organization, these skills and experiences will be put to good use.

Even more significantly, though, your mate will learn hard but incredibly valuable lessons about leadership and character. Many start-ups are felled by outside forces, like recessions or competition or changes in government regulation, but just as many are brought down by the founder's approach to leadership or decision-making. Maybe he held on too tightly to control or he made some poor hires. Perhaps he didn't prioritize tracking his cash flow or lowering his costs.

Once an entrepreneur experiences the negative consequences of her mistakes, she will be able to more clearly see her strengths, weaknesses, and any changes she needs to make. She will better understand the most effective ways she can lead and the most effective ways she can empower others to support her.

Some of these skills could be learned through classes or trainings, but this kind of on-the-job, trial-by-fire learning is far more effective. There's even an educational theory around it called *desirable difficulties*, a term coined by UCLA research psychologist Robert Bjork. The theory "suggests that introducing certain difficulties into the learning process can greatly improve long-term retention of the learned material."[10] And there may be no learning process more difficult than starting a company, building it up, and watching it die. That's why even entrepreneurs who couldn't successfully sustain a venture find themselves in high demand by other organizations.

What, then, is your role in supporting your entrepreneur through this learning process? One approach is to simply encourage him to talk about what happened and what he learned. As Bjork writes, ". . . the act of retrieving information is itself a potent learning event. Retrieved information, rather than being left in the same state it was in prior to being recalled, becomes more recallable in the future than it would have been otherwise, and competing information associated with the same cues can become less recallable in the future."[11]

The learnings from an experience as stark as losing a business are so invaluable, in fact, that this supposed "failure" may end up being one of the best things that happens to your mate. George Kembel, who was an entrepreneur and venture capitalist before founding the Hasso Plattner Institute of Design at Stanford University, talks about how being an entrepreneur almost destroyed his marriage. At the age of twenty-seven, he was working on his second company when he married his wife, Alice. He did the typical entrepreneurship thing: he never turned off and never fully stepped away from the job. Alice, like many of us, felt incredibly resentful and accused her husband of having an affair with his company.

Today, Kembel says, "I think I'm lucky that that second company failed. . . . It saved my marriage."[12] When his company was doing well financially, he became much more focused on multiplying that success, giddy at the thought that he could retire early and provide for his parents, his wife, and his children for the rest of their lives. "Because the company failed, I realized that I almost lost everything that I was doing it for. And that's not worth it. And I think I was lucky to learn that in two years. I think most people . . . learn that in a career."[13]

No matter how dark the season of failure may feel for you or your entrepreneur, remember that you are both getting a lifetime of learning out of it. It's impossible to put a price on that kind of wisdom and experience, and both your family and your beloved's future career will undoubtedly benefit from it.

That being said, I'm sure we all hope that our significant others can eventually hit upon an idea that flourishes. In fact, I'm sure most of us wouldn't mind that ultimate prize of a big acquisition or IPO as a reward for everything our family has sacrificed for the business. But that kind of success comes with its own major risks. If you want your relationship and family to stay intact, preparing for success is just as critical as preparing for failure.

20

Surviving Success

A woman I'll call Penelope thought her family had reached the promised land. After ten exhausting years of supporting her husband and his start-up, including raising two young children mostly on her own, the end had arrived. Her husband's company had been acquired by a large corporation, and they were suddenly rich beyond their wildest dreams.

Penelope envisioned a lovely future for their family, with years of happy partnership, co-parenting, and domestic bliss ahead of them. To some degree, that vision came true. Her husband was around more. He could help out with the kids and the household chores. Penelope felt like she finally had her partner back, and their family was together in a way they hadn't been before.

But then, not too long after the acquisition, her husband suddenly asked her for permission to sleep with other women. Stunned, Penelope immediately said no. He backed off and didn't ask again.

Yet, for Penelope, the idea that her husband would even consider such an arrangement remained immensely painful. The more she thought about it, the more certain she was that his deep betrayal was related to his successful exit. "There's a fantasy that gets portrayed," she told me. "One day he'll be done with his company, we'll ride into the sunset, and everything will be hunky-dory. But that's just not real."

What was real were the accolades and acclaim that were suddenly being showered upon Penelope's husband. He had gone from being a fairly obscure entrepreneur to someone that everyone wanted to meet. Rich and powerful people told him how amazing he was and how he could do anything he wanted.

The effect on his ego was not pretty. The man who had been Penelope's best friend and closest partner for fifteen years became someone she no longer recognized. His request to sleep around was only one of the problems that came up. The many fissures that had formed in their relationship over the past decade came boiling to the surface. They fought constantly. At one point, Penelope told him, "I don't think I can respect you anymore. You're a jackass now."

Unfortunately, Penelope's experience isn't that unique. Executive coach Julien Adler explains that money and fame tend to have a peculiar effect on people. "Money and fame magnify all areas of you, the good and the ugly. It magnifies what's going on in an individual. If someone is well balanced, they will certainly grow. If someone is not balanced, they will also grow but there is a lot of collateral damage," Adler explained. And that collateral damage is likely to strike your marriage and family first.

Contrary to what we tend to think, reaching the pinnacle of success for entrepreneurs—that big exit—doesn't mean you are set for the rest of your life. If anything, it means you have that much more responsibility to manage your new wealth and the impact it will have on your life. It means you have to be that much more careful about who you are and how you use your financial resources.

You've no doubt heard the many stories of lottery winners who have blown through their winnings within months and ended up bankrupt. Others have lost friendships, struggled with substance abuse, gotten sucked into criminal activity, or even become so depressed that they committed suicide.[1]

These individuals have experienced what psychologists Stephen Goldbart and Joan Indursky DiFuria, founders of the Money, Meaning & Choices Institute, call *Sudden Wealth Syndrome* (SWS).[2] Typical symptoms of SWS include stress, isolation, guilt, and fear of losing money.[3] At the root of SWS is a deep, expansive identity crisis: the rapid shift from being a typical hardworking individual to a person of extraordinary privilege and status. How an individual sees himself, and how others see him, has been transformed overnight.

Though financially successful entrepreneurs typically work harder for their money than lottery winners, they are just as susceptible to the stressors and challenges that come with a massive and abrupt change in wealth and standing. Your beloved may be average Joe or Jane entrepreneur one day, and then be featured on the cover of *Forbes* magazine the next. She may be toiling in an unmarked office building this week, and treated as a celebrity the next. This change is not necessarily negative in and of itself, but if you and your entrepreneur don't prepare well for this possibility, the consequences of a big exit could get really ugly, really fast.

Even if you are not directly involved in the business, you are not immune to these impacts either. Where you fit in society, who wants to be your friend and who doesn't, what unfamiliar opportunities open up for you, how your material possessions measure up to your peers'—these are all fresh challenges that you will likely need to deal with almost immediately after your family's material worth skyrockets.

There's a catchphrase that Google likes to use in many of its employee communications: "Scarcity brings clarity."[4] Though I'm willing to bet that Google employees only experience artificially created scarcity, this is still a useful maxim. When there is less to go around, we are forced to choose what and who matters most to us. In what will we invest our valuable resources—whether it be time, money, energy, or skill—if we have only a little bit to share? These are the questions most entrepreneurs and their families wrestle with for much of the start-up journey.

It makes sense, then, that an overabundance of resources would create confusion. When you are swimming in wealth, it's easy to forget your priorities and what you value or who matters most to you. It seems like you can do anything you want, whenever and in whatever manner you desire. If you need more time or energy, you can simply buy it by paying other people to help you. If you need a particular skill, you could hire for it. Or take some classes. Or attend a conference. Or get a private coach or teacher. Or self-fund a project to figure it out yourself. The options are endless—which can actually be a dreadful thing.

Psychologist Barry Schwartz, who specializes in memory and learning, explains that having choices provides individuals with an important sense of freedom and self-determination. "But as the number of choices keep growing, negative aspects of having a multitude of options begin to appear," Schwartz writes in *The Paradox of Choice: Why More Is Less*. "As the number of choices grows further, the negatives escalate until we become overloaded. At this point, choice no longer liberates, but debilitates. It might even be said to tyrannize."[5] Unsurprisingly, the symptoms of choice over-load that Schwartz cites are the same as that of Sudden Wealth Syndrome: anxiety, stress, dissatisfaction, and clinical depression.[6]

So, can money bring any measure of happiness? Based on decades of research, scientists have found a clear and consistent correlation between money and happiness—but only up to a point.[7] Those who have enough money to provide for their basic needs and live comfortably are typically happier than those who are struggling to make ends meet. However, after a certain threshold—in 2010, one research team said it was $75,000—more money doesn't produce proportionally more happiness.[8] Affluent individuals are only marginally happier than those who have a lot less. "The surprising truth is that we all reach a saturation point when it comes to money," Goldbart and DiFuria write.[9]

Here's more bad news about money: having a lot of it can fundamentally change your character, and usually for the worse. Recent studies have shown that the more wealth someone has, the less generous and empathetic he or she will be. Those who are more affluent, despite all their material advantages, tend to lie, cheat, and act less ethically than people with less. They commit adultery more often.[10] They're more willing to cut off other drivers on the road and to take candy from children.[11] While it would be perfectly logical to argue that the wealthy need less help and fewer perks, they instead end up feeling like they are exempt from the rules and entitled to more.

I say this not to wag my finger at people who happen to have more material resources than I. My point is that we are *all* susceptible to these pitfalls. Ned's company hasn't had an exit yet, and I don't know when or if that will come. But our household income has ticked up gradually over the years as d.light has grown, and that alone has been enough to cause changes in my behavior. There are subtle ways in which I have become less empathic and more entitled. I get more frustrated with having to wait in line; I am less patient with others; I'm more likely to interrupt when someone is talking or to ignore an email I don't feel like responding to. If I continued on this trajectory long enough without checking myself, I'd probably end up taking candy from children too.

Sadly, this is the direction human nature tugs us in when we have relatively more power and resources than others. No matter how grounded and compassionate and humble you and your entrepreneur are now, if you suddenly find yourself with a few extra zeros in your bank account balance, there will be powerful forces pulling you toward arrogance, selfishness, and entitlement.

Even one of the most noble reasons people have to pursue wealth—to provide for their children and future generations—isn't all it's cut out to be. It turns out that children who grow up in extremely privileged households struggle with certain challenges far more than the average population. According to psychologist and Stanford professor Madeline Levine, who has provided clinical counseling for high-income families in Silicon Valley for decades, "American's newly identified at-risk group is preteens and teens from affluent, well-educated families. In spite of their economic and social advantages, they experience among the highest rates of depression, substance abuse, anxiety disorders, somatic complaints, and unhappiness of any group of children in this country."[12]

Levine has found that the many privileges provided by affluent families, plus the pressure to perform and achieve that often comes from successful parents, can form young adults who are less resilient, disconnected from others, and have underdeveloped interests and passions.[13] No wonder, then, that some of the world's richest people are deciding to leave only a tiny fraction of their wealth to their children.[14]

On top of that, because many newly affluent adults don't actually have the financial know-how to manage their own finances or the tools to talk to their children about it, 70 percent of wealthy families lose their fortune by the second generation. By the third generation, a whopping 90 percent have frittered away their financial resources.[15]

Yet most of us are in denial about the detrimental impact that large amounts of money can have on us and our families. Despite the broad range of research documenting the challenges that come from wealth, the majority of us persist in thinking that more money will bring us that much more life satisfaction. We also assume that those who have fewer financial resources are a lot more unhappy than they actually are.[16]

This mismatch between expectation and reality probably explains much of the emotional turmoil that can come in the wake of sudden wealth. Like Penelope, you may expect all your hardships to disappear when that IPO happens.

Instead, aside from helping with practical matters of survival, money tends to make life more complicated. A wildly successful start-up can threaten your marriage as much as a failed start-up may. Remember how conflict over finances is one of the top causes of divorce? Unfortunately, couples can fight just as much about an abundance of money as they can about a shortage of money.

The bottom line: money is not, in fact, the be-all and end-all that we often make it out to be. It is a valuable tool, but like any tool, what matters most is how we choose to use it. It can do great good or cause great harm, depending on what role it plays in our lives and decisions.

Given all that is at stake for your well-being and family, I would contend that it makes sense to approach preparing for an IPO or acquisition with as much deliberation and care as you might prepare for bankruptcy. If you see a business-related windfall coming in the next few years—or even if you don't—now would be a great time for you and your mate to begin discussing and planning for this possibility. Before your judgment is clouded by all those dollar signs, before you have too many voices vying for your attention and trying to sway your decision-making, it's a good idea to figure out what matters most to you and how you would want to use your increased wealth.

Perhaps your mate's business is not the kind that's going to be acquired or to go public. Your family is doing fine financially but you don't see any possibility of a sudden payout coming your way. Or you set up your company as a lifestyle business from the beginning and have no interest in selling it off. That doesn't mean that you are exempt from all these risks. If your family's income is trending upward, it just means you have a little bit longer to adjust to your new economic status.

A man I'll call Mitchell took over his company when it was small and floundering, and has painstakingly built it up over a decade. He and his wife Vivien's affluence has come gradually. But because most people in their social circles have remained in the same socioeconomic class during that time, the dynamic of most of their friendships has changed quite a bit over the last few years.

"The people who have always been my peers and friends have very different economic lives," Vivien told me. "We have a really nice house now. People make assumptions because of that. There's an inherent awe and jealousy that people have because of our supposed status." Vivien has felt a lack of understanding from others who think that she has only "first-world problems," and she doesn't feel able to share openly about challenges related to the business because word might get back to some of Mitchell's employees.

As a result, Vivien actually feels more isolated now than earlier in Mitchell's career. When friends do approach her, she can't be entirely sure of their motivations. "People see us and think what they can get out of us. They're inviting us to fundraising dinners," she explained. "We're still us, but there's this added thing. 'Come to my this,' 'donate to my that.' It feels like we have this identity that people see but we don't project."

Vivien and Mitchell feel challenged to find peers who fully understand their situation and whom they can confide in. They have encountered friends who are wealthy but don't understand the start-up life; others are entrepreneurial but they haven't been as financially successful. They try to be generous with their resources, but that can sometimes feed into the image that they are extraordinarily wealthy with money to spare.

Money can buy a lot, but it can't bring relationships or personal contentedness. As a team of psychologists from Harvard, the University of Virginia, and the University of British Columbia reported, "Money is an opportunity for happiness, but it is an opportunity that people routinely squander because the things they think will make them happy often don't."[17]

According to Goldbart and DiFuria, almost everyone goes through a honeymoon phase as they adjust to their newly minted status as affluent people.[18] In that initial period of euphoria, of feeling like you can do anything and be anything you want because you have so much money, you are most at risk of making bad financial decisions. You may make large, spontaneous purchases; you may give lavishly (but not particularly thoughtfully) to family and friends; you may try your hand at investing without doing the proper due diligence.

A good place to start, then, is to make sure you take things slowly. Don't go and buy yourself a Tesla right away. Don't promise every family member a new house. Don't immediately enroll your children in the best private school in the area. Don't tell your childhood friend that you'll be the first investor in his new company.

This may be harder than it sounds, as you'll likely have both friends and strangers approaching you for favors or to present you with new and exciting opportunities. Ned told me once that, each time d.light closes an investment round, he gets a slew of emails and catalogs from random (and sometimes fairly aggressive) individuals with requests to help manage his finances, pitches about new business opportunities, and advertisements for large-scale luxury purchases like yachts and vacation homes. If you or your significant other are impulsive or have trouble saying no, it could be particularly challenging for you to fend off the many requests that will come your way.

Instead, it may be a good idea for your family to just keep living life at the same pace and spending rate that you were before. Both of you are going to need some time just to get used to this major shift in your reality. The people around you—your family and friends and colleagues—may also need time to get used to your new status, and are likely watching you carefully to see how you will change. Keeping as many things constant in your life as possible will only help in that adjustment period.

The priorities that we discussed in chapter 7, for example, shouldn't change even if you have a sudden explosion of wealth. Perhaps the number of priorities that you can act upon expands a bit, but ultimately what was important to you when you had less money should still be what's important to you when you have more.

The challenge is that when we have a lot of wealth, we may forget about the other currencies that we used in the past to build contentment, like daily practices and rhythms to keep us grounded or authentic friendships that have no strings attached. The two of you can help gently remind one another what your priorities were and still are, regardless of how much you're worth on paper.

Another reason to take it slow? As strange as it may sound, you need to learn how to be a person of considerable financial means. You may find yourself being inundated with invitations to new social circles and investment opportunities. And now that you have the option to spend your money on more things, you need to figure out the best use of those funds that will feel most meaningful to you. For example, studies have found that a majority of people derive more satisfaction and happiness from purchasing experiences rather than things, and from spending on others instead of themselves.[19]

You will likely also need to consider areas of financial management that you never knew about before: trusts, estates, wills, philanthropy, and different tax laws. One couple I spoke with had to delve into international tax law when the husband's company was acquired. His wife had the opportunity to enter her dream graduate program in Europe, but she decided to turn it down when they discovered that they would have to pay $250,000 in wealth tax if they moved abroad.

To evaluate and understand each of these new areas, it would be a good idea to ask for as much help as you need. In general, entrepreneurs can benefit from sound financial advice, and this is even more the case when their finances are beyond what they know how to manage. It's never too early to engage the services of a trusted financial adviser. You and your mate may also want to work with a coach, therapist, or spiritual leader to develop a robust sense of self-worth outside of any material success. If you haven't yet gotten your big windfall, I'd suggest investing deeply in friendships now, such that your bonds become resilient enough to withstand a sudden widening in the economic differences between you. Or, if you're already awash in cash, try connecting with someone who has been through a similar acquisition in wealth and could offer you helpful advice.

In the process of learning how to be a responsible, kind, and grounded person of wealth, I cannot say too much about the importance of humility. No one succeeds, or remains successful, alone. Your significant other likely had many supporters along the way to her big payout: cofounders and business partners, investors and funders, employees and contractors, clients and customers. She has also had you and your children and the rest of your family.

Similarly, you will continue to need the help of others even after you become millionaires or billionaires. You may not need the advice, encouragement, or friendship of others for survival, but you will need it for the well-being of your soul and spirit. And you and your significant other will probably need to depend on one another more than ever to act as the sandpaper to one another's egos, gently nudging each other toward greater maturity and groundedness.

An important part of that is ensuring that your entrepreneur's sense of identity and self-worth remain distinct from his financial assets and social status. Just as being defined by failure is harmful to our character, so is being defined by success. As many entrepreneurs can attest, success can be fleeting and fickle. Your wealth and status are subject to change depending on factors far outside of your control, such as government regulations or the state of the economy.

But even if you remained wealthy for the rest of your life, your contentedness about your status would likely wane. After a while, you and your mate might start worrying that it's been too long since you had your last big success; you might fall into the habit of comparing yourselves to even richer individuals and feel like you need more to be happy. Therefore, it's important to remember that the two of you have value far beyond the size of your most recent buyout, no matter what your peers, the media, or other successful people may tell you.

If you hope to get rich without damaging your family, your integrity, or your soul, the odds are actually stacked against you. But it *is* possible to walk with your entrepreneur through this transition wisely and relatively unscathed, as long as you hold on to your values and priorities and sense of identity, and limit your expectations on what money will do for you. Perhaps then you'll be able to follow in the footsteps of the remarkable humanitarian work of Bill and Melinda Gates, or the generosity and down-to-earth family life of Warren Buffett.[20]

But the best news of all may be the fact that you and your entrepreneur don't need to strike it rich to have a full and contented life. Living with purpose while surrounded by loved ones is a far more reliable recipe for a meaningful existence with few regrets. You can, in essence, create your own happiness and well-being, no matter the valuation, acquisition potential, or eventual fate of the start-up in your family.

In fact, as I've reflected on my experience as an entrepreneur's spouse, and the many other stories I have heard from others, I've come to the encouraging conclusion that you and your mate have a very good chance of being okay. In fact, you may even be better than okay. This thrilling, unpredictable ride that our beloved innovators and leaders have taken us on is truly one of a kind, and there is every reason to believe that we can come out of this as uniquely mature and experienced individuals.

Conclusion

There's a daydream I like to indulge in occasionally: Ned and I are semiretired, living off the funds we got when he cashed out on his d.light shares. We are still involved in doing meaningful things, of course, but there's not the pressure to build it from the ground up or to constantly secure funding or to worry about everyone's jobs. Maybe we work or volunteer twenty hours a week, but the rest of the time we read books, go to the movies, and make spontaneous weekend getaways to the beach or the mountains. We spend plenty of time together as a family, playing board games and going hiking and regularly taking our son on exotic vacations.

As much as I savor this dream, I know it's never going to happen. That kind of life is not compatible with the man I married. He doesn't ever want to stop innovating and learning and stretching himself. By extension, I don't expect that he will ever stop stretching me.

Among the dozens of couples I interviewed for this book, the most well-adapted significant others all had one thing in common: they accepted who their entrepreneurs were, warts and all, and accepted the kind of impacts the start-up life would have on their existence. They didn't try to resist the uncertainty and instability. Instead, they figured out how to operate within the ups and downs, creatively thinking around them and courageously trying different things to ensure that their bond and family life would continue to thrive.

I think it's no coincidence that acceptance is the fifth and final stage of grief. Coming to a place of acceptance requires a letting go of the way you wish things were but can't be. It is right and healthy to grieve the loss of dreams and hopes you may have carried into your relationship. It takes time to release our long-held expectations. Yet grief is only the beginning, not the end destination.

I've seen many a significant other give in to the temptation to stay in their grief and milk it as much as they can, laying the guilt and resentment on their entrepreneurs' shoulders as thickly as possible. I have done this many times over the course of our marriage and still occasionally mourn how life with Ned will never resemble a Thomas Kinkade painting. Oftentimes, I find myself doing this when I want Ned to fix everything. He's the one who made the mess, I think, so it follows that he should make it right again.

Entrepreneurs, for all their positivity and innovative energy, can fall into a similar rut of despair. *It's not possible to balance a start-up and family*, they argue. *I have to give this business everything I can in order for it to succeed. I don't have anything left for family. I can't do anything more.*

If there is any message that you take away from this book, I hope it is this: there are plenty of things you can do to make things better for your family.

There is, however, no magic formula that will work for every couple all the time. Much of the work comes in figuring out what strategies are most effective for your relationship in the particular circumstances that you find yourselves in. And those strategies will change over time, as the business grows and falters, and as you and your partner enter and exit different life stages. Adapting, pivoting, adjusting, experimenting, innovating—these will all be required by you and your beloved entrepreneur at some point to ensure that you are still investing in one another.

It turns out that the stubborn persistence, creativity, and grit that enable company founders to be successful are exactly what your family needs as well.

Of course, it is ideal if both partners recognize the importance of investing in the relationship and are willing to change and sacrifice to improve your marriage. But even if only one person in the relationship—whether the entrepreneur or the significant other—chooses to prioritize family, there are still many options for making the most of this unpredictable journey. And more likely than not, the actions of one partner will eventually influence the behavior of the other.

I know that Ned chose to be with me, and chooses every day to remain with me, not because I enable and indulge his every whim, but because I support his dreams while also keeping him grounded. My broken-record insistence that he pay more attention to his own well-being, our marriage, and our family has no doubt irritated him over the years. Yet he has witnessed firsthand how everyone in our family is healthier, happier, and more well connected when he is fully present to us. And that, in turn, gives him more energy and focus to be a strong leader and manager for his first baby, d.light.

But what if that's not the case? What if your entrepreneur

refuses to change, and the stressors on your marriage and family only worsen over time? When is getting out of the relationship the best course of action?

Every marriage-family therapist, executive coach, and relationship expert I interviewed for this book, who have cumulatively worked with thousands of couples, was surprisingly reluctant to recommend separation or divorce, even for the most unhappy spouse. There are some behaviors that they agreed were unacceptable in a marriage, such as physical or emotional abuse, or chronic addictions that remain untreated. One therapist cited irreconcilable values systems as another consideration for ending a marriage. But in general, they agreed, one after the other, regardless of their faith background or personal experience, that divorce is a much-higher-risk proposition than we often like to think it is.

"The devastation that divorce causes is generally huge and life-long," therapist Chris Bruno told me. This is especially the case if children are involved. Social science research has consistently shown that children from divorced parents are more likely to have behavioral, psychological, and academic challenges. The only benefits children may experience are if a separation takes them out of a chronic high-conflict household environment, full of regular shouting, arguing, and other aggressive behavior.[1]

The financial side of divorce can also be complicated for entrepreneurs and their spouses, especially when both partners have a financial stake in one or more companies. I've heard a fair number of stories about spouses who waited until the big acquisition or IPO payout, and then immediately filed for divorce. Some entrepreneurs have had their earnings gutted and their businesses destroyed by a separation from their spouse.[2] Investors, for better or worse, are becoming more savvy about this, requiring soon-to-be-married entrepreneurs to sign prenuptial agreements with their significant others as a condition of investment. Ned and I had already been married for several years when d.light received its first investment; even then, I had to sign papers agreeing not to try to take over the company if Ned and I ever divorced.

The stark reality, though, is that the majority of couples who choose to separate do not do so because of abuse, irreconcilable values, financial difficulties, or even infidelity. "Most people divorce because they feel like the magic or spark is gone," research psychologist Ty Tashiro explained. "That's the most prevalent category of divorce."

Guess what? The spark will go out at some point even if your mate has the most predictable nine-to-five job and its accompanying cost-of-living salary increase each year. The spark will disappear when you have children, or it will fizzle out if you never have children. The spark will be snuffed out from stress, exhaustion, conflict, busyness, and boredom—whether your beloved is an entrepreneur or not. This is the challenge that all couples face, no matter their professional choices or career trajectories.

But the spark, if you let it, also has a very good chance of coming back. One recent study in the UK found that 70 percent of couples who reported being unhappy when their first child was born felt fulfilled ten years later.[3] And, as we've discussed, there is plenty you can do to re-create romance and intimacy in your relationship, no matter how busy or stressed the two of you are feeling. "There can be a value in defaulting to staying," one therapist told me.

Choosing to separate or divorce is, of course, a very personal decision, and the circumstances in most entrepreneurial relationships are highly complex. I cannot tell you what the best decision is for you and your entrepreneur. I can only encourage you to make such a weighty decision slowly and with caution. The truth is that, in the vast majority of relationships, it can, in fact, get better, if we're willing to keep trying.

In all honesty, my marriage with Ned no longer has the same heated romance of our first few years together. But our relationship is far more mature and robust, carved and polished by the many hardships we have endured into something beautiful and lasting. My love for him today is deeper and full of greater respect and unconditional acceptance than our heady days as dating teenagers. We have seen the very best and worst of one another, we know all about one another's shortcomings, and yet we remain wholly committed to each other. It is, to put it simply, a relationship worth fighting for and staying for.

That said, our life together is anything but predictable. Ned and his ongoing entrepreneurial adventures always keep me on my toes and compel us to keep working to strengthen our bond. The challenge for us to stay connected and on the same page about our priorities and life plans will likely remain with us for as long as Ned has that entrepreneurial bug.

If you happen to be married to an entrepreneur who really, truly is ready to hang up her founder hat, the journey to grow together is just as worthwhile. When you are faced with an empty business nest, the past investments you have made in your relationship mean that you still have a strong marriage to turn back to. You will hopefully delight in the opportunity to spend extra time together and to dream about other, slightly less wild escapades you want to go on together. It won't be about rebuilding, but building on the reliable foundation you already have.

The journey to figure out a healthy and sustainable balance for your relationship is by no means straightforward. It will include false starts and restarts; mistakes, mishaps, and misadventures; conflicts and compromises; tears and heartache. But, as a number of entrepreneurs reminded me over the course of writing this book, nothing that is truly worthwhile is ever easy. Figuring out how to pursue your biggest professional dreams, while also nurturing your marriage and family life, can enrich you and your loved ones in immeasurable ways. I can think of fewer things more worthwhile than that.

As an entrepreneur's spouse, I have had a heck of a time accepting the fact that I cannot control my husband or the craziness he brings into my life. I can't alleviate the constant fundraising pressure or stop sudden pivots in business strategy. I can't make all of d.light's partners, employees, and customers behave in a way to make Ned's life as painless as possible. What I can fully control, though, is how I respond to the circumstances around me. Even when things are hard and exhausting and uncertain, they can still be *good*.

Despite everything—through severe anxiety and depression, through seasons of intense doubt and conflict, through many surprising and abrupt turns in our fate—the truth of the matter is that I wouldn't have it any other way. Though Ned has not been able to provide me with quiet nights and planned vacations, his work has taken us on some remarkable adventures. He has stretched and challenged me far beyond where I would have gone myself. His courage, tenacity, and risk-taking have inspired me to live with more grit and purpose.

I am an entirely different person because of who Ned is and how his pursuits have impacted my choices. My life story, in the end, is so much richer because of my entrepreneurial spouse.

It starts, of course, with your commitment to one another, and your shared determination to make this unconventional road into something good for both of you. There is enough time for both of you to do what you love. There is enough space in life for both of you to flourish.

Now, go, and try to make it happen. And if you can't figure it out the first time, get up, dust yourselves off, and keep trying. You and your relationship are well worth it.

Acknowledgments

Birthing a book is not unlike launching a business, full of risks and unknowns, rejections and failures, surprising opportunities and a healthy dose of divine intervention. It also requires numerous supporters, cheerleaders, and collaborators each step of the way.

At the very beginning of my writer's journey were three women who took my earliest efforts to transform my life into story and molded those words with kindness, humor, and endless grace. Sue Eitemiller, Irene Bennett, and Darien Tso, your friendship and companionship as fellow writers have been such a gift to me.

I am so grateful to my agent, Carric Pestritto, for her wise guidance and persistent positivity. Thank you for never giving up on this book. Thank you to my editor, Christina Boys, for believing in the importance of this topic and being an absolute pleasure to collaborate with, and to the Center Street team for applying their considerable talents into making this book what it is today. Thanks also to Meg and Gary Hirshberg for being trailblazers in this subject and for so generously providing their warm and sincere support in the foreword.

Many thanks to Audrey Kalman and Cara Meredith for giving me invaluable feedback on the earliest drafts of this book. I am also deeply fortunate to be part of several communities of smart, dedicated, and generous writers, particularly the Redbud Writers Guild and the Her.manas. Thank you, ladies, for your constant inspiration, encouragement, wisdom, and practical assistance.

Thanks to the editors and staff at Inc.com and the *Unreasonable* blog, who were among the first to recognize the value of empowering entrepreneurs to prioritize their families, and provided avenues for me to begin sharing the lessons I have learned. I am grateful also to the numerous editors I have worked with at *Christianity Today*, *The Well*, *Asian American Women on Leadership*, and other publications, who have all made me a better and more honest writer.

This book is built upon the wisdom of many, many people. I am grateful to the therapists, coaches, psychologists, business school staff, investors, and other professionals who generously shared their expertise with me. I am particularly grateful to the individuals and couples who shared their personal stories. Opening up one's marriage and family to the scrutiny of others is never easy, particularly in the image-conscious start-up world. But I am confident that their courage and vulnerability will serve many couples and may save more than a few relationships.

So many family members, friends, and colleagues have cheered me on through the writing of this book. Thank you, loved ones, for every hug, thoughtful comment, encouraging word, and heartfelt prayer that you have extended to this writer's thirsty soul. You are each so precious to me.

It is quite obvious that this book would not exist without my husband, Ned. The challenges of our marriage may have been the impetus for this book, but it was Ned's unyielding love, support, encouragement, and utter confidence in me that allowed it to come to fruition. Ned, thank you for taking me on the adventure of a lifetime—and for letting me tell the world about it. I love you more with every wild, unexpected turn in our lives.

Endnotes

INTRODUCTION

1 Vivek Wadhwa, Raj Aggarwal, Krisztina "Z" Holly, and Alex Salkever, *The Anatomy of an Entrepreneur: Family Background and Motivation* (Ewing Marion Kauffman Foundation, July 2009), 5, http://www.kauffman.org/~/media/kauffman_org/research%20 reports%20and%20covers/2009/07/anatomy_of_entre_071309_final.pdf.

2 Ibid.

3 Ibid.

4 Martin Ruef, Howard E. Aldrich, and Nancy M. Carter, "The Structure of Founding Teams: Homophily, Strong Ties, and Isolation among U.S. Entrepreneurs," *American Sociological Review* 68, no. 2 (April 2003): 195–222.

5 Rose Leadem, "Stressed and Exhausted? More than Half of Founders Say They Never 'Switch Off,'" Entrepreneur.com, June 2, 2017, accessed June 2, 2017, https://www.entrepreneur.com/article/295299.

CHAPTER 1

1 Wadhwa et al., *Family Background and Motivation*, 6.

2 Scott A. Shane, *The Illusions of Entrepreneurship: The Costly Myths That Entrepreneurs, Investors, and Policy Makers Live By* (New Haven, CT: Yale University Press, 2008), 44.

3   Wadhwa et al., *Family Background and Motivation*, 6.

4   Gillian B. White, "Women Are Owning More and More Small Businesses," *The Atlantic*, April 17, 2015, accessed May 19, 2017, https://www.theatlantic.com/business/archive/2015/04/women-are-owning-more-and-more-small-businesses/390642/; "Women Business Owner Statistics," the website of National Association of Women Business Owners, accessed February 3, 2017, https://www.nawbo.org/resources/women-business-owner-statistics.

5   "Pay Equity & Discrimination," Institute for Women's Policy Research, accessed February 3, 2017, http://www.iwpr.org/initiatives/pay-equity-and-discrimination; Matt Egan, "Still Missing: Female Business Leaders," *CNN Money* online, March 24, 2015, accessed November 16, 2015, http://money.cnn.com/2015/03/24/investing/female-ceo-pipeline-leadership/.

6   Kerry Miller, "Can Your Relationship Survive B-School?" BusinessWeek.com, February 13, 2007, accessed August 21, 2014, http://www.businessweek.com/stories/2007-02-13/can-your-relationship-survive-b-school-businessweek-business-news-stock-market-and-financial-advice.

7   Menachem Wecker, "Business Schools Welcome Students' Partners, Spouses," *U.S. News & World Report*, January 23, 2012, accessed February 6, 2017, http://www.usnews.com/education/best-graduate-schools/top-business-schools/articles/2012/01/23/business-schools-welcome-students-partners-spouses.

8   Shane, *Illusions of Entrepreneurship*, 101.

9   Guy Kawasaki, *The Art of the Start: The Time-Tested, Battle-Hardened Guide for Anyone Starting Anything* (New York: Portfolio, 2004), 3.

10   Ashlee Vance, *Elon Musk: Tesla, SpaceX, and the Quest for a Fantastic Future* (New York: HarperCollins, 2015), 17 (suspension points in the original).

11   Shane, *Illusions of Entrepreneurship*, 98, 109.

12   José Ernesto Amorós and Niels Bosma, *Global Entrepreneurship Monitor: 2013 Global Report*, (Concepción, Chile: Global Entrepreneurship Monitor), 11.

13   Vivek Wadhwa, Raj Aggarwal, Krisztina "Z" Holly, and Alex Salkever, *The Anatomy of an Entrepreneur: Making of a Successful Entrepreneur* (Ewing Marion Kauffman Foundation, November 2009), 6, http://www.kauffman.org/~/media/kauffman_org/research%20reports%20and%20covers/2009/07/makingofasuccessfulentrepreneur.pdf.

14   Shane, *Illusions of Entrepreneurship*, 103–5.

15   Trisha Garek Harp, "Spousal Satisfaction in Entrepreneurial Couples: The Role of Congruity of Family and Business Goals" (master's thesis, Ohio State University, 2007), 12, https://harpfamilyinstitute.com/wp content/uploads/2016/06/Spousal-Satisfaction-in-Entrepreneurial-Couples.pdf.

CHAPTER 2

1   Will Yakowicz, "5 Things to Know about Doing Business in Shenzhen," Inc.com, February 24, 2015, accessed November 17, 2015, http://www.inc.com/will-yakowicz/shenzhen-city-of-electronics.html.

2   Shane, *Illusions of Entrepreneurship*, 68.

3   Robert P. Singh, Gerald E. Hills, Ralph C. Hybels, and G.T. Lumpkin, "Opportunity Recognition through Social Network Characteristics of Entrepreneurs," *Garland Studies in Entrepreneurship*, 1999, http://fusionmx.babson.edu/entrep/fer/papers99/X/X_B/X_B.html.

4   Caron Beesley, "How to Estimate the Cost of Starting a Business from Scratch," *Starting a Business* (blog), U.S. Small Business Administration, last modified September 27, 2016, accessed February 3, 2017, https://www.sba.gov/blogs/how-estimate-cost-starting-business-scratch.

5   Valentina Zarya, "Venture Capital's Funding Gender Gap Is Actually Getting Worse," Fortune.com, May 13, 2017, accessed May 26, 2017, http://fortune.com/2017/03/13/female-founders-venture-capital/.

6   J. McGrath Cohoon, Vivek Wadhwa, and Lesa Mitchell, *The Anatomy of an Entrepreneur: Are Successful Women Entrepreneurs Different from Men?* (Ewing Marion Kauffman Foundation, May 2010), 7, http://www.kauffman.org/~/media/kauffman_org/research%20reports%20and%20covers/2009/07/successful_women_entrepreneurs_510.pdf.

7   "Stats," Kickstarter, accessed May 26, 2017, https://www.kickstarter.com/help/stats.

8   Jonathan T. Eckhardt, Scott Shane, and Frederic Delmar, "Multistage Selection and the Financing of New Ventures," *Management Science* 52, no. 2 (February 2006), 220–232.

9   Howard Marks, "Dare to Be Great" (memo to Oaktree Clients, September 7, 2006), 4, accessed February 3, 2017, https://www.oaktreecapital.com/docs/default-source/memos/2006-09-07-dare-to-be-great.pdf?sfvrsn=2.

10   Kawasaki, *Art of the Start*, 14.

11   Scott Shane, "Startup Failure Rates—The REAL Numbers," SmallBizTrends.com, April 28, 2008, accessed February 3, 2017, https://smallbiztrends.com/2008/04/startup-failure-rates.html.

12   Shane, *Illusions of Entrepreneurship*, 7.

13   Henry Blodget, "Dear Entrepreneur: Here's How Bad Your Odds of Success Are," *Business Insider*, May 28, 2013, accessed September 4, 2014, http://www.businessinsider.com/startup-odds-of-success-2013-5.

14   Malcolm Gladwell, *Outliers: The Story of Success* (New York: Little, Brown, 2008), 41.

15   Shane, *Illusions of Entrepreneurship*, 73.

CHAPTER 3

1   Jack Torrance, "Entrepreneurs Work 63% Longer than Average Workers," *RealBusiness*, August 13, 2013, accessed January 12, 2015, http://realbusiness.co.uk/article/22838-entrepreneurs-work-63-longer-than-average-workers.

2   Rose Leadem, "Stressed and Exhausted? More Than Half of Founders Say They Never 'Switch Off,'" Entrepreneur.com, June 2, 2017, https://www.entrepreneur.com/article/295299.

3   "Americans Stay Connected to Work on Weekends, Vacation and Even When Out Sick," American Psychological Association, September 4, 2013, accessed November 19, 2015, http://www.apa.org/news/press/releases/2013/09/connected-work.aspx.

4   Mandy Oaklander, "Answering Emails After Work Is Bad for Your Health," *TIME*, November 6, 2014, accessed November 14, 2014, http://time.com/3560203/stress-work-email/.

5   "U.S. Travel Answer Sheet (2016)," U.S. Travel Association, accessed May 22, 2017, https://www.ustravel.org/answersheet.

6   Noam Scheiber, "The Brutal Ageism of Tech," *New Republic*, March 23, 2014, accessed February 5, 2017, https://newrepublic.com/article/117088/silicons-valleys-brutal-ageism.

7   Meg Cadoux Hirshberg, *For Better or For Work: A Survival Guide for Entrepreneurs and Their Families* (New York: Inc., 2012), Kindle edition, 2.

8   Jessica Bruder, "The Psychological Price of Entrepreneurship," Inc.com, September 2013, accessed February 5, 2017, http://www.inc.com/magazine/201309/jessica-bruder/psychological-price-of-entrepreneurship.html.

9   Kelly McGonigal, *The Upside of Stress: Why Stress Is Good for You, and How to Get Good at It* (New York: Avery, 2015), Kindle edition, xxi.

10   *Wikipedia*, s.v. "Richard Lazarus," accessed November 20, 2015, https://en.wikipedia.org/wiki/Richard_Lazarus.

11   *Wikipedia*, s.v. "Eustress," accessed November 20, 2015, https://en.wikipedia.org/wiki/Eustress.

12   Harry Mills, "Types of Stressors (Eustress v. Distress)," MentalHelp.net, November 18, 2015, accessed November 20, 2015, https://www.mentalhelp.net/articles/types-of-stressors-eustress-vs-distress/.

13   *Wikipedia*, s.v. "Eustress."

14   "Understanding Chronic Stress," American Psychological Association, accessed November 20, 2015, http://www.apa.org/helpcenter/understanding-chronic-stress.aspx.

15   Christopher Bergland, "Chronic Stress Can Damage Brain Structure and Connectivity," *Psychology Today*, February 12, 2014, accessed November 14, 2014, http://www.psychologytoday.com/blog/the-athletes-way/201402/chronic-stress-can-damage-brain-structure-and-connectivity.

16   "Holmes-Rahe Stress Inventory," American Institute of Stress, accessed January 20, 2015, http://www.stress.org/holmes-rahe-stress-inventory/.

17   Bruder, "The Psychological Price of Entrepreneurship."

18   Michael A. Freeman, Sheri L. Johnson, Paige J. Staudenmaier, and Mackenzie R. Zisser, *Are Entrepreneurs "Touched with Fire"?*, pre-publication manuscript, April 17, 2015, 3, http://www.michaelafreemanmd.com/Research_files/Are%20Entrepreneurs%20Touched%20with%20Fire%20(pre-pub%20n)%204-17-15.pdf.

19   Laura A. Pratt and Debra J. Brody, *Depression in the U.S. Household Population, 2009–2012*, U.S. Department of Health and Human Services, Centers for Disease Control and Prevention, December 2014, 1, https://www.cdc.gov/nchs/data/databriefs/db172.pdf.

20   *Wikipedia*, s.v. "Creativity and Mental Illness," accessed September 25, 2015, https://en.wikipedia.org/wiki/Creativity_and_mental_illness.

21   Ben Horowitz, "The Struggle," Andreessen Horowitz website, June 15, 2012, accessed February 5, 2017, http://www.bhorowitz.com/the_struggle.

22   Adelaide Lancaster, "Why Entrepreneurs Are Bound for Burnout," *Forbes*, October 7, 2011, accessed February 16, 2015, http://www.forbes.com/sites/thebigenoughcompany/2011/10/07/why-entrepreneurs-are-bound-for-burnout/.

23   Ibid.

24   Robert W. Fairlie, E. J. Reedy, Arnobio Morelix, and Joshua Russell, *The Kauffman Index: 2016 Startup Activity: National Trends* (Ewing Marion Kauffman Foundation, August 2016), 5,

http://www.kauffman.org/~/media/kauffman_org/microsites/kauffman_index/startup
_activity_2016/kauffman_index_startup_activity_national_trends_2016.pdf.

25   Richard Branson's Facebook page, January 14, 2013, accessed February 5, 2017, https://
www.facebook.com/RichardBranson/photos/a.10150152138395872.292541
.31325960871/10151189368195872/?type=1&theater.

26   Steve Wozniak and Gina Smith, *iWoz: Computer Geek to Cult Icon: How I Invented the
Personal Computer, Co-Founded Apple, and Had Fun Doing It* (New York: W. W. Norton,
2006), Kindle edition, 300.

27   Laura Stampler, "Science Says Stress Is Contagious," *TIME*, May 1, 2014, accessed January
6, 2016, http://time.com/84080/stress-contagious/.

28   Rebecca L. Brock and Erika Lawrence, "A Longitudinal Investigation of Stress Spillover in
Marriage: Does Spousal Support Adequacy Buffer the Effects?" *Journal of Family Psychology*
22, no. 1 (February 2008), 11–20.

CHAPTER 4

1   Jacquelyn Smith, "Steve Jobs Always Dressed Exactly the Same. Here's Who Else Does,"
Forbes, October 5, 2012, accessed November 25, 2015, http://www.forbes.com/sites
/jacquelynsmith/2012/10/05/steve-jobs-always-dressed-exactly-the-same-heres
-who-else-does/.

2   Eugene Kim, "Here's the Real Reason Mark Zuckerberg Wears the Same T-Shirt Every
Day," *Business Insider*, November 6, 2014, accessed November 25, 2015, http://www
.businessinsider.com/mark-zuckerberg-same-t-shirt-2014-11.

3   Daniel J. Levitin, *The Organized Mind: Thinking Straight in the Age of Information Overload* (New York: Plume, 2014), 4.

4   Ibid., 7.

5   Ibid., 6.

6   Hirshberg, *For Better or For Work*, 9.

7   Names and details have been changed.

8   *Wikipedia*, s.v. "List of Countries by GDP (PPP) Per Capita," accessed January 13, 2015, http://en.wikipedia.org/wiki/List_of_countries_by_GDP_(PPP)_per_capita.

9   Andrew Moravcsik, "Why I Put My Wife's Career First," *The Atlantic*, October 2015, accessed November 9, 2015, http://www.theatlantic.com/magazine/archive/2015/10/why-i-put-my-wifes-career-first/403240/.

10   Steven Stosny, "Chains of Resentment: Can You Name the Chains You Drag Through Life?" *Psychology Today* (blog), September 9, 2011, accessed December 8, 2015, https://www.psychologytoday.com/blog/anger-in-the-age-entitlement/201109/chains-resentment.

11   Stephen R. Covey, A. Roger Merrill, and Rebecca R. Merrill, *First Things First* (New York: Fireside, 1995), 37. Used by permission of FranklinCovey Co., approved on January 30, 2017.

12   Ibid., 33, 35.

13   Jasmin Palacios, "Divorce in America," Daily Infographic, October 24, 2013, accessed September 30, 2014, http://dailyinfographic.com/divorce-in-america-infographic; "New Survey Sheds Light on How and Why Couples Call It Quits (INFOGRAPHIC)," *Huffington Post*, March 25, 2014, accessed September 30, 2014, http://www.huffingtonpost.com/2014/03/25/divorce-survey_n_5029740.html.

CHAPTER 5

1   Richard Rohr and Andreas Ebert, *The Enneagram: A Christian Perspective* (New York: Crossroad, 2009), 3.

2   Valerian J. Derlega and John H. Berg, ed., *Self-Disclosure: Theory, Research, and Therapy* (New York: Plenum, 1987), 63.

3   Arthur Aron, Edward Melinat, Elaine N. Aron, Robert Darrin Vallone, and Renee J. Bator, "The Experimental Generation of Interpersonal Closeness: A Procedure and Some Preliminary Findings," *Personality and Social Psychology Bulletin* 23, no. 4, 364.

4   John M. Gottman and Nan Silver, *The Seven Principles for Making Marriage Work: A Practical Guide from the Country's Foremost Relationship Expert* (New York: Three Rivers Press, 2015), Kindle edition, 3. Excerpt(s) from THE SEVEN PRINCIPLES FOR MAKING MARRIAGE WORK by John Gottman, Ph.D., copyright © 1999 by John M. Gottman, Ph.D. and Nan Silver. Used by permission of Crown Books, an imprint of the Crown Publishing Group, a division of Penguin Random House LLC. All rights reserved.

5   Ibid., 48.

6   Daniel Jones, "The 36 Questions That Lead to Love," *Modern Love* (blog), *New York Times,* January 9, 2015, accessed May 24, 2017, http://www.nytimes.com/2015/01/11/fashion/no-37-big-wedding-or-small.html?_r=0.

7   Bryan E. Robinson, *Chained to the Desk: A Guidebook for Workaholics, Their Partners and Children, and the Clinicians Who Treat Them*, 2nd ed. (New York: New York University Press, 2007), Kindle edition, 7.

8   Ibid., 17.

CHAPTER 6

1   Name and personal details have been changed.

2   "Grade Your Marriage," *For Your Marriage* (blog), accessed January 22, 2016, http://www.foryourmarriage.org/%20everymarriage/grade-your-marriage/.

3   Gottman and Silver, *Seven Principles for Making Marriage Work*, 27.

4   Ibid., 23.

5   Ibid., 19.

6   Ibid., 20.

7   Harville Hendrix, *Getting the Love You Want, 20th Anniversary Edition: A Guide for Couples* (New York, Henry Holt, 2001), Kindle edition, 5.

8   "Dr. Gary Chapman Explains the 5 Love Languages," *Verily*, April 23, 2013, accessed May 24, 2017, http://verilymag.com/dr-gary-chapman-explains-the-5-love-languages/.

CHAPTER 7

1   "Figure Out What's Important to You," Action for Happiness, accessed May 22, 2015, http://www.actionforhappiness.org/take-action/figure-out-whats-important-to-you.

2   "The R.I.P Report—Startup Death Trends," CB Insights, January 18, 2014, accessed September 4, 2014, http://www.cbinsights.com/blog/startup-death-data/.

3   Name has been changed.

4   Tara Parker-Pope, "Your Nest Is Empty? Enjoy Each Other," *New York Times*, January 19, 2009, accessed May 6, 2015, http://www.nytimes.com/2009/01/20/health/20well.html?_r=0.

5   Mark Lino, Kevin Kuczynski, Nestor Rodriguez, and TusaRebecca Schap, *Expenditures on Children by Families, 2015*, United States Department of Agriculture, Center for Nutrition Policy and Promotion, January 2017, ii, https://www.cnpp.usda.gov/sites/default/files/expenditures_on_children_by_families/crc2015.pdf.

6   "How Much You'll Spend on Childcare," Baby Center, accessed May 22, 2015, http://www.babycenter.com/0_how-much-youll-spend-on-childcare_1199776.bc.

7   JP, "How Much Will You Need to Send Your Child to College in 2030?" *U.S. News & World Report*, July 25, 2012, accessed May 21, 2015, http://money.usnews.com/money/blogs/my-money/2012/07/25/how-much-will-you-need-to-send-your-child-to-college-in-2030.

8   Ann Carrns, "Assessing the Costs of Caring for an Aging Relative," *New York Times*,

August 28, 2013, accessed May 21, 2015, http://www.nytimes.com/2013/08/28/your
-money/assessing-the-costs-of-caring-for-an-aging-relative.html?_r=0.

9   *Wikipedia*, s.v. "Lifestyle Business," accessed June 2, 2015, http://en.wikipedia.org
/wiki/Lifestyle_business.

CHAPTER 8

1   "Another Side of the Story," *Startup* (podcast), season 2, episode 3, Gimlet Media, accessed
November 7, 2016.

2   Ray Hennessy, "Don't Let the Loneliness of Entrepreneurship Kill You," *Entrepreneur*, January
5, 2016, accessed November 10, 2016, https://www.entrepreneur.com/article/254641.

3   Brené Brown, *Daring Greatly: How the Courage to Be Vulnerable Transforms the Way We
Live, Love, Parent, and Lead* (New York: Penguin, 2012), Kindle edition, 25–26.

4   The Data Team, "How Marriage Makes People Healthier," *The Economist*, January 13,
2015, accessed February 6, 2017, http://www.economist.com/blogs/economist-explains
/2015/01/economist-explains-0.

5   David Brooks, *The Road to Character* (New York: Random House, 2015), Kindle edition, 1.

CHAPTER 9

1   *Wikipedia*, s.v. "Sex Tourism," accessed May 5, 2015, http://en.wikipedia.org/wiki
/Sex_tourism.

2   John Gottman, "John Gottman on Trust and Betrayal," *Greater Good: The Science of a
Meaningful Life*, October 29, 2011, accessed February 9, 2017, http://greatergood.berkeley
.edu/article/item/john_gottman_on_trust_and_betrayal.

3   "Venture Capital: Sand Hill Road Rules the Valley," *Bloomberg*, December 4, 2014,

accessed February 11, 2017, https://www.bloomberg.com/news/articles/2014-12-04
/venture-capital-sand-hill-road-rules-silicon-valley.

4   Ellyn Bader, Peter T. Pearson, and Judith D. Schwartz, *Tell Me No Lies: How to Stop Lying to
     Your Partner–and Yourself–in the 4 Stages of Marriage* (New York: Skylight Press, 2000), 14.

5   Ibid., 2. Italics in original quote.

6   Ibid., 37.

7   Ibid., 6.

8   Gottman, "John Gottman on Trust and Betrayal."

9   David Richo, *How to Be an Adult in Relationships: The Five Keys to Mindful Loving* (Boston:
     Shambhala, 2002), 89.

10   David Bedrick, "Building & Repairing Trust: Keys to Sustainable Relationship,"
     Psychology Today, October 31, 2013, accessed February 11, 2017, https://www
     .psychologytoday.com/blog/is-psychology-making-us-sick/201310/building
     -repairing-trust-keys-sustainable-relationship.

11   Patrick Lencioni, *The Five Dysfunctions of a Team: A Leadership Fable*, 1st ed. (San Fran-
     cisco: Jossey-Bass, 1994).

12   Jennifer Wieselquist, Caryl E. Rusbult, Craig A. Foster, and Christopher R. Agnew, "Com-
     mitment, Pro-Relationship Behavior, and Trust in Close Relationships," *Journal of Per-
     sonality and Social Psychology* 77 no. 5, November 1999, 942, http://psycnet.apa.org
     /psycinfo/1999-01257-004.

CHAPTER 10

1   Dorothy Littell Greco and Christopher Greco, *Making Marriage Beautiful: Lifelong Love,
     Joy, and Intimacy Start with You* (Colorado Springs, CO: David C. Cook, 2017), 23.

2   Mark Goulston, *Just Listen: Discover the Secret to Getting Through to Absolutely Anyone* (New York: AMACOM, 2015), Kindle edition, 16.

3   "Modern Marriage," Pew Research Center, July 18, 2007, accessed November 17, 2016, http://www.pewsocialtrends.org/2007/07/18/modern-marriage/.

4   Wendy Klein, Carolina Izquierdo, and Thomas N. Bradbury, "The Difference Between a Happy Marriage and a Miserable One: Chores," *The Atlantic*, March 1, 2013, accessed February 11, 2017, https://www.theatlantic.com/sexes/archive/2013/03/the-difference -between-a-happy-marriage-and-miserable-one-chores/273615/.

5   Ibid.

6   Alexandra Sifferlin, "How Family Ties Keep You Going, in Sickness and in Health," *TIME*, February 13, 2017, 20.

7   Gary Chapman, *Now You're Speaking My Language: Honest Communication and Deeper Intimacy for a Stronger Marriage* (Nashville: B&H, 2014), Kindle edition, 8.

8   Ibid., 2.

9   Richo, *How to Be an Adult in Relationships*, 174.

10 Ibid., 142–3.

CHAPTER 11

1   Kevin Daum, "6 Things Entrepreneurs Wish Family, Friends and Employees Understood," Inc.com, April 7, 2014, accessed September 4, 2014, http://www.inc.com/kevin -daum/6-things-entrepreneurs-wish-family-friends-and-employees-understood.html.

2   Brad Feld and Amy Batchelor, *Startup Life: Surviving and Thriving in a Relationship with an Entrepreneur* (Hoboken, NJ: John Wiley & Sons, 2013), Kindle edition, Preface.

3   Ibid.

4   Henry Cloud and John Townsend, *Boundaries in Marriage: Understanding the Choices That Make or Break Loving Relationships* (Grand Rapids, MI: Zondervan, 1999), Kindle edition, 17.

5   Ibid., 22. Italics in original text.

6   Ibid., 196.

7   Brigid Schulte, *Overwhelmed: Work, Love, and Play When No One Has the Time* (New York: Sarah Crichton Books, 2014), Kindle edition, 88.

8   Mandy Oaklander, "Answering Emails after Work Is Bad for Your Health," *TIME*, November 6, 2014, accessed November 14, 2014, http://time.com/3560203/stress-work-email/.

9   Carmen Binnewies, Sabine Sonnentag, and Eva J. Mojza, "Recovery During the Weekend and Fluctuations in Weekly Job Performance: A Week-Level Study Examining Intra-Individual Relationships," *Journal of Occupational and Organizational Psychology* 83, no. 2, June 2010, 419–41, http://onlinelibrary.wiley.com/doi/10.1348/096317909X418049/abstract.

10 Brandon W. Smit, "Successfully Leaving Work at Work: The Self-Regulatory Underpinnings of Psychological Detachment," *Journal of Occupational and Organizational Psychology* 89, no. 3, September 2016, 493–514, http://onlinelibrary.wiley.com/doi/10.1111/joop.12137/abstract.

11 Maria Baratta, "Compartmentalizing: A Tool for Achieving Balance Between Work and Home," *Psychology Today*, July 13, 2013, accessed January 20, 2016, https://www.psychologytoday.com/blog/skinny-revisited/201307/compartmentalizing-2.

12 Smit, "Successfully Leaving Work at Work."

13 Gottman and Silver, *Seven Principles for Making Marriage Work*, 259–61.

14 Brigid Schulte, "Making Time for Kids? Study Says Quality Trumps Quantity," *Washington Post*, March 28, 2015, accessed June 5, 2015, http://www.washingtonpost.com/local/making-time-for-kids-study-says-quality-trumps-quantity/2015/03/28/10813192-d378-11e4-8fce-3941fc548f1c_story.html.

15 Bronnie Ware, *The Top Five Regrets of the Dying: A Life Transformed by the Dearly Departing* (Carlsbad, CA: Balboa, 2011), Kindle edition, 37, 70.

16 Susie Steiner, "The 5 Things People Regret Most on Their Deathbed," *Business Insider*, December 5, 2013, accessed June 12, 2015, http://www.businessinsider.com/5-things-people-regret-on-their-deathbed-2013-12#ixzz3ctHsxGaD.

17 Schulte, *Overwhelmed*, 79.

18 Oaklander, "Answering Emails after Work Is Bad for Your Health."

19 "Accretive Accelerates Value Creation," Accretive Solutions, accessed February 11, 2017, http://www.accretivesolutions.com/accretive-accelerates-value-creation.

20 Schulte, *Overwhelmed*, 88.

CHAPTER 12

1 Kristen P. Mark, Erick Janssen, and Robin R. Milhausen, "Infidelity in Heterosexual Couples: Demographic, Interpersonal, and Personality-Related Predictors of Extradyadic Sex," *Archives of Sexual Behavior* 40, no. 5, October 2011, 971–82; Weekend Edition Sunday, "Sorting Through the Numbers on Infidelity," NPR, July 26, 2015, accessed May 24, 2017, http://www.npr.org/2015/07/26/426434619/sorting-through-the-numbers-on-infidelity.

2 Richard A. Friedman, "Infidelity Lurks in Your Genes," *New York Times*, May 22, 2015, accessed February 9, 2017, https://www.nytimes.com/2015/05/24/opinion/sunday/infidelity-lurks-in-your-genes.html?_r=0.

3 Amanda M. Maddox Shaw, Galena K. Rhoades, Elizabeth S. Allen, Scott M. Stanley, and Howard J. Markman, "Predictors of Extradyadic Sexual Involvement in Unmarried Opposite-Sex Relationships," *The Journal of Sex Research* 50, no. 6, 2013, 598–610, https://www.ncbi.nlm.nih.gov/pubmed/22524318.

4 Elizabeth S. Allen, Galena Kline Rhoades, Scott M. Stanley, Howard J. Markman, Tamara Williams, Jessica Melton, and Mari L. Clements, "Premarital Precursors of

Marital Infidelity," *Family Process* 47, no. 2, June 2008, 243–59, http://onlinelibrary.wiley
.com/doi/10.1111/j.1545-5300.2008.00251.x/full.

5   Harry T. Reis and Phillip Shaver, "Intimacy as an Interpersonal Process," *Handbook of Personal Relationships*, ed. Steve Duck (Chichester: John Wiley & Sons, 1988), 367–89, http://
depts.washington.edu/uwcssc/sites/default/files/Reis%20%26%20Shaver,%201988.pdf.

6   Esther Perel, "YPO NorCal Chapter Forum" (lecture, Lafayette Park Hotel, Lafayette, CA,
February 10, 2016).

7   Neil Rosenthal, *Love, Sex and Staying Warm: Creating a Vital Relationship* (Boulder, CO:
Flagstaff Mountain Press, 2016), Kindle edition, 137.

8   Michele Weiner Davis, *The Sex-Starved Marriage: Boosting Your Marriage Libido: A Couple's Guide* (New York: Simon & Schuster Paperbacks, 2003), Kindle edition, 64.

9   Ty Tashiro (author and relationship expert), interview with the author by phone, February
8, 2017.

10   Esther Perel, *Mating in Captivity: Unlocking Erotic Intelligence* (New York: HarperCollins,
2009), Kindle edition, 37.

11   Weiner Davis, *The Sex-Starved Marriage*, 35–36. Italics in original text.

12   Benny Luo, "Renowned Sex Therapist: Are Successful Men More Likely to Cheat?" *NextShark*, September 11, 2014, accessed December 14, 2016, http://nextshark.com/are
-successful-men-more-likely-to-cheat/.

13   Dan Hurley, "How Sex Affects Intelligence, and Vice Versa," *The Atlantic*, January 13,
2014, accessed December 9, 2016, http://www.theatlantic.com/health/archive/2014
/01/how-sex-affects-intelligence-and-vice-versa/282889/.

14   Erica R. Glasper and Elizabeth Gould, "Sexual Experience Restores Age-Related Decline
in Adult Neurogenesis and Hippocampal Function," *Hippocampus* 23, no. 4, April 2013,
303–12, https://www.ncbi.nlm.nih.gov/pubmed/23460298.

15   Jong-In Kim, Jae Won Lee, Young Ah Lee, Dong-Hun Lee, Nam Soo Han, Yang-Kyu Choi,

Boo Ram Hwang, Hyung Joon Kim, and Jin Soo Han, "Sexual Activity Counteracts the Suppressive Effects of Chronic Stress on Adult Hippocampal Neurogenesis and Recognition Memory," *Brain Research* 13, no. 1538, November 2013, 26–40, https://www.ncbi .nlm.nih.gov/pubmed/24041775.

16 Hurley, "How Sex Affects Intelligence, and Vice Versa."

17 Nick Drydakis, "The Effect of Sexual Activity on Wages," Institute for the Study of Labor, Discussion Paper no. 7529, July 2013, https://www.econstor.eu/bitstream/10419 /80661/1/766234657.pdf.

18 Michelle Castillo, "Study: People Who Have Sex Four or More Times a Week Make More Money," CBS News online, August 15, 2013, accessed February 12, 2017, http://www .cbsnews.com/news/study-people-who-have-sex-four-or-more-times-a-week-make -more-money/.

CHAPTER 13

1 Mark Karpel, "Individuation: From Fusion to Dialogue," *Family Process* 15, no. 1, March 1976, 65–82, https://www.ncbi.nlm.nih.gov/pubmed/1026435.

2 Robert Firestone, *The Fantasy Bond: Structure of Psychological Defenses* (Santa Barbara, CA: Glendon Association, 2014), Kindle edition, Introduction.

3 Richo, *How to Be an Adult in Relationships*, 25.

4 Robert Firestone, "The Fantasy Bond: A Substitute for a Truly Loving Relationship," *Psychology Today*, December 5, 2008, accessed December 19, 2016, https://www.psychologytoday .com/blog/the-human-experience/200812/the-fantasy-bond-substitute-truly-loving -relationship.

5 "How the Arts Affect Your Health," *NIH News in Health*, June 2008, accessed December 20, 2016, https://newsinhealth.nih.gov/2008/june/docs/01features_01.htm.

6   Amanda Enayati, "A Creative Life Is a Healthy Life," CNN.com, May 26, 2012, accessed December 20, 2016, http://www.cnn.com/2012/05/25/health/enayati-innovation -passion-stress/index.html.

7   Robert Grimm, Jr., Kimberly Spring, and Nathan Dietz, *The Health Benefits of Volunteering: A Review of Recent Research* (Washington, DC: Corporation for National and Community Service, April 2007), accessed December 20, 2016, 1, https://www.nationalservice .gov/sites/default/files/documents/07_0506_hbr.pdf.

8   *Reference*, s.v. "Why Are Hobbies Important?" accessed February 10, 2017, https://www .reference.com/world-view/hobbies-important-92e267882082e5d2.

9   "What Role Do Religion and Spirituality Play in Mental Health?" American Psychological Association, March 22, 2013, accessed February 12, 2017, http://www.apa.org/news /press/releases/2013/03/religion-spirituality.aspx.

CHAPTER 14

1   "Impact," Kiva, accessed April 5, 2017, https://www.kiva.org/about/impact.

2   Amanda Palmer, *The Art of Asking: How I Learned to Stop Worrying and Let People Help* (New York: Grand Central, 2014), Kindle edition, Introduction.

3   M. Nora Klaver, *Mayday!: Asking for Help in Times of Need* (San Francisco: Berrett-Koehler, 2007), 190.

4   Ibid.

5   Brown, *Daring Greatly*, 37. Italics in original text.

6   Amanda Palmer, "The Art of Asking," TED video, filmed February 2013, 13:47, https:// www.ted.com/talks/amanda_palmer_the_art_of_asking#t-569931.

7   Garret Keizer, *Help: The Original Human Dilemma* (New York: HarperCollins e-books, 2009), Kindle edition, 4.

CHAPTER 15

1   John Eldredge and Stasi Eldredge, *In Love and War: Finding the Marriage You've Dreamed Of* (New York: Doubleday Religion, 2009), 115.

2   Matthew J. Lindquist, Joeri Sol, and Mirjam van Praag, "Why Do Entrepreneurial Parents Have Entrepreneurial Children?" *SSRN Electronic Journal* 33, no. 2, April 2015, https://www.researchgate.net/publication/254405707_Why_Do_Entrepreneurial_Parents_Have_Entrepreneurial_Children.

3   Name has been changed.

CHAPTER 16

1   *Wikipedia*, s.v. "SMART criteria," accessed February 12, 2017, https://en.wikipedia.org/wiki/SMART_criteria.

2   Henriette Anne Klauser, *Write It Down, Make It Happen: Knowing What You Want—and Getting It!* (New York: Scribner, 2001), Kindle edition, 19.

3   Ibid., 16.

CHAPTER 17

1   Matt Fitzgerald, "The Art of Pacing Yourself in Running," Competitor.com, last updated January 18, 2016, accessed February 12, 2017, http://running.competitor.com/2014/04/training/the-art-of-pacing-yourself-in-running_52927.

2   Angela Lee Duckworth, "Grit: The Power of Passion and Perseverance," TED video, filmed April 2013, 6:12, https://www.ted.com/talks/angela_lee_duckworth_grit_the_power_of_passion_and_perseverance.

3   Wadhwa et al., *Family Background and Motivation*, 5.

CHAPTER 18

1   Timothy Keller and Kathy Keller, *The Meaning of Marriage: Facing the Complexities of Commitment with the Wisdom of God* (New York: Penguin, 2011), 154.

2   "Lao Tzu Quotes," Goodreads, accessed January 25, 2017, http://www.goodreads.com /quotes/256029-he-who-knows-others-is-wise-he-who-knows-himself.

3   Sarah Begley, "The Fallacy of Finding Your One True Love," *TIME*, January 12, 2017, accessed February 13, 2017, http://time.com/4632654/how-choose-partner-susan-quilliam/.

4   Prov. 27:17 (New International Version).

5   Don Richard Riso and Russ Hudson, *The Wisdom of the Enneagram: The Complete Guide to Psychological and Spiritual Growth for the Nine Personality Types* (New York: Bantam, 1999), 45.

6   Ibid., 27.

CHAPTER 19

1   John C. Maxwell, *Failing Forward: Turning Mistakes into Stepping Stones for Success* (Nashville, TN: Thomas Nelson, 2000), Kindle edition, 14.

2   Adrian Chen, "Why Did This 22-Year-Old Entrepreneur Commit Suicide?" *Gawker*, November 14, 2011, accessed November 18, 2016, http://gawker.com/5859366/why-did -this-22-year-old-entrepreneur-commit-suicide.

3   Amrit Mann, "Failure Is Not Flowery," *Entrepreneur India*, July 3, 2016, accessed November 18, 2016, https://www.entrepreneur.com/article/278518.

4   Anne C. Mulkern, "Solyndra Bankruptcy Reveals Dark Clouds in Solar Power Industry," *New York Times*, September 6, 2011, accessed February 10, 2017, http://www.nytimes.com /gwire/2011/09/06/06greenwire-solyndra-bankruptcy-reveals-dark-clouds-in-sol-45598 .html?pagewanted=all.

5   Ori Brafman and Rom Brafman, *Sway: The Irresistible Pull of Irrational Behavior* (New York: Doubleday, 2008), 30.

6   Ibid., 21–22.

7   Maxwell, *Failing Forward*, 78–80.

8   Bruder, "The Psychological Price of Entrepreneurship."

9   Brooks, *The Road to Character*, Introduction.

10   Jeffrey K. Bye, "Desirable Difficulties in the Classroom," Psychology in Action, January 4, 2011, accessed November 23, 2016, http://www.psychologyinaction.org/2011/01/04/desirable-difficulties-in-the-classroom/.

11   Robert Bjork, "Desirable Difficulties Perspective on Learning," in *Encyclopedia of the Mind*, ed. Harold Pashler (Los Angeles: Sage, 2013), 243.

12   "Interviewing the Co-Founder of Stanford's d.school," Unreasonable Institute video, 74:19, July 20, 2014, accessed February 13, 2017, https://unreasonable.is/fireside-chat-with-founder-of-stanford d school-co-leader-of-unreasonableea/#video-1.

13   Ibid.

CHAPTER 20

1   Jen Doll, "A Treasury of Terribly Sad Stories of Lotto Winners," *The Atlantic*, March 30, 2012, accessed December 6, 2016, http://www.theatlantic.com/national/archive/2012/03/terribly-sad-true-stories-lotto-winners/329903/.

2   Alina Dizik, "Loneliness Often Follows Sudden Wealth," BBC News online, October 17, 2016, accessed November 23, 2016, http://www.bbc.com/capital/story/20161014-loneliness-often-follows-sudden-wealth.

3   "Signs of Sudden Wealth Syndrome," WebMD, April 17, 2000, accessed November 29, 2016, http://www.webmd.com/balance/features/sudden-wealth-syndrome.

4   "Google's Mayer: Staying Innovative in a Downturn," Bloomberg.com, December 15, 2008, accessed May 25, 2017, https://www.bloomberg.com/news/articles/2008-12-14/googles -mayer-staying-innovative-in-a-downturnbusinessweek-business-news-stock-market-and -financial-advice.

5   Barry Schwartz, *The Paradox of Choice: Why More Is Less, Revised Edition* (New York: HarperCollins e-books, 2009), Kindle edition, 2.

6   Ibid., 3.

7   Elizabeth W. Dunn, Daniel T. Gilbert, and Timothy D. Wilson, "If Money Doesn't Make You Happy Then You Probably Aren't Spending It Right," *Journal of Consumer Psychology* 21, no. 2, April 2011, 115–125, http://www.sciencedirect.com/science/article/pii /S1057740811000209.

8   "The Price of Happiness: $75,000," *The Week*, September 7, 2010, accessed February 13, 2017, http://theweek.com/articles/491307/price-happiness-75000.

9   Stephen Goldbart and Joan Indursky DiFuria, *Affluence Intelligence: Earn More, Worry Less, and Live a Happy and Balanced Life* (New York: Da Capo, 2011), Kindle edition, Introduction.

10   Jane Weaver, "Many Cheat for a Thrill, More Stay True for Love," NBC News, April 16, 2007, accessed February 13, 2017, http://www.nbcnews.com/id/17951664/ns/health -sexual_health/t/many-cheat-thrill-more-stay-true-love/#.WKIGdbYrKHo.

11   Mitch Moxley, "Why Being Rich Might Make You a Jerk," *Slate*, May 2014, accessed December 2, 2016, http://www.slate.com/articles/news_and_politics/uc/2014/05 /_why_being_rich_might_make_you_a_jerk.html.

12   Madeline Levine, *The Price of Privilege: How Parental Pressure and Material Advantage Are Creating a Generation of Disconnected and Unhappy Kids* (New York: HarperCollins, 2008), paperback edition, 17.

13   Ibid., 4–5.

14   Kathleen Elkins, "Billionaires Warren Buffett and Bill Gates Have Similar Ideas about How Much Money You Should Leave Your Kids," CNBC.com, September 26, 2016, accessed February 15, 2017, http://www.cnbc.com/2016/09/26/warren-buffett-bill-gates-have-similar-ideas-on-how-much-money-to-leave-kids.html.

15   Chris Taylor, "70% of Rich Families Lose Their Wealth by the Second Generation," *TIME*, June 17, 2015, accessed December 6, 2016, http://time.com/money/3925308/rich-families-lose-wealth/.

16   Lara B. Aknin, Michael I. Norton, and Elizabeth W. Dunn, "From Wealth to Well-Being? Money Matters, but Less Than People Think," *The Journal of Positive Psychology* 4, no. 6, 2009, 523–527, http://dx.doi.org/10.1080/17439760903271421.

17   Dunn et al., "If Money Doesn't Make You Happy Then You Probably Aren't Spending It Right."

18   Roger Reynolds, "A Refreshing Twist to the Pitfalls of Sudden Wealth Syndrome," Coldstream Wealth Management, July 17, 2012, accessed February 13, 2017, http://www.coldstream.com/2012/07/17/a-refreshing-twist-to-the-pitfalls-of-sudden-wealth-syndrome/.

19   Dunn et al., "If Money Doesn't Make You Happy Then You Probably Aren't Spending It Right."

20   Marco della Cava, "Bill Gates Explains His Optimism: 'Things Are Tending to Improve,'" *USA Today*, February 14, 2017, accessed February 15, 2017, http://www.usatoday.com/story/tech/talkingtech/2017/02/14/bill-gates-explains-his-optimism-things-tending-improve/97853116/; Kathleen Elkins, "Warren Buffet's Youngest Son Describes What It Was Like Being Raised by a Billionaire," *Business Insider*, December 3, 2015, accessed February 15, 2017, http://www.businessinsider.com/warren-buffett-son-describes-childhood-2015-12.

CONCLUSION

1   Paul R. Amato, Jennifer B. Kane, and Spencer James, "Reconsidering the 'Good Divorce,'" *Family Relations* 60, no. 5, December 2011, 511–24.

2   Meg Cadoux Hirshberg, "Why So Many Entrepreneurs Get Divorced," Inc.com, November 1, 2010, accessed February 13, 2017, http://www.inc.com/magazine/20101101/why-so-many-entrepreneurs-get-divorced:html.

3   Rozina Sabur, "Staying in an Unhappy Marriage Could Be the Best Thing You Do, New Study Suggests," *Telegraph*, February 8, 2017, accessed February 13, 2017, http://www.telegraph.co.uk/news/2017/02/08/staying-unhappy-marriage-could-best-thing-do-new-study-suggests/.